REVOLUTIONARY REHEARSALS

EDITED BY COLIN BARKER

nous sommes le pouvoir

Haymarket
Books

Revolutionary Rehearsals
By Ian Birchall, Colin Barker, Mike Gonzalez,
Maryam Poya and Peter Robinson

This edition: Copyright 2002 by Haymarket Books,
P.O. Box 180165, Chicago, IL 60618.

Original publication: Bookmarks
(London, Chicago, and Melbourne), 1987.

ISBN: 1-931859-02-7

ISBN 13: 978-1-931859-02-8

HAYMARKET BOOKS is a project of the Center for Economic
Research and Social Change, a nonprofit 501(c)3 organization.
    We take inspiration—and our name—from the Haymarket Mar-
tyrs, who gave their lives fighting for a better world. Their struggle
for the eight-hour day in 1886 gave us May Day, the international
workers' holiday, a symbol for workers around the world that ordinary people can organize and struggle for their own liberation.
    Write us at P.O. Box 180165, Chicago, IL 60618, or visit
www.haymarketbooks.org on the Web.

CONTENTS

THE AUTHORS

All the authors are members of the Socialist Workers Party in Britain.

Ian Birchall is senior lecturer in French at Middlesex Polytechnic in London. Among his previous publications are **France: The Struggle goes on** (with Tony Cliff, London 1968) and **Bailing out the System: Reformist Socialism in Western Europe 1944-1985** (Bookmarks, London 1986).

Colin Barker teaches social science at Manchester Polytechnic. Among his previous publications is **Festival of the Oppressed: Solidarity, reform and revolution in Poland 1980-81** (Bookmarks, London 1986).

Mike Gonzalez writes on Latin America for **International Socialism** journal and is the author of **Nicaragua: Revolution under siege** (Bookmarks, London 1985). He teaches Spanish at Glasgow University.

Maryam Poya was in Iran during the events of 1979. She writes on the Middle East for **Socialist Worker Review** and has translated several books from English into Farsi.

Peter Robinson played an active role in Portugal in 1974-75. Now a teacher in Derby, he is working on a thesis on the Portuguese revolution for the Open University.

INTRODUCTION

THE HEART of socialism is the struggle to abolish human exploitation and oppression across the globe. Karl Marx, classically, gave this vision its most coherent expression. He presented the core of his ideas in the Founding Rules of the First International, back in 1866.[1]

The emancipation of the working class, those Rules declared, must be won by the working class itself. The significance of the battle for working-class self-emancipation is that it embodies the struggle to abolish all class rule. At the root of all social misery in modern society is the worker's economic subjection to those who monopolise the means of production. Hence, all modern political movements must aim at the economic emancipation of the working class, learning from previous defeats. The emancipation of labour is not a merely national issue, but the great international social problem of the epoch.

Over the past hundred years, a variety of pundits have regularly declared that vision to be old hat, dead and finished. Equally, they have declared irrelevant the account of capitalism that accompanied it. Capitalism, they have explained, is *not* inherently crisis-ridden; its inner contradictions do not produce vast social, economic and political convulsions, whether wars or revolutionary situations.

Quite as regularly, these pundits have been proved wrong, in practice. Eduard Bernstein at the turn of the century preached the self-abolition of capitalism's contradictions: the First World War was capitalism's fierce judgement on his theory. Daniel Bell in the USA in the 1950s announced the 'end of ideology': the civil rights movement and the Vietnam war were America's reply. Only two years before the French working class erupted in 1968 into the largest general strike in world history, Andre Gorz was carefully explaining why never again would they do any such thing.

Every temporary capitalist stabilisation and every defeat of the left brings such people forward. Their work does not last, for they have nothing very serious to say: they are the mayflies of depression.

The mid-1980s, too, have seen a whole host of new pundits emerging, to play a set of variations on the old themes.[2] These years have seen a down-turn in the level and intensity of working-class struggle across the world. This is not, however, the first such period in international working-class history, nor (yet) the most serious in its consequences.

As a whole, though, if any century deserves the title, the twentieth has been the 'century of revolutions'. And the past two decades have been no exception.

Not all revolutions, however, contain within themselves the seeds of a socialist alternative. For Marx's vision of socialism to become reality, something more must be present than simply an insurgent 'people'. Central to Marx's argument, and still crucially relevant today, is an emphasis on the independent, conscious activity of the *working class*, in pursuit of its own 'economic emancipation'.

In that more precise sense, the last two decades have seen five major occasions when the specifically *socialist* argument has revealed, and measured, its possibilities. They were: the strike movement that engulfed France in May and early June 1968, the workers' movement under the Allende government in Chile in 1972 and 1973, the Portuguese revolution of 1974 to 1975, the Iranian revolution of 1979, and the 'Solidarity' movement in Poland in 1980 to 1981.[3]

Those five sets of events are the subject of this book. We do not discuss in these pages other important popular revolutions of recent years, such as those in Vietnam, in the former Portuguese colonies of Mozambique, Guinea and Angola, in Nicaragua or the Philippines. For while all involved extensive revolutionary struggles against highly oppressive regimes, none had the special vivifying element of extensive independent working-class activity and organisation that marked the events discussed here. In that sense, none of them contained the same possibilities for *socialist* revolution.

When these five movements occurred in France, Chile, Portugal and Poland, they provided an immense inspiration to socialists everywhere. They continue to do so. But they were also full of bitter lessons. No workers' movement that does not learn from its defeats will ever succeed. And every one of these movements, despite their power and their potential, was defeated. Two of them — in France and Portugal — ended with a disappointed retreat of the revolutionary forces back into the normal routines of bourgeois democracy. The movements in Chile and Poland were crushed and repressed by counter-revolutionary military intervention, which took a particularly murderous form in Chile. In Iran, the working class and other popular forces were bloodily swamped by an 'anti-imperialist' Islamic counter-revolution.

Each of these movements contained major possibilities for socialist advance. In every one, the working class posed a massive challenge to the continued hegemony of capitalist social relations. In each, workers built their own class organisations and formulated and fought for their own class demands, independently of other social forces. From a socialist standpoint, these five sets of events are dramatic and exciting revelations of the continuing, and strengthened, validity of revolutionary Marxist ideas.

In each of them, also, the classic question of 'reform or revolution' was posed as a practical problem of immense significance. Each movement arrived at a critical turning point, where it must either go forward and challenge the existing structures of state power and property, or be driven back. As in every potentially revolutionary crisis this century, major reformist political forces were on hand in each case to lead the way in containing and demobilising the popular upsurge. Those forces varied in character: union leaders, intellectuals, socialists, communists, priests, even guerrillas. All proposed to the workers' movement strategies and tactics which led to their defeat.

In all the variety of particular local circumstances, another common element unites these experiences: the practical and theoretical weakness of the socialist left. In no case did a significant revolutionary socialist party offer an alternative path to that taken. In our view, that missing element played a major part in the destruction of these movements.

Mindless inspiration is of little use to socialism. A hard look at our real forces and weaknesses, nationally and internationally, is a vital precondition of future advance. So too is a critical consideration of the major opponents of socialism in the contemporary world. In particular, the politics of reformism — in all its variety of local hues — has prevented potential advances by the workers' movement time and again.

If socialists are to be effective, we must come to terms with both the possibilities and the history of our own period. Two inseparably inter-connected problems confront us today: the need to reduce the weight of reformist politics and to develop a powerful revolutionary socialist current within the world working class. If we persuade a few readers to work towards these ends, this book will have succeeded.

Colin Barker
Ian Birchall
Mike Gonzalez
Maryam Poya
Peter Robinson

Acknowledgements

The editor and authors, individually and collectively, owe thanks to many people for their encouragement and critical comment, first of all to each other, but also to Daniel Birchall, Alex Callinicos, Norah Carlin, Tony Cliff, Chris Harman, Phil Marshall, Annie Nehmad, John Rose, Kara Weber, Steve Wright, Andy Zebrowski. A special debt is owed to Pete Marsden, without whom . . .

ONE

FRANCE 1968

'All power to the imagination!'
Ian Birchall

IN MAY 1968 that highly class-conscious weekly **The Economist** published a special supplement by Norman Macrae, entitled 'Old France in a Hurry', to mark ten years of Gaullist rule in France. Macrae delivered a sustained, if not uncritical, eulogy of the French economy. French living standards were equivalent to those in Britain; indeed, the French ate more meat and owned more cars than the British. France had the 'great national advantage' that its trade unions were 'pathetically weak'.

In particular Macrae paid tribute to what one Frenchman had called 'our purposive educational revolution', which meant that the quality of managers and technicians in France was higher than in Germany. He then went on to examine the machinery for 'indicative planning' of the economy in France, which had been much admired in Britain by such Labour cabinet members as Tony Benn and Peter Shore, and showed how the French economy had achieved a desirable balance between interventionist planning and free market forces. Looking to the future beyond de Gaulle's death or retirement, Macrae concluded that 'a French swing to industrial expansion and modernisation and intelligent economic liberalism after de Gaulle could yet astonish the world.'[1]

Within a week of Macrae's article hitting the newsstands France was indeed astonishing the world — with the biggest general strike in the whole of human history. More than nine million workers were involved, in all the branches of French industry, and in every reach of society from the Meudon Observatory to the Folies Bergères. In most cases workers were not simply striking, but challenging the sacred heart of property relations by occupying their workplaces.

It was not only bourgeois commentators like Macrae who found their assumptions rudely shattered; the left were equally stunned. In January 1968 the year's issue of the **Socialist Register** had carried an article by one of France's best-known Marxist theorists, André Gorz, who declared that 'in the foreseeable future there will be no crisis of European capitalism so dramatic as to drive the mass of workers to revolutionary general strikes or armed insurrections in support of their vital interests.'[2]

The events of May 1968 produced a flood of comment and analysis. By the end of 1968 more than a hundred books and innumerable articles had appeared in French.[3] Around the world the French strike was a source of inspiration and euphoria; the mood of the time was captured by the **Black Dwarf**,[4] which filled its front page with the slogan: 'WE SHALL FIGHT, WE SHALL WIN, PARIS LONDON ROME BERLIN'.

May 1968 in France was part of a world-wide wave of student and youth radicalisation which formed a whole political generation. As so many of that generation have drifted to reformism or made their peace with the old order, they have become somewhat embarrassed by their political roots. The May events are now little discussed; to the best of my knowledge, there is now no book in print in English dealing with France in 1968.

Yet May 1968 deserves to be remembered. Since 1968 Europe has seen further upsurges; Portugal in 1974-75 and Poland in 1980-81 both experienced workers' actions which in many ways went further, and created more original forms of organisation, than France had done in 1968. Yet both these countries lacked a tradition of bourgeois democracy and of reformist workers' organisations. Portugal suffered from the legacy of an archaic colonialism; Poland from the specific problems of state capitalism and the Russian threat. Hostile critics will try to claim that both are irrelevant to Britain in the 1980s. The argument that socialist revolution is a realistic option for the coming decades in advanced capitalist democracies such as Britain, West Germany or the United States must still to a considerable extent rest on the experience of France in May 1968.

The looming crisis

From the workers' standpoint France at the beginning of 1968 did not look as rosy as it did to Norman Macrae. Indeed, the preceding twenty years had seen a long period of downturn. In the late 1940s the French Communist Party had led a wave of highly militant strikes; but the party was motivated more by the needs of the Cold War than by a clear strategy for working-class advance in France, and by the early 1950s there was considerable demoralisation among workers. When the Algerian War broke out in 1954 the French labour movement failed to put up any effective resistance, and the small number of leftists who opposed the war became increasingly isolated.

In 1958 the Fourth Republic collapsed under the strain of the war, and de Gaulle was able to take power with relatively little opposition. As president he preserved the trappings of bourgeois democracy, but in a form that concentrated power in his own hands. He not only brought the Algerian War to an end, but continued and accelerated the work of the Fourth Republic in modernising French capitalism; he was able to do this with little opposition from a largely dormant and demoralised working class.[5]

By the late 1960s French workers still faced many grave problems. Real wages were rising and had more or less reached British levels, but a large section of the working class still suffered from low pay. A quarter of all wage earners were getting less than 500 francs a month (about £46), and a million and a half unskilled workers and agricultural labourers were still getting around 400 francs a month (about £33). Unemployment had risen to over half a million, a high figure for what was still the long post-war boom. Young people were particularly affected; in the Burgundy region 29 per cent of those under 25 were jobless.[6]

The weakness of the trade unions (with only about three million workers unionised, as against seven million in 1945) meant poor conditions in the workplace. Some of France's biggest employers were able to ride roughshod over the most elementary trade union rights. Michelin boasted they had talked to strikers only three times in thirty years. In June 1967 Peugeot called in riot police and two workers were killed. Citroën effectively refused all recognition to *bona fide* trade unions.[7]

And in the summer of 1967 the government had made another successful attack on workers' standards by reorganising the Social Security system, cutting the reimbursement of medical expenses and reducing workers' involvement in the running of the system.

The organised trade union movement had done little to help workers to fight back. French unions were divided into three federations: the Confédération Générale du Travail (CGT — effectively controlled by the Communist Party), the Confédération Française Démocratique du Travail (CFDT — originally a Catholic union, but moving closer to the reformist left), and Force Ouvrière (FO — a Cold War split-off from the CGT, and, at leadership level, virulently anti-Communist). The division meant that the majority of workers did not trouble to pay dues to any union, though they would often join in particular actions. The main strategy used by the union leaderships to keep control of the movement and to bolster up their negotiating position was that of partial strikes. Time and again stoppages for a single day — and even for periods of one hour — were called in order to make a symbolic show of force to back up negotiations, and in order to defuse any potential all-out confrontation.

Yet in the years preceding 1968 there were signs of discontent seething below the surface. Early in 1963 there was a miners' strike lasting two and a half months. Despite foot-dragging by the CGT (which wanted partial action and a secret ballot), and an unsuccessful attempt by the government to legally compel a return to work, the miners won at least a partial victory and gave the government a psychological setback.[8] The presidential election of December 1965, when François Mitterrand got a surprisingly high vote in opposition to de Gaulle, was a further indication of workers' impatience with the regime.

In 1967 and the early months of 1968 there was a whole wave of strikes and lock-outs, involving engineers, carworkers, the steel and shipbuilding industries, as well as a wide range of public sector workers. Between the beginning of March 1968 and early May there were no fewer than eighty cases of trade union action at the Renault Billancourt plant, with demands for higher wages, shorter hours and better conditions.[9] A long-running struggle took place at the Rhodia-ceta synthetic fibres factory in Lyons. In March 1967 a 23-day strike had involved a total of 14,000 workers. At the end of the year management responded to a further strike over jobs and bonus levels with a partial lock-out and the sacking of ninety-two militants. The struggle continued into 1968 with further lock-outs and mass demonstrations.[10] Slowly but surely pressure was building up for a massive social explosion.

The Student Detonator

But the explosion did not result from a simple quantitative increase in working-class militancy. Instead history took a detour through another sector of society — France's growing student population.

The massive expansion of higher education in the 1960s was an intrinsic part of the Gaullist regime's effort to modernise French capitalism. In the article quoted above, Norman Macrae cited one French view of the process (prior to the beginning of May):

'Germany in its apprentice schools is turning out skilled workers for the industries of yesterday,' purred one Frenchman happily, 'while France in its universities is producing technicians for the industries of tomorrow'.[11]

The sheer figures were impressive. Between 1958 and 1968 the number of students in higher education in France rose from 175,000 to 530,000. In Paris alone the figure rose from 68,800 in 1958 to 130,000 in 1967. In six years up to 1968 the total area occupied by university premises was more than doubled; yet even so overcrowding was chronic and facilities woefully inadequate.[12]

Student revolt, which had appeared earlier in the 1960s at Berkeley in California and the London School of Economics, had become a world-wide phenomenon by 1968. It was particularly acute in France because of the hectic rush to expand to catch up with other advanced countries, and because of the highly centralised and conservative structures of the French education system. But the crisis of higher education was part of the crisis of capitalism, not something extraneous to it. Those who saw the student movement as autonomous from the class struggle tended either, like Herbert Marcuse and his followers, to exalt students as a new revolutionary vanguard replacing an integrated and apathetic working class, or, like the Communist Parties, to dismiss the student radicalism as something alien to the working class. Others, however, stressed the social roots of the student movement:

> The central contradiction of capitalism is that between the production of what Marx called use-values, and the production of values. The first are natural, the second are specific to the capitalist order of society. In the university this is reflected as a contradiction between the ideal of unlimited intellectual development, free from social, political and ideological restraint, and the tight intellectual reins imposed by capitalism. The liberal mystique of education clashes with its social content.[13]

Before the Second World War students had been a relatively small elite, training to become members of the ruling class or its well-paid agents (lawyers, professors, priests, scientists, etc). But with the vast expansion of the universities, most students were destined to become technicians and administrators, perhaps a little more privileged than the working class, but not radically separate from it. Indeed, since the expansion had been rapid and unplanned, many of the students were unable to get any kind of employment relevant to their studies. Naturally disaffection and criticism became rife.

New problems required new organisational forms. The French national students' union (UNEF), which had played a militant and creditable role during the Algerian war, was in decline. Its membership had fallen to 50,000, a quarter of the figure at the start of the decade, despite the rise in student numbers.[14] But a new wave of students were being radicalised by new issues, both international and domestic. On the one hand opposition to the American war in Vietnam led many to enthusiasm for the Third World, for Che Guevara (murdered in autumn 1967) and for the Chinese Cultural Revolution. Many others were infuriated by the conservatism which dominated French academic life. At Nanterre, in the Paris suburbs, students set up a 'critical university' to attack the ideological content of the lecture courses.[15] Perhaps the issue which provoked most activity was the demand for 'free circulation', the right of male and female students to visit each others' rooms in the university hostels. For two or three years before 1968 this issue produced protests and demonstrations.

Out of the new issues new leaders began to emerge. In January 1968 the Minister of Youth and Sports, François Missoffe, went to Nanterre to inaugurate a new swimming-pool. He was confronted by a student militant called Daniel Cohn-Bendit who was to become internationally notorious within a few months:

> 'Mr Minister, you've drawn up a report on French youth 600-pages long (a reference to a ministry document which had just appeared). But there isn't a word in it about our sexual problems. Why not?'
> 'I'm quite willing to discuss the matter with responsible people, but you're clearly not one of them. I myself prefer sport to sexual education. If you have sexual problems, I suggest you jump in the pool.' The Minister had lost his temper.
> 'That's what the Hitler Youth used to say,' Cohn-Bendit retorted brazenly.[16]

From this time on the level of struggle escalated rapidly. One demonstration followed another, on Vietnam or on student issues. The victimisation of militants led simply to further demonstrations of protest. By the beginning of May the situation in Paris was almost out of control. On 3 May the authorities decided to close the Sorbonne. Obviously they hoped that since the examination period was approaching, most students would be busy revising, and it would be possible to pick off the militants without too much trouble. But this proved to be a colossal miscalculation. Over the next week there were student demonstrations and clashes with the police every day. The extreme right also began to emerge; fascists from the Occident group set fire to a student union office at the Sorbonne.[17]

The crunch came on the night of 10 May. Students who had been battered by police over the preceding days decided to stand their ground and fight. By midnight they found themselves holding the Latin Quarter, and in order to ward off police attacks they began to build barricades. The streets of Paris were still paved with cobbles; one account has it that a passing builder showed the students how to use a pneumatic drill to tear them up.[18] From then on the situation developed at great speed; many by-standers joined the students, and on-the-spot radio reports told others what was going on and brought them out to join in. One eye-witness recounts:

> Literally thousands help build barricades (Europe No. 1 Radio reported that *more than 60* barricades were built in different streets), women, workers, bystanders, people in pyjamas, human chains to carry rocks, wood, iron. A tremendous movement is started. Our group (most have never seen the others before, we are composed of six students, ten workers, some Italians, by-standers and four artists who joined later; we never even knew each other's names) organises the barricade at the angle of Rue Gay Lussac and St Jacques. One hundred people help carry the stuff and pile it across the street. From then on I was so busy coordinating work at our barricade that I don't know what happened elsewhere. Witnesses say it all happened at the same time and more or less in the same way all over the Latin Quarter. Our barricade is double: one three-foot high row of cobble stones, an empty space of about twenty yards, then a nine-foot high pile of wood, cars, metal posts, dustbins. Our weapons are stones, metal, etc found in the street.[19]

The scene was an echo of Paris's long tradition of insurrectionary barricades. The Belgian Trotskyist Ernest Mandel is said to have climbed on to a barricade and declared 'How beautiful! It's the Revolution!' He was watching his own car burn.[20]

But the barricades were no Romantic gesture. For a week the Paris police had been exercising systematic violence against the students. As well as vicious clubbing they used tear-gas grenades and, it eventually transpired, CS gas as used in Vietnam. Cafes and private homes in which students took refuge were forcibly entered; photographers had their films destroyed; pregnant women were beaten.[21] On the night of 10 May a special meeting of ministers instructed the head of the Paris police to use all necessary force against the students. Recognising the potential consequences, the police chief, Grimaud, asked for the instruction to be put in writing. This was done.[22]

But by the next day the government was to find itself in a serious dilemma. The students' courage and the gross brutality of the police had turned public sympathy in their direction. The trade union federations called a one-day strike for the following Monday, 13 May, to be accompanied by a mass demonstration in Paris.

The government now had no choice but to retreat. The prime minister, Georges Pompidou, who had been travelling abroad, returned to Paris on 11 May. He immediately ordered the Sorbonne be reopened and indicated that the imprisoned students would be released. He had little choice; as he was to write in his memoirs:

> Some people . . . have thought that by reopening the Sorbonne and having the students released I had shown weakness and set the agitation

going again. I would simply answer as follows: let's suppose that, on Monday 13 May the Sorbonne had remained closed under police protection. Who can imagine that the crowd, swarming towards Denfert-Rochereau, would have failed to break in, carrying everything before it like a river in flood? I preferred to give the Sorbonne to the students than to see them take it by force.[23]

Yet by making the concessions Pompidou showed that the police action of the previous week had been not only brutal but futile. If the concessions had been made a day earlier, the 'night of the barricades' — and all that followed — might never have happened. The government was losing credibility fast, and the initiative was going to its opponents.

In this situation the demonstration of 13 May took place. While it is virtually impossible to get an accurate assessment of its size, it seems probable that something like a million people marched across Paris. An eyewitness described the intoxicating nature of the experience:

> Endlessly they filed past. There were whole sections of hospital personnel, in white coats, some carrying posters saying *'Où sont les disparus des hôpitaux?'* ('Where are the missing injured?'). Every factory, every major workplace seemed to be represented. There were numerous groups of railwaymen, postmen, printers, Metro personnel, metal workers, airport workers, market men, electricians, lawyers, sewermen, bank employees, building workers, glass and chemical workers, waiters, municipal employees, painters and decorators, gas workers, shop girls, insurance clerks, road sweepers, film studio operators, busmen, teachers, workers from the new plastic industries, row upon row upon row of them, the flesh and blood of modern capitalist society, an unending mass, a power that could sweep *everything* before it, if it but decided to do so.[24]

The unions had tried to use their well-established tactic yet again; one day's action to defuse the situation, then back to the negotiating table. But this time it had not worked; after this glimpse of mass power, the movement had to go on.

The General Strike

In some phases of the class struggle, confidence is more important than consciousness. It is not that workers do not know that the system is rotten, and that they are exploited. But they have no faith in their collective ability to change things. Such was the situation with many French workers before 13 May 1968. Ironically, the way in which the left had stressed the exceptional nature of Gaullist rule in its propaganda had probably helped to reinforce the idea that de Gaulle was invincible.

But now things were changing. The students had shown that the regime could be forced to make concessions; the one-day action on 13 May had given workers a sense of their power.

The centre of the action now shifted from Paris to Nantes in Western France. On 14 May workers at the Sud-Aviation aircraft factory decided that one-day action was not enough, and resolved to go into indefinite strike with occupation of the factory. In a sense the action was spontaneous; no national union or political organisation had called for all-out action. But the spontaneity had its roots in a long history of militancy at the plant, and more specifically in the fact that over several months a small group of Trotskyists in the FO union branch had been pushing for more generalised forms of struggle.[25]

Initially the Sud-Aviation occupation made little impact. The national press, whether of left or right, gave it scant attention. But within days similar occupations were launched in workplaces up and down France. Often the beginnings of such action were unplanned and spontaneous. A young worker from the Sorting Office of a Paris railway station describes how his particular occupation began:

> On 17 May, when we came in to work on the night shift at 6.30pm, we heard that the Montparnasse railway workers were on strike. We did not need a vote to decide and do the same, enthusiastically. It is true that the night shift is composed of a majority of young people. The first evening, we did not even think of occupying the office for lack of experience. The next morning, some of the day shift workers wanted to come in. We had to convince them. We then understood that we had to occupy the place and protect it with a strike picket.[26]

Contemporary accounts lay much stress on the spontaneity of the strike, and it would be wrong to deny this. No national executive or central committee imagined the strike, let alone called for it; it was the initiative and determination of thousands of nameless militants that made it possible. Yet no action is purely spontaneous; millions of workers do not move unless a lead is given. In the early days a crucial role was played by thousands of political activists who, by one means or another, sought to extend the strike. As one historian of the strike recounts:

> The psychological effect of the Renault complex being part of the strike movement was decisive for the small plants around the Flins Renault factory; to this one must add the practical efforts of groups of young workers who went on a round tour of all the small factories and were instrumental in bringing them out. Elsewhere, it was the efforts of determined political militants; the Trotskyist OCI who, in Nantes, kept plugging the idea of a General Strike of students, workers and teachers from the beginning of May if not before; or the Maoist students in Lyons

who discussed with the in-going and out-going shifts at the Richard-Continental heavy machinery plant, some workers staying out to discuss the matter with a group of 200 to 300 students.[27]

As the strike spread the union bureaucrats, especially those of the CGT who had been initially taken aback by the movement, stepped in to encourage it so that it should not completely escape their control. Remorselessly the strike spread to affect even workplaces with no traditions of struggle; the Citroën (Javel) plant had its first strike since 1952.[28]

Within a fortnight more than nine million workers were on strike.[29] Every sector was involved; as one eye-witness reported: 'On Wednesday the undertakers went on strike. Now is not the time to die.'[30]

A general strike inevitably poses the question of power — power at the level of the factory, of society and of the state. The fact that French workers followed the students' example and occupied their workplaces[31] added a new dimension to the strike; the sacred right of property, and management's right to manage, were under threat. This was very clear in the most militant occupations, for example at Sud-Aviation:

> In the case of Sud-Aviation, a group of twenty members of management was detained for over a fortnight, in spite of repeated appeals by unions to release them. They were locked up in the offices and had the use of a terrace. Their families were allowed to bring them food and sleeping bags, etc, and they had the use of a telephone. A group of over twenty strikers stood guard outside, in two-hour shifts, sitting on the floor in gloomy surroundings. At first a loudspeaker blared out the *Internationale* as 'an effective way for bosses to learn the *Internationale* without ideological effort', but this was discontinued when the workers themselves could no longer stand it. Various pressures on the management included granting permission to go the lavatory only under escort and restrictions on bringing food so that they shared the same fare as the strikers instead of eating chicken, etc. At every general meeting a vote was taken on whether to release them or not.[32]

But the enormous power unleashed by a general strike also poses problems. In an ordinary sectional strike the goal is generally a total halt to production, resisting the blandishments of employers or bureaucrats who want exceptions to be made. But if the whole working class stops work simultaneously it simply condemns itself to starvation. The general strike therefore necessarily raises the question of control; some production and services must continue, but workers must decide which ones and in what form.

The last weeks of May therefore brought these questions to the fore. In a number of cases striking workers continued to provide full or partial services. Gas and electricity workers joined the strike, but maintained supplies; there were a few brief power cuts of a warning nature.[33] Water workers ensured supplies for Paris under the direction of their strike committee.[34] After brief interruptions agreements were made which ensured that food supplies reached Paris as normal.[35] The postal workers' strike committee in cenrral Paris agreed to transmit urgent telegrams where human life was at stake.[36] CGT printworkers issued a statement saying that, in view of the gravity of the situation they did not want the television and radio, tightly controlled by the government, to have a monopoly over information; they therefore agreed to allow newspapers to continue to appear as long as the press 'carries out with objectivity the role of providing information which is its duty.'[37] In a few cases print-workers insisted on changes to headlines or even refused to print an issue when right-wing papers such as **Le Figaro** or **La Nation** breached this condition.[38]

It is difficult to make a retrospective judgment on all the tactical decisions involved in the continued provision of services. The crucial fact was that workers, and their organisations, were deciding; *they* determined what was an emergency, what was objective reporting. The necessities of life, normally taken for granted, now appeared visibly as the products of human labour.

Yet it is impossible to resist the conclusion that in some cases workers did not go all the way in exploiting the power that lay in their hands. Far more could have been made of at least the threat of cutting off electricity supplies. Print-workers could have silenced the bourgeois papers completely and used the occupied presses to print a paper giving the workers' point of view. (In the circumstances, of course, this would have posed an insoluble dilemma; what to do with **L'Humanité**, paper of the Communist Party, which slandered the students and manipulated the return to work.)[39] The union bureaucrats, who wanted to settle the strike in the framework of negotiations, clearly did not want to see the power of the rank and file unleashed in a head-on confrontation with the system.

In a few cases workers went beyond the stage of simply providing full or partial services and tried to take the whole productive process into their own hands. Some key examples are listed in an article by Ernest Mandel:[40]

> . . . at the CSF factory in Brest, the workers decided to carry on production, but they produced what they themselves considered important, notably walkie-talkies to help the strikers and demonstrators to defend themselves against the forces of repression;
>
> . . . at the Mureaux Cement Works, the workers voted in a general assembly to remove the manager. They refused to accept the employers'

proposal for a new vote. The manager in question was thereupon sent off to a different branch of the same Cement Works, where, out of solidarity with the lads from Mureaux, the workers immediately came out on strike — for the first time in the history of the factory;

. . . at the Wonder Batteries factory, at Saint-Ouen, the strikers elected a strike committee, and, in order to show their disapproval of the reformist line of the CGT, they barricaded themselves inside the factory and refused to let the union officials in;

. . . at Saclay, the workers of the nuclear energy centre requisitioned materials from the factory in order to carry on the strike;

. . . at the Citroën factories, in Paris, a first modest and embryonic attempt was made to requisition lorries for the purpose of supplying the strikers.

In some places a very high level of involvement by the strikers was achieved and the running of the strike was taken completely into the hands of the workers. Thus a young militant describes the strike at the Renault Flins plant:

In all there were about a thousand people who took part in the strike pickets, but every morning we had a meeting of a smaller or greater number; as long as the coach service was running, we can say we got a minimum of about five thousand chaps every morning. (The total labour force was around 10,500.)[41]

At the Orly-Nord airport maintenance plant an active strike committee assumed the running of the strike:

The strike lasted 21 days (17 May - 6 June) and was actively supported by a majority of workers of all categories. The elected inter-union strike committee met every day, with representatives of shop-floor committees in increasing numbers as the strike developed. A general meeting every morning, of up to 3,500 workers, heard reports by various union representatives who had made proposals and these were voted on by show of hands. Lists of demands were made on proposals from shop-floor committee representatives as well as from union officials. It was in this way that the continuation of the strike was decided upon. Each shop-floor committee was responsible in the shop for organisation of duty rotas, safety, guarding of one entry or post, organising the collection of food, petrol coupons, etc. But, at the same time, each union retained its own framework which continued to function. At shop floor and plant levels, each union member or delegate was therefore making proposals which had been elaborated and discussed previously within their organisation. It is clear that the unions were thus firmly in control of the movement. Organisation was reported to have been efficient, machinery well looked after, more so than in 'normal' conditions, they said, if this can openly be stated in the servicing of planes! Efficiency and discipline were unquestionable in this case. An interesting example of strike committee initiative was a call for women workers to get together at plant level and form their own 'action committee'.[42]

Unfortunately, this was not the whole story. For if May 1968 gives us some unparalleled examples of workers' power, it also shows all too clearly the cramping effect of bureaucracy in the labour movement. For the union leaderships — above all the CGT — were determined that the strike should not get out of their control and develop in directions contrary to their political intentions. By strengthening their own grip on the strike, they stifled the enormous potential for working-class creativity that the strike had unleashed.

Only in a very few workplaces was the strike run by a democratically elected strike committee. In most places a strike committee was imposed by the union machine; inevitably it would consist of those who were already union activists and representatives. There was no role for those newly radicalised and inspired by the strike, although they might have been the most imaginative and active. Known members of revolutionary socialist groups were also carefully excluded.

This was doubly unfortunate since in many workplaces only a minority of workers were union members. Out of nine million strikers, only some three million were trade unionists. A general strike was no time to moralise with these workers that they should have joined the union before. On the contrary, everything should have been done to draw them into activity; at the very least many of them would have been recruited to the unions. But the bureaucrats preferred to cling to the control they had as if by divine right.

Moreover, the bureaucrats had no enthusiasm for the idea of regular mass meetings in the factories. In their eyes these would simply offer a forum for revolutionary elements who might challenge their strategy. Maximum involvement in picketing, likewise, would expose large numbers of workers to possible encounters with revolutionary students. So in many cases the strike committee itself ensured the continuation of the occupation, and the rest of the workforce were simply sent home, where, of course, they were exposed to the bourgeois press and the government-controlled radio and television.

In this situation it is not surprising that, even where they were not actually excluded, many younger workers turned their backs on the factories. They found more stimulation in joining the student demonstrations and attending the continual mass meetings at the Sorbonne and other universities. The factories, instead of being the fortresses of the working class, were often empty shells inhabited by a small clique of union functionaries.[43] In many ways, therefore, May 1968 was less developed than June 1936, when the election of a

Popular Front government was followed by a mass strike with factory occupations. Then the trade union movement had been less well established, and spontaneous organisation had gone much further.

Not surprisingly, by the end of May there began to be a decline in morale. The bureaucrats had got what they wanted — at the price of demobilising what was potentially one of the most powerful workers' movements in history.

Groping for Power

If democratically elected strike committees had existed in most workplaces, they would have provided the basis for a network of workers' councils (the *soviets* of Russia 1917). In their absence, the growing desire for democratic control took the form of action committees. These bodies were rapidly improvised from the middle of May onwards; they claimed no delegate or representative status, and no formal relation to union organisations. They were based on small groups of activists who came together for practical and political tasks, often at the initiative of revolutionary militants. Some were based in localities, some in workplaces, while others were set up explicitly as joint worker-student bodies.[44]

As the general strike spread, the number of action committees grew rapidly. At an assembly held on 19 May in Paris some 148 action committees were represented, and by the last week of May there were some 450 action committees in Paris alone, and hundreds more in the rest of the country. (This does not include action committees set up by the Communist Party and the United Socialist Party, which were mere projections of their own organisations.) Various assemblies and co-ordinating bodies linked the action committees, though these were of their nature rather fragile and short-lived.

The action committees did not have formally defined tasks; rather they responded to the needs of the situation. Basically their activities fell into two categories. Firstly they did practical jobs made necessary by the strike. They cleared rubbish that had accumulated in the streets; organised lifts in cars where public transport was not running; collected money for strikers' families. Most important of all, in some areas they took on the organisation of food supplies, on occasion making direct links with peasants and cutting out the profiteering middle-men. Secondly they took on the task of producing information and propaganda; huge numbers of leaflets were written, duplicated and distributed; posters were made and fly-posted; street meetings were organised, films shown and photographic exhibitions (for instance on police violence) set up.[45]

The activities of some of the Paris action committees are described by a participant:

> To begin with the activities of these committees had to be geared to the vagaries of the battles raging in Paris itself and sometimes as far away as Flins. To that end, we had to make sure that information was passed on quickly and efficiently. The only way in which the students involved in the struggle could spread their message and break out of their isolation was to communicate with as many of the local people as possible. Now, once the people had seen the police at work, they were only too anxious to express their solidarity, and to participate in future actions. To begin with, they helped to tend the wounded, collected funds, and above all saw to the provisioning of the stay-in strikers: in the Thirteenth *Arrondissement* alone, almost two tons of fruit and vegetables were distributed each week. We also ran solidarity meetings and gave direct support to the strikers, by reinforcing their pickets, and by printing posters for them.
>
> At the local level, we carried on with permanent information and discussion centres in well-known places. Every day, people who had been out on demonstrations gave an account of what had happened to them personally, of what was going on in the rest of Paris, and of how the strikers were faring . . . When necessary, several thousand militants could be assembled within an hour (between 2,800 and 3,500 were called out by the Permanent Factory Mobilisation Committee at 9am on Monday 3 June and stayed until 1pm on Wednesday 5 June).[46]

The spontaneity of the action committees was their strength — and also their weakness. Activists were naturally unwilling that the committees should be taken over or manipulated by any political organisation. But this attitude often extended to a hostility to political organisation as such. As a result action committees, which could have flourished as united front bodies bringing together members of different organisations, found themselves trying to act as a substitute for political parties. Once the movement began to go down, they were often paralysed by political disputes — for example, what position to take on the Russian invasion of Czechoslovakia in August 1968. The action committees were born of the upsurge in struggle, but died along with it.[47]

It was at Nantes that the movement had first passed out of the hands of the students into those of the workers, and it was at Nantes that the movement was to reach its highest level. For a week at the end of May workers' organisations effectively ran the city; the police and the administration simply looked on powerlessly. It was a case of dual power in one city.

On 24 May peasants from the countryside around Nantes put up road-blocks on all the main roads leading into the city as part of the 'day of warning' called by their union in support of their own demands and in solidarity with workers and students.[48] These barricades were then taken over by transport workers — lorry-drivers and others — who, together with school and university students, controlled all traffic in and out of the city for the next week.

Workers also took control of petrol supplies. No petrol tankers were allowed into the city without workers' authorisation, and a picket was put on the only functioning petrol pump in town, with supplies being reserved for the use of doctors.[49]

Contact was made with peasant organisations in the surrounding region, and food supplies were arranged; by cutting out intermediate stages of distribution it was possible to get some sharp reductions in prices. A litre of milk sold for 50 *centimes* as against the normal 80; a kilo of potatoes was cut from 70 *centimes* to 12, a kilo of carrots from 80 to 50.[50] To ensure that others did not profiteer during the period, shops were obliged to display stickers on their windows stating: 'This shop is authorised to open. Its prices are under permanent supervision by the unions.' The stickers bore the signature of the three unions CGT, CFDT and FO who made up the Central Strike Committee which had effectively taken over the administration of the town from the municipal authorities.[51]

Since the schools were closed, teachers, together with students and others, organised nurseries, play-groups, free meals and other activities for strikers' children. Women were notably active, not only as strikers, but as housewives; committees of strikers' wives were set up, and these took a leading role in the organisation of food supplies.

The experience of Nantes (and to a lesser extent of other towns)[52] shows the potential power of working people to run their own lives without bureaucrats and without profiteers. There were limits — notably the fact that there was no development of workers' control inside the factories — and the whole experience came to an end by the last days of May. None the less, the Nantes experience will live as an example of the revolutionary potential that exists at the heart of an ordinary provincial city.[53]

A Society in Ferment

One of the most exciting things about May 1968 in France was the way in which ideas and attitudes were rapidly communicated from one section of the population to another. The radicalism of the student milieu quickly infected young workers who were exposed to it. As one Renault worker recounted:

In the first few days of May every evening I took five or six workers —
quite often members of the Communist Party — in my car to the
Sorbonne. When they returned to work next day they were completely
changed people. Through the students and the 'groupuscules' they got
the political education they did not get from the CP. There was a
completely libertarian atmosphere at the university, so different from
the totalitarian atmosphere at the factory. The student demonstration
created an environment in which people were free to coin their own
slogans. In the official trade union demonstrations, only certain, centrally
determined, slogans were permitted. When Renault was occupied, the
workers experienced a change from control by the management which
uses modern manipulative techniques, to control by the CP bureaucracy,
which is completely totalitarian. In Renault their freedom was alienated.
In the Sorbonne they felt free. When a worker went to the Sorbonne he
was recognised as a hero. Within Renault he was only a thing. In the
university he became a man. This atmosphere of freedom in the sense of
being considered human gave great combativity to the young workers.[54]

A slogan on the wall of the Paris Faculty of Medicine read:
'Those who are afraid will be with us if we remain strong.'[55] In any
class struggle there are people caught in the middle, frightened or
corrupted by the pressures of society. A social movement that is going
forward will take these people with it, and indeed help them to
envisage their own liberation. But if it stops half-way then they will
scuttle back to the camp of the established order. France in 1968 is a
text-book example of this process.

Thus the May general strike involved not only traditional sectors
of industrial workers, but many who in calmer times would identify
themselves as 'middle class', 'professional' or what have you. Thus
there was a well-developed strike movement, raising not only trade-
union issues, but fundamental questions of power and control, at the
nuclear research centre at Saclay, where the majority of the 10,000
employees were researchers, technicians, engineers or graduate scientists.[56] There was a heated debate in the medical profession, calling
into question the outdated traditions of hierarchy in the hospitals and
medical schools. The debate even infected the Church and in Paris
young Catholics occupied a church in the Latin Quarter and demanded
a debate instead of mass.[57] After the end of the strike this radicalism
evaporated or was incorporated into a purely reformist process of
modernisation; but for a moment the enormous potential for revolutionary change in these sectors of society had been glimpsed.

Education, sport, entertainment and the mass media were all
affected. A movement which began among university students soon
involved students in the lycées (secondary schools) and sparked off a

process of challenge to the ultra-centralised and formalistic structures of French education at all levels. On 22 May footballers occupied the headquarters of the French Football Federation, locking up the general secretary and putting up a red flag and a sign reading 'Football for the footballers'.[58] Three hundred dancers, stage-hands and dressing-room staff at the Folies Bergères struck and occupied the theatre.[59]

A general strike not only challenges the basis of capitalist exploitation; it also brings to the surface the various forms of oppression inherent in society. In May 1968 this meant in particular the oppression of immigrant workers and of women.

In France in 1968 there were some three million immigrant workers — from Southern Europe, North Africa and the West Indies. Their conditions were explicitly designed to impede any development of militancy. Many were lodged in company hostels, where overcrowded and insanitary conditions were accompanied by draconian discipline (no visits, no newspapers, in one case no speaking at the meal table).[60] At Citröen immigrant workers were arranged on the production line by nationality, so that one worker was never next to another who spoke the same language.[61] If immigrant workers proved too militant, the companies would simply get the police to remove their work permits.[62]

Yet despite these pressures immigrant workers played a considerable role in the movement. When the strike pickets were first set up at Renault Flins they included a high proportion of immigrant workers.[63] On the 13 May demonstration in Paris there was an unprecedentedly large number of West Indian workers and groups of Portuguese workers chanting 'Franco, de Gaulle, Salazar murderers'.[64]

Threats of victimisation meant that later there was a decline in immigrant involvement but the struggle continued. At the end of May the 'Action Committee of Workers and Students from Countries under French Colonial Domination' occupied the Paris headquarters of the BUMIDOM,[65] a state body which organised the immigration into France of workers from the West Indies, Réunion and French Guyana. The occupiers accused the BUMIDOM of running a 'new slave trade' by bringing thousands of young workers to France, thus impeding development of their native countries, and encouraging low wages and unemployment in France.[66] A 'Maghrebin Action Committee' issued a leaflet urging North African workers to support the strike and denouncing the dictatorships in Tunisia, Algeria and Morocco (though it is impossible to know what base actually existed for such a committee).[67]

Certainly the strike strengthened bonds between French and immigrant workers. One immigrant at Renault Flins said that he welcomed the strike even if nothing was won by it, since before it he had been completely isolated, whereas now he knew everyone.[68] On 19

June there were stoppages at Renault to defend immigrant workers against the threat of non-renewal of contracts.[69] The general mood of internationalism in May was well summed up by the student slogan 'We are all German Jews' in response to right-wing attacks on Cohn-Bendit.

The issue of women's oppression, however, was much less prominent. The tone of many revolutionary slogans had *macho* overtones ('The more I make the revolution, the more I want to make love') and some were overtly sexist ('Long live rape and violence'),[70] while the desegregation of lavatories and cloakrooms at Nanterre cannot be given much political importance.[71] In a situation where workers were being sent home from occupied factories little was done to involve non-working wives in the movement; the closure of schools and public transport probably made many women even more housebound than usual.

Nonetheless, where the struggle was at its highest women were deeply involved. Observers commented on the large number of female students fighting at the barricades on 10 May;[72] as we have seen, women played a key role in the activities of the Nantes strike committee; and at the Orly-Nord airport maintenance plant the strike committee attempted to get women workers to form their own action committee.[73]

The ideas of 'women's liberation' had not really hit France in 1968, and in the frantic atmosphere of May they had little chance to develop; but there can be no doubt that the spirit of May, its emphasis on liberation and self-organisation, helped prepare the ground for the women's movement that was to develop in France over the next few years.

For many students a source of inspiration was the Chinese 'Cultural Revolution' (or what they imagined it to be) and it can be argued that a kind of cultural revolution took place in France during May. Traditional cultural practices were thrown into crisis. Orchestras went on strike and the Cannes Film Festival was cancelled; artists, writers and musicians set up discussions to re-evaluate their role in society.[74] Writers such as Jean-Paul Sartre, Marguerite Duras and others addressed the Sorbonne students in solidarity.[75] The Odéon theatre was occupied and turned into a permanent forum, visited by Jean Genet among others, under the slogan 'When the National Assembly becomes a bourgeois theatre, all bourgeois theatres must become national assemblies.'[76] The Sorbonne Commission of Cultural Agitation narrowly rejected a proposal to plaster over a pseudo-classical frieze by mid-nineteenth century painter Puvis de Chavannes.[77]

But more significant than these challenges to traditional culture was the way the movement began to create its own cultural forms.

Action committees countered the lies of the official media by producing wall-newspapers to be posted in streets and tube stations.[78] Striking television journalists and technicians produced films to be shown at political meetings. Art students established 'Popular Workshops', which turned out over 100,000 copies of 350 different posters.[79] A more individual creativity, but one typical of May 1968, was shown by the slogans which covered the walls of the Paris universities,[80] some neatly encapsulating the spirit of the movement ('it is forbidden to forbid'), others giving an ironic twist to political orthodoxy ('I am a Marxist of the Groucho tendency').[81] Many slogans came from surrealist poets such as André Breton, or from the writings of those cultural revolutionaries of the 1960s, the Situationists.

The State under Threat

Society was in deep ferment, but Capital still ruled. Hierarchies of power were being challenged in the workplaces and on the streets, but the state machine was as yet untouched. By the last week of May the movement had reached a critical juncture; if it was to continue to go forward, it would have to confront the whole apparatus of class rule. As prime minister Pompidou noted in his memoirs, the stakes were very high:

> The crisis was infinitely more serious and more profound; the regime would stand or be overthrown, but it could not be saved by a mere cabinet reshuffle. It was not my position that was in question. It was General de Gaulle, the Fifth Republic, and, to a considerable extent, Republican rule itself.[82]

Economically the system was in deep trouble. People were crossing the borders to Belgium and Switzerland with suitcases filled with currency; commercial banks throughout the world were refusing to deal in the French franc; and 'nobody was quite certain who would be answering the telephone at the Bank of France'.[83] Over the weekend of 25-26 May the government had concluded extensive negotiations with the union leaders; substantial concessions had been made in the hope of ending the strike. But on Monday 27 May workers first at Renault, then at other big plants, rejected the offers as inadequate. The union leaders had no alternative but to continue the strike.

On 24 May de Gaulle had resorted to a device he had used more than once since 1958 to maintain his authority: the calling of a referendum. A rather vague and anodyne set of promises for educational, social and economic reform, including the notorious Gaullist panacea of 'participation', were to be offered to the people; de Gaulle made it clear that the whole exercise was a vote of confidence in himself, and that he would resign if defeated.[84]

The unions did not propose a formal boycott of the referendum, although they made it clear that they saw it as no solution; Séguy of the CGT declared that 'the workers are not demanding a referendum but better living and working conditions.'[85] However in practice the referendum proved impossible. Not a single printshop in France would print the ballot papers needed, and when an attempt was made to get them printed in Belgium, the Belgian printers refused in solidarity.[86] In a broadcast on 30 May de Gaulle had to admit that the situation was 'materially preventing' the holding of the referendum and that it would have to be postponed.[87]

The government's options were narrowing; a head-on confrontation between the workers and the forces of state repression seemed ever more likely. Here too there would be problems for the regime. Certainly the government had a substantial array of 'armed bodies of men'. There were some 144,000 police (armed) of various categories, including 13,500 of the notorious CRS riot police, and some 261,000 soldiers stationed in France or West Germany. This was apparently an imposing force, but it could hardly do the jobs of nine million workers, nor yet compel them all to work at gun-point. Moreover, the army consisted largely of conscripts, most of whom would have strikers in their own families, and who would be reluctant to be used as strikebreakers. Only when the movement was going down and becoming fragmented would it be possible to use armed force to smash particular workplace occupations.

Moreover, there were throughout May indications of considerable discontent in the ranks of the police and armed forces. During the second and third weeks of May representatives of police unions made a number of statements critical of the government's handling of the situation.[88] There was particular dissatisfaction at Pompidou's statement of 11 May. Many police felt that by climbing down the government was repudiating those whom it had ordered to go into action. On 13 May a police union body representing 80 per cent of uniformed personnel issued a declaration that it

> . . . considers the prime minister's statement to be a recognition that the students were in the right, and as a total disavowal of the actions by the police force which the government itself had ordered. In these circumstances, it is surprised that an effective dialogue with the students was not sought before these regrettable confrontations took place.[89]

Later the same week one of the leaders of the Paris police union told listeners to Radio Luxembourg that he had 'been almost instructed by a general meeting to launch a police strike against the prime minister's attitude.'[90] The police also had their own sectional claims to make, and **The Times** reported that 'the branch dealing with intelligence about student activity has been deliberately depriving the government of information about student leaders in support of an expenses claim.'[91]

Of course there can be no suggestion that the Paris police were on the point of going over to the revolution. Many would doubtless have liked nothing better than authorisation to make completely uninhibited use of armed force against the students. But a discontented and demoralised police force was hardly likely to prove a reliable support for the government in a policy of strike-breaking.

Discontent in the armed forces, where there were no trade union rights, is harder to document, but it seems clear that the spirit of May did not leave the armed forces untouched. There are reports of a mutiny on the aircraft carrier *Clemenceau*, which at the end of May was bound for the French nuclear test in the Pacific but was brought back to Toulon. Three families were informed that their sons had been 'lost at sea'.[92] There were some moves to form action committees in the army (forerunners of the soldiers' committees of the mid-1970s), as is shown by a leaflet issued by members of the 153rd RIMECA (mechanised infantry regiment) stationed at Mutzig, near Strassburg, part of which read:

> Military instruction must be an equal right for all. Military instruction and sex education must be administratively, geographically and chronologically integrated into the whole system of National Education from the earliest age, and controlled according to the same principles now demanded in Universities and schools: dialogue and joint management . . .
>
> Like all conscripts, we are confined to barracks. We are being prepared to intervene as repressive forces. The workers and youth must know that the soldiers of the contingent WILL NEVER SHOOT ON WORKERS. We Action Committees are opposed at all costs to the *surrounding of factories* by soldiers.
>
> Tomorrow or the day after we are expected to surround an armaments factory which three hundred workers who work there want to occupy. WE SHALL FRATERNISE.
>
> Soldiers of the contingent, form your committees![93]

It would be wrong to underestimate either the strength of the bourgeois state, or the ruthlessness of those who command and deploy that strength. No socialist revolution can succeed without taking these on. But likewise, no socialist revolution can succeed that succumbs to the blackmail of the threat of civil war. If we wait for the bourgeois state to disarm itself we shall wait for ever. The French state was in relative disarray at the end of May 1968; a movement bold enough to go forward in unity could have confronted it without fear.

The recognition of the weak position of the state penetrated the highest levels of government. It was an open secret that during May and June there was considerable friction between president de Gaulle and prime minister Pompidou. (Pompidou's memoirs, published by his wife on the basis of notes written before his death in 1974, give a clear account of this, though obviously recounted in such a way as to show Pompidou in the best light.)[94]

Symptomatic of the government disarray in this period is the strange story of de Gaulle's disappearance on 29 May. In the morning of that day de Gaulle and his wife left Paris by air, supposedly heading for their country home at Colombey. Later that day it became clear that they had not gone to Colombey, and no one — not even the prime minister — knew where they were. Soon it was learnt that de Gaulle had gone to Baden-Baden in West Germany, where he had a meeting with General Massu, notorious for his use of brutality and torture during the Algerian War, especially in the famous 'Battle of Algiers'. According to Pompidou, de Gaulle had been the victim of an 'attack of demoralisation' and had intended to withdraw from political life and stay in West Germany. Had he done so, of course, the impact on the situation would have been overwhelming; if the students and strikers had believed they had dislodged de Gaulle, their confidence would have grown to such an extent that the government would have found it impossible to stop them.

According to Pompidou,[95] Massu succeeded in persuading de Gaulle to return to Paris and take a tough line. Massu has confirmed the main lines of Pompidou's account,[96] though others closely associated with de Gaulle have challenged it.[97] Since everyone concerned is defending their own reputation or that of their political faction, it is unlikely that the full truth will ever be known. The alternative scenario is that de Gaulle's disappearance was a calculated move to show his government colleagues and the whole people just how indispensable he was. Even if this were true, it would have been a risky manoeuvre and an indication of just how difficult the regime's situation had become.

For three or four days in the last week of May 1968 there was a power vacuum in France. The government had lost effective control of the situation and had no quick way to regain it. The possibilities open to a movement with an audacious leadership were immense. This is not, however, to suggest that there was an immediately revolutionary situation in existence. The idea that the Communist Party was on the verge of establishing a 'People's Democracy' belonged only to the fantasy world of right-wing journalists.[98]

In fact the Communist Party later boasted that it had not attempted the revolutionary road; but it too distorted the nature of the alternatives that existed. According to Waldeck-Rochet, the party's general secretary:

In reality the choice to be made in May was the following:

— Either to act in such a way that the strike would permit the essential demands of the workers to be satisfied, and to pursue at the same time, on the political level, a policy aimed at making necessary democratic changes by constitutional means. This was our party's position.

— Or else quite simply to provoke a trial of strength, in other words move towards an insurrection: this would include a recourse to armed struggle aimed at overthrowing the regime by force. This was the adventurist position of certain ultra-left groups.[99]

This was a false alternative. Certainly there was no question of storming the Elysée Palace on 29 May. And although there were indeed some genuine ultra-lefts among the students, few of them believed that this was the option. After all one of the students' favourite slogans — 'It's only a beginning; let's continue the fight' — precisely posed the perspective of a prolonged struggle.

The real option was whether the movement should go forward or go back. The crucial question in the last week of May was not insurrection. It was how to establish genuine strike committees based on the rank and file in every workplace, and link these up into local, regional and national councils of workers' representatives. This would have raised further questions — in particular, the physical defence of the workplaces and the attempt to resume production under workers' control.

Class consciousness is not static. It is undoubtedly true that most workers saw the general strike in terms of higher wages and better conditions, and not in terms of state power. But there is no rigid dividing line between the economic and the political. A whole range of issues — such as union rights and limitations on the power of management — link the two. As long as the movement went on rising, more and more workers were learning from their own experience that the stakes were much higher than pure trade-union demands.

Of course, it can be no more than speculation to ask what might have happened if the strike had continued to develop. Even if a compromise had had to be made a few weeks later, it would have been on immeasurably better terms for the workers — bigger economic gains, much stronger workplace organisation and the departure of de Gaulle. At best, a process could have begun which in a period of months could have put insurrection on the agenda.

But none of this was to be. For while the state was in disarray the workers too lacked decisive leadership. The gap was filled by reformist leaders who were almost as frightened of workers' power as was the ruling class.

The bureaucrats duck out

The strongest organisation on the French left in 1968 was without doubt the Communist Party (PCF). The PCF had been excluded from the government in 1947, and over the intervening twenty-one years had played no part in any of the governmental alliances that were formed. It had maintained its strength as a result of its powerful implantation in the CGT, which gave its members access to many positions of responsibility in trade union and welfare organisations in the workplaces; moreover, its control of a number of working-class municipalities made it a significant dispenser of jobs.

The PCF in 1968 was still much more resolutely pro-Russian than its counterpart in Italy (its first major break with Russia would come in August 1968, when it opposed the Russian invasion of Czechoslovakia). Central to its political strategy was the aim of returning to parliamentary power. This it could achieve only through electoral alliances with the non-Communist left (grouped in the Left Federation, the FGDS), with a view to eventual participation in a coalition government. This in turn meant that the PCF had to prove itself to be a party committed to parliamentary methods and to respect for constitutional procedures.[100]

The rise of a revolutionary current within the student movement was therefore a matter of considerable concern to the PCF leadership. Firstly, it wished to preserve its claim to be the only Marxist party and the only legitimate representative of the working class in France. Secondly, if French politics moved on to the path of violence, the PCF would risk either losing its reputation for legality, or being outflanked on its left.

As a result, from the very beginning of May, the PCF leadership was anxious to draw a clear line between itself and the leftist students. On 3 May 1968 Georges Marchais — soon to become the party leader — published an article vigorously denouncing the leftist *groupuscules* (little groups):

> Not content with the agitation they are carrying on in student circles — agitation which goes counter to the interests of the mass of students and favours fascist provocations — these pseudo-revolutionaries are now claiming to give lessons to the working-class movement. More and more they are to be found at the factory gates or in immigrant workers' centres giving out leaflets and other propaganda material.

These false revolutionaries must be vigorously unmasked, for objectively they are serving the interests of the Gaullist government and of the big capitalist monopolies.

. . . The ideas and activities of these 'revolutionaries' are laughable. All the more so because in general they are the sons of the upper bourgeoisie — contemptuous towards students of working-class origin — who will soon damp down their 'revolutionary flame' to go and manage Daddy's company and exploit the workers there in the best traditions of capitalism.

However, it would be wrong to underestimate their pernicious activity which tries to sow confusion, doubt and scepticism among workers and especially among youth . . . By developing anticommunism, the leftist *groupuscules* are serving the interests of the bourgeoisie and of big capital.[101]

The PCF preserved this line of attack against the revolutionary students in its press, and, even more viciously, by word of mouth. At the same time, it had to ensure that it was not outflanked on its left. After the mass demonstrations of 13 May the PCF had to recognise that the students had won considerable sympathy by their courage in resisting the police, and that to attack them too blatantly would mean isolating itself. There was a certain shift of tone.

The general strike certainly began outside the control of the PCF. The first day of the Sud-Aviation occupation earned just seven lines in the PCF's daily paper, tucked away on page nine.[102] By Thursday 16 May the CGT felt itself obliged to respond to the growing wave of strikes, while scrupulously refraining from actually giving a militant lead, let alone launching a general strike call:

The CGT salutes the workers, especially those of the National Renault Company who, in response to its call, have decided to strike and occupy.

It calls on all workers to hold workplace meetings, and to determine, with their union officials, on what conditions they will join the struggle and what demands to fight for.

It calls on all its militants to immediately take any initiative necessary to raise the level of struggle on the basis of broad consultation of workers and in trade union unity.[103]

This carefully worded statement hedged the CGT's (and the PCF's) bets. While carefully avoiding 'adventurism' it warned its militants to make sure the movement was under their control. On the ground the CGT's tactics were to appoint strike committees of loyal members, to demobilise the rank and file and to exclude revolutionary students from the workplaces. Fine words about unity often covered up a sectarian practice on the ground. In at least one case CGT members occupied a factory telephone switchboard so as to cut the CFDT representatives off from contact with their departmental office.[104]

By the end of May the PCF was forced to confront the question of power. On 29 May its daily paper bore a banner headline: 'The workers demand: A popular government of democratic union with Communist participation.'[105] This was much more modest than calling for the revolution; unfortunately it was much more ambitious than what was actually achieved. Once again the PCF proved that 'realists' are often the greatest utopians.

The constant concern of the PCF was to avoid 'provocations'. One critic compared it to a woman deciding to thwart a rapist by consenting to his advances, thus making the act no longer 'rape'.[106] Often the police returned the compliment by letting the large PCF demonstrations pass off peacefully, reserving violent attacks for the leftists. It suited the authorities to keep the PCF firmly inside the constitutional fold.[107]

In its own terms the PCF did not do badly out of May 1968. Its claim that it signed up 15,000 new members in the month after 13 May may not be hopelessly exaggerated, since in many places it did seem to be leading the movement.[108] Its conduct in the general strike demonstrated both its massive industrial power and its commitment to legality. In order to make such a demonstration, of course, it had to stifle one of the greatest spontaneous mass movements in history; but in the eyes of its leaders this was doubtless a cheap price to pay.

The political weight of the social-democratic left was far smaller than that of the PCF. The Socialist Party (SFIO), under its treacherous leader Guy Mollet, had been widely discredited by its support for the Algerian War and for the accession of de Gaulle. When the 13 May demonstration passed by the SFIO headquarters there were chants of 'Guy Mollet to the museum'.[109] Mollet and his party made no significant intervention during May 1968.

However two reformist politicians who did have some impact were former ministers from the Fourth Republic, François Mitterrand and Pierre Mendès-France (who as prime minister had ended the Indochina war in 1954). Both had opposed de Gaulle from the beginning, and Mitterrand had put up a good fight in the 1965 presidential election.

Unlike the PCF, they did not have a mass base to worry about and could therefore take rather more risks in expressing sympathy with the students. At the same time they knew that, while in a straight electoral context between de Gaulle and the PCF the former would always win, a left centre figure could cobble up a majority by winning support from both PCF and disgruntled or leftish Gaullists. This was the logic behind Mitterrand's announcement on 28 May that he was a candidate for the presidency, and that Mendès-France should be asked to form a provisional government.[110]

Mitterrand's campaign was purely opportunist. When de Gaulle spoke of a 'third way' between capitalism and communism, Mitterrand responded that the only political force offering the third way was the Left Federation which combined socialism and liberty.[111] Yet he was able to appeal to leftist students in a way that the PCF dared not. Even the anarchist Cohn-Bendit went so far as to say: 'François Mitterrand isn't an ally, but if necessary he can simply be of use to us.'[112]

Mitterrand's account of why he wanted Mendès-France to head a provisional government likewise shows the policy of co-option and collaboration pursued by both men:

> He had real prestige with the protesting students through the medium of the United Socialist Party and the National Union of French Students, a prestige increased by his presence at the Charléty rally. His financial orthodoxy reassured moderate circles. Monsieur Abelin, leader of the Democratic Centre, had expressed this tendency by asking General de Gaulle to entrust him with the task of resolving the crisis. *A priori*, then, he had more chance than anyone else of pulling together a broad range of public opinion and of working for the reconciliation of French people which I had been appealing for.[113]

During May Mendès-France worked with a small committee of academics and lawyers which maintained contact on the one hand with the government and police authorities, and on the other with the student leaders, in an effort to prevent any escalation of violence.[114] But on Monday 27 May Mendès-France attended a rally of some 50,000 people at the Charléty stadium (sitting on the platform, but without speaking). This was an attempt to regroup the currents to the left of the Communist Party, and the various revolutionary *groupuscules* were present and active. Mendès-France was clearly there to prevent the emergence of a non-parliamentary left leadership; as he is reported to have commented afterwards: 'We can't cut ourselves off from those who represent the youth.'[115]

Mendès-France was able to retain his credibility with the leftists, though he had little in common with their politics, by the fact of his membership of the United Socialist Party (PSU). The PSU had originated from a split with the SFIO by those who could not stomach its position on the Algerian War. In many ways the PSU was a classically centrist organisation, containing within its not very well disciplined ranks both advocates of revolutionary socialism and left reformists. It veered from Marxist rhetoric to orientation on technocrats and the production of counterplans. The PSU swung sharply to the left during May and Mendès-France resigned from it the following month.

Neither Mitterrand nor Mendès-France achieved anything significant in May (though Mitterrand doubtless acquired a little credit for later use). But, like the PCF, they helped to maintain the movement within constitutional channels and thus impeded the emergence of an independent revolutionary leadership.

The Fragmented Vanguard

A massive social movement can begin spontaneously; but for it to realise its full potential is quite another matter. The absence of a revolutionary party able to lead a challenge to the centralised power of the state was one of the main reasons why the enormous creativity and militancy developed in May 1968 was largely frittered away in June.

It would be both easy and futile to indulge in a circular argument about the missing party (why was there no revolutionary party? Because the class struggle had not reached a high enough level to produce one. Why had the class struggle not reached a high enough level? Because there was no revolutionary party). The answer to both questions can be found only in a detailed account of subjective and objective factors stretching right back to 1917.

But without such futile speculation it can be argued quite simply that throughout May 1968 the working class never broke away from reformist leadership, and that because it did not, it was led to make a compromise within the framework of the existing system. A revolutionary party rooted in the working class would have drawn on the spontaneous wave of militancy and tried to generalise from it; it would have communicated experience with the aim of raising every struggle to the level of the most developed; it would have produced a centralised newspaper that could respond immediately to the lies and distortions of the bourgeois media; it would have at once called the bluff of the authorities when they threatened armed force or civil war.

The revolutionary current that did exist showed great courage and initiative, but it was simply not in a position to take on these tasks. Not only was it small, but it had suffered years of isolation from the mainstream of the labour movement; it was largely, if not exclusively, confined to the student milieu; and it was deeply divided along political and organisational lines.

Among the myriad small and very small *groupuscules* it is possible to identify three main currents — anarchists, Maoists and Trotskyists.[116] The anarchists of one brand and another made an enormous contribution to the spirit of May; their libertarianism and contempt for the old order were a vital element in the upsurge. But their very volatility prevented them from playing a consistent role, and their politics was marked by a rejection of the very idea of a revolutionary party. Daniel Cohn-Bendit, the most conspicuous of the anarchists, often seemed to regard 'Bolshevism' in its various manifestations as a greater danger than the Gaullist regime.[117] Not only did this make it easy for the PCF to pin the 'anti-communist' label on him, but it disqualified him from the crucial task of trying to build a revolutionary organisation.

The Maoists, some of whom had split from the PCF as it moved towards an ever more parliamentary orientation, also made their specific contribution to the spirit of May. They had taken from the Chinese Communist Party's attempt to industrialise by its own boot-straps a voluntarist approach to politics which contrasted healthily with the jaded 'realism' of the reformists. But they had also inherited a profound ambiguity to the whole tradition of Stalinism. As a result they drew slogans rather haphazardly from the past, veering from 'Third Period' sectarianism to Popular Frontism.[118] They contributed a great deal of dedication but little in the way of strategy.

Within the Trotskyist segment of the spectrum there were three main groupings. The most visible were probably the Jeunesse Communiste Révolutionnaire (Revolutionary Communist Youth). The JCR had originated from a split in the PCF student organisation in 1966; their leadership were closely linked to the PCI, the French section of the Fourth International. The JCR played a key role in the street fighting and mass demonstrations, but tended to accommodate overmuch to the moods and attitudes of the student milieu. Also active were the OCI, often known as 'Lambertists' after their main leader. Their student front, the FER, was subjected to some derision for refusing to join the barricade fighting on 10 May;[119] but it was OCI militants who initiated the Sud-Aviation occupation at Nantes.[120] A third grouping, around the paper **Voix Ouvrière**, had the most systematic approach to workplace organisation, but its ultra-Bolshevik and semi-clandestine style made it somewhat unfitted to mass work.

The achievements of the revolutionary left in May 1968 should not be underestimated. In many cases it was individual revolutionary militants from one tendency or another who successfully pushed for occupations after 13 May, often reaping the benefit of long periods of thankless revolutionary agitation and propaganda.[121] For example, at Renault Billancourt it was members of **Voix Ouvrière** and the FER who succeeded in defeating opposition from the CGT to win support for occupation.[122]

But the revolutionary left had two grave weaknesses that could not be overcome in the short time at its disposal. Firstly, despite the non-sectarian spirit shown by many (if not all) militants in the day-to-day struggle, it was not possible to overcome the deep divisions within the revolutionary left.[123] No one group had the size to establish itself as a credible alternative pole of attraction to the reformists.

Secondly, much of the revolutionary left showed a serious tendency towards ultra-leftism. The contempt for reformism among the *groupuscules* was refreshing, but reformism will not disappear simply by being denounced. To break the grip of the PCF and the other reformists, a serious application of the united front strategy would have been necessary, with the revolutionaries proposing joint action against the government to the reformist leaders, hoping thus to win the support of the reformist rank and file. But the divided and strategically uncertain far left was incapable of this.[124] So the revolutionaries were unable to resist the right-wing backlash when it came.

The Right regroups

On the afternoon of Thursday 30 May, de Gaulle broadcast to the nation. It was a short message, four and half minutes in duration,[125] and de Gaulle's continuing weakness was shown by the fact that his speech could not be televised due to strike action at French Television.[126] But de Gaulle's tone was confident and defiant. The proposed referendum was to be dropped, and parliamentary elections were to be held. De Gaulle threatened that if the PCF ('a party which is a totalitarian enterprise') obstructed the election, 'other means' would be used to preserve the Republic, and he appealed for the immediate organisation of 'civic action'. Behind the cryptic language de Gaulle was threatening the use of armed force (there were reports of troop movements around Paris and tanks were seen in the countryside)[127] and was calling on his supporters to use extra-parliamentary measures against the left.

De Gaulle's strategy was shrewd. The PCF and reformists had been able to denounce the referendum as a typical authoritarian device which de Gaulle had used before to reinforce his personal power; but they could not reject parliamentary elections without abandoning wholesale the entire logic of their political strategy. Since that was inconceivable, they were now obliged to play the game on de Gaulle's terms.

The same evening a million people demonstrated through the streets of Paris in support of the government. The extreme right, dormant for the last couple of weeks, now crept out of the woodwork. Car horns sounded the rhythm that meant 'Keep Algeria French' (the theme tune of the far right), and sections of the demonstration chanted 'Cohn-Bendit to Dachau'.[128] To further ingratiate himself with the extreme right de Gaulle released from jail General Salan and other leaders of the notorious Secret Army Organisation (OAS), which had run a murderous campaign to keep Algeria French; he also imposed a legal ban on all the main revolutionary *groupuscules*. The PCF and other reformists were so anxious to prove their constitutional credentials that they raised scarcely a cheep of protest.

Meanwhile the Gaullist 'civic action' began to develop. In the course of the election PCF offices and left militants were attacked by Gaullist thugs with iron bars and even guns,[129] and in Arras a young PCF militant was murdered while flyposting.[130] Yet the reformists were so concerned with their parliamentary image that they kept on whining that it was leftist violence that was losing them votes; as a result the Gaullists were able to combine thuggery on the streets with the projection of a 'law and order' image.

The strike was now an embarrassment to both the government and the bureaucrats of the labour movement. The government began to use force to break occupations; on the early morning of 31 May armed police repossessed the occupied post office at Rouen.[131] Further attacks on occupations by the CRS riot police followed; on 10 June a student was killed at Flins and on 11 June a young worker at Sochaux.[132]

At the same time economic concessions were made. Settlements were made separately in different workplaces, but in general there were wage rises of 10 per cent or more, cuts of an hour in the working week, and extensions of trade union rights in the workplace.[133] Obviously these were real gains and showed that revolutionary action is the most effective way of winning reforms. Yet certain qualifications must be made. The wage increases were at a level that could easily be borne by the system, or at least by its stronger sections. Some of the bigger employers welcomed the wage increases on the grounds that they would drive small employers out of business and accelerate industrial concentration.[134] The permanent value of the wage rises was in any case doubtful since the government made it clear that there would be no effective price control.[135] Citroën simply waited until the elections were safely over and then sacked some 925 employees.[136]

In the light of all this the PCF daily paper was somewhat rash in its claim on 6 June in a banner headline: 'Victorious return to work in unity'.[137] In fact it was the strategy of the PCF and the CGT which made the return far less victorious than it need have been. The policy of allowing each sector of workers to settle separately broke the unity and solidarity of the movement and ensured that some groups won less than they might have done if the movement had stayed united. There were still enormous reserves of militancy, and some workers stayed out until almost the end of June; but the CGT's policy pushed even the most combative workers into isolation. Bourgeois leaders made their usual cries for secret ballots,[138] but the CGT showed consummate skill in manipulating the votes on the return to work, as the following account shows:

> The role of the CGT in these votes was at best confusing and at worst criminal. At Citroën, on the occasion of the first vote, organised by the management by secret ballot outside the factory, the CGT took no action but simply declared 'people are free to vote.' At the second vote, different coloured ballot papers were used, and CGT observers carefully scrutinised how workers voted. At Polymécanique (Pantin) the CGT confused the issue by announcing that the vote was not for or against a return, but for or against the management proposals. At Crédit Lyonnais Paris, there was no supervision of the ballot so one could vote several times. At Thomson-Gennevilliers, before the ballot took place, the CGT distributed a leaflet and sold **L'Humanité**, both declaring that Thomson had returned to work having gained great advantages. To make sure their declarations would be proved correct, they allowed non-strikers to vote. At Sev-Marchal, Issy-les-Moulineaux, not only non-strikers but also foremen and supervisors and even management were allowed to participate in the vote on the return.
>
> In this situation of fragmented return, the role of information was crucial, for obviously the decision whether or not to return was dependent on decisions elsewhere. The bourgeois state and press combined its efforts with the CGT. Teachers first learnt that they were to return to work by a radio announcement. A standard technique of the CGT was to announce in one factory that other factories had decided to return.
>
> In Paris transport — underground and buses — the trade union representatives were the only ones who went from one depot to another. To the workers of each depot they said: 'You are against the return to work, but you are on your own. Everybody else wants to return to work.' Thus, while the depot at *rue* Lebrun had voted to carry on the strike, other depots had been told that it had voted for a return. After talking to the union officials, the elected strike committee at Lebrun, hearing that all the other depots were back at work, ordered a return, ignoring the vote already taken. At last, as a result of this method, after four weeks of strike, the transport workers were demoralised enough to vote for a return to work.[139]

The elections held at the end of June were a triumph for de Gaulle's strategy. The Gaullists and their close allies increased their parliamentary representation from 240 to 358 (out of 487); the PCF fell from 73 deputies to 34 and the Left Federation from 118 to 57. The PCF's vote fell by around 600,000 and the Left Federation's by some 570,000. The one bright spot was the fact that the PSU, the only party which had clearly identified with the students and the action committees, got an extra 379,000 votes, 75 per cent more than its score in the 1967 elections, although it lost all its three deputies. The revolutionary left did not present candidates and in general opposed participation in the elections.[140]

At first sight it seems incomprehensible that a social movement as profound as that of May 1968 could be followed so rapidly by a landslide electoral victory for the right. Certainly it is true that various factors mean that the simple figures are deceptive. The result in terms of parliamentary seats grossly overstated the actual trend of voting: there was a Gaullist deputy for every 27,000 Gaullist voters, but 135,000 Communist voters were needed for each PCF deputy.[141] The most militant elements in May had been students and young workers, but there were no votes for those under twenty-one. One can only speculate how five million young people between sixteen and twenty-one might have voted if they had had the chance. Two million immigrant workers also had no votes. Communists who tried to give election material to servicemen were arrested, while Gaullist propaganda was circulated inside a naval base.[142]

But while these facts clarify the picture, we are still left with the indisputable reality that the left did very badly in the elections. A major part of the explanation must lie in the fact that the reformist leadership of the workers' movement was still in full retreat by the time of the elections. Many of those who had been frightened by the May events, but who had dared do nothing but keep their heads down while the movement was advancing, now flocked to the polls to vote for law and order. The extreme right-wing tone of de Gaulle's campaign and his gestures to the ex-OAS leaders undoubtedly won him some extreme right-wing votes he had not had in previous elections. Meanwhile some Communist voters abandoned their party in disgust at its opportunist role during the strike. Some turned to the PSU; others simply did not bother to vote. The left also paid for its failure to involve non-working women, many of whom probably swelled the total of right-wing votes.[143]

The most basic lesson of all, however, is that the working class was wrong to take on de Gaulle on the terrain of elections. Workers' unique strength lies in the workplaces, not in the ballot-box. Not only the particular disadvantages listed above, but the whole context of electoral politics necessarily favours the right. The electoral catastrophe was merely the confirmation of a defeat that had in fact taken place in the first days of June as the return to work began.

The Legacy

May 1968 in France remains a crucial date in the history of the international working class. It is an experience from which a number of simple but vital lessons can be learnt.

Firstly, it showed that even in a highly sophisticated advanced capitalist country the working class has the power and the potential to call the whole system into question.

Secondly, it showed how a mass strike penetrates into every sector of society, and raises demands that go far beyond the confines of trade unionism to make questions of control central to the struggle.

Thirdly, it showed that, in the absence of a revolutionary leadership, reformism can regain control of even the most radical movement and pull it back into the framework of the existing order.

Moreover, May 1968 opened up a period of struggle between reformism and revolutionary politics that is still not completed. It redrew the map of the French left.

The first casualty of the events was the Left Federation which broke up in November 1968. Initially the PCF seemed much more resilient, regaining its lost electorate in the 1969 presidential election; indeed its membership continued to grow until the mid-1970s. But in fact 1968 saw the beginning of a long-term decline for the PCF. After 1968 it could no longer make any claim to be a revolutionary organisation; it had firmly declared itself to be a constitutional and parliamentary party. Yet the more the PCF tried to look like a social democratic party, the more the electors preferred the real social democrats — better a real sheep than a wolf in sheep's clothing. François Mitterrand's newly regrouped Socialist Party remorselessly outflanked and overtook the PCF during the 1970s. Mitterrand's record of openness to the left in 1968 clearly stood him in good stead with the younger generation of activists and voters.

When Mitterrand was elected president in 1981 many observers compared the scenes of public celebration to the events of 1968. But if Mitterrand had co-opted many of the militants of 1968, he had also picked up some of their enemies. His first government contained as industry minister Pierre Dreyfus, who had been managing director of Renault during the 1968 strike, and a senior position in the ministry of the interior went to Maurice Grimaud, head of the Paris police during 1968.

The revolutionary left derived a major impetus from May 1968. Ideas which had previously been the property of tiny groups now gained a wider credibility and influence. The modest but significant scores since obtained by revolutionary electoral candidates shows that the ideas of 1968 still have an audience.[144]

Yet 1968 also left the revolutionary left with a deep problem. Revolutionaries who, in 1968, had seen the question of state power appearing on the agenda, often found it difficult to recognise that the level of struggle had fallen again. Hence a part of the post-1968 left collapsed into wild ultra-leftism, trying to keep insurrection alive by pure will-power; thus the Maoist **La Cause du Peuple** was banned in 1970 for advocacy of murder, theft, pillage and arson. For others the concern to keep politics on the level of broad national solutions led to a preoccupation with running election campaigns or calling for governmental combinations between Socialists and Communists. Such activity often seemed more glamorous than getting involved in small strikes; yet it led revolutionaries to stray from the real task of developing their roots in the working-class movement. At times it seemed that the brief moment of glory in 1968 had become an albatross around the neck of the revolutionary left.

Yet amid a downturn that still has the whole world in its grasp, and after the five bleak years of 'socialist' government in France, the memory of May 1968 burns bright. It reminds us that there are moments when even the wildest dreams of revolutionaries become reality. For that, if for nothing else, it should never be forgotten.

TWO

CHILE 1972-73
The workers united
Mike Gonzalez

ON 27 OCTOBER 1972 Chile's lorrymen locked their vehicles, in a conscious act of class hostility. These were not wage-earners, but lorry *owners*, some of them with whole fleets that transported goods along the roads of this long thin country. This was a bosses' strike.

The limited size of the national railway network gave the lorrymen a crucial economic role,[1] and a real power — if they chose to use it. That October, the government's decision to nationalise a small transport firm in the far south of the country, at Aysen, provided the pretext for them to act. The decision to strike was announced by Leon Vilarin, the leader of the lorrymen's organisation. Vilarin himself, a lawyer, was a well-known politician of the extreme right;[2] but the strike was not the product of a small right-wing conspiracy. It was a key move in a whole strategy in which the lorrymen were allotted the role of shock troops for a whole class, set on clawing back the control over the Chilean state which it felt it had lost.

The October strike began a second stage in that political and economic strategy. The previous months had seen a rising level of middle-class mobilisation and a number of political victories against the government. By October, the leaders of the right-wing opposition had judged the time was right to move to the offensive and bring down the government.

As it turned out, events took a direction as unexpected for the Chilean bourgeoisie as it was for the government of Salvador Allende. Allende's victory in the 1970 presidential elections set the whole chain of events in motion. Allende had been carried to power on a wave of working-class activity to which the bourgeoisie had been able to offer no response. Officially assuming the presidency in December 1970, Allende initiated a series of fairly limited measures of social and economic reform. In themselves the reforms were offensive only to the most entrenched sectors of the old ruling class.[3] But the Chilean bourgeoisie saw them as a massive political threat — not because of their *content*, but because of the context in which they were carried through. Allende's election had been the result of a growth of political confidence in the working class, and the victory enhanced that confidence and strength. For the first nine months of the new government the bourgeoisie's political leadership was in disarray: its political response was limited to blocking actions in courts and parliament, to acts of protest and demonstrations of discontent designed to rally its own class.

But by late 1972, the active leaders of the right — such as Vilarin — judged that Allende's working-class support was waning. The economic successes of the first year had given way to a deepening economic crisis expressed in inflation, disinvestment and a deliberate slowdown in production.[4] The Allende government found itself increasingly in conflict with the workers and pesants who had voted for it as, with growing desperation, it sought to reassure the bourgeoisie that it was prepared to make concessions over any and all further reforms. The economic situation was becoming more and more difficult, and the defensive strategies of the ruling class — basically a systematic go-slow in both production and distribution, coupled with a refusal to invest — were now giving way to a more sustained attempt to create economic chaos. The lorrymen's strike was part of this effort.

And it might have succeeded — had the working class not erupted on to the political stage and taken control of the streets and the factories. Twice in less than twelve months, the organisations of the working class seized the political initiative and defeated the mobilised bourgeoisie in direct confrontation. And twice the workers' traditional political leaders, who shared control of the state with Salvador Allende, proved themselves more afraid of the Chilean workers' strength and organisation than of their class enemies.

The events in Chile offer a dramatic paradox. The working class exercised its power directly in defence of its gains; yet, as that defence began to grow into a challenge to the bourgeois state itself, so the response of the traditional political leadership of the working-class movement was to call in the military to restore the power of that state. Thus was the context created in which a frightened ruling class would move to the most barbaric and brutal resolution to the class struggle — the military coup of 11 September 1973.

In the years since the coup, the Chilean example has been used around the world, by Communist and Social Democratic parties alike, as evidence that in today's conditions any process of change must be limited to what is acceptable to the bourgeoisie — the 'historic compromise'. Chile, in these terms, has been used to justify those parties' renunciation of the struggle to bring the working class to power.[5] Yet the conclusion those parties drew involved falsifying and rewriting the actual experience of that dramatic period in the class struggle.

The limited promise of Popular Unity

Salvador Allende had come to power as the representative of a coalition of six parties called Popular Unity (UP); it was his sixth appearance as the candidate of a broad front of this kind. The major components of UP were the Socialist Party, of which Allende was a member, and the Chilean Communist Paty. Both organisations could justly claim to be the political leadership of the Chilean working class. Their hegemony was the product of a consistent history of proletarian struggle, beginning with the heroic strikes of the nitrate workers in the first decade of the century.

The Chilean Communist Party was founded in 1920 by Luis Emilio Recabarren, one of Latin America's most important revolutionary organisers. The Socialist Party,[6] formed in the early 1940s, also claimed revolutionary credentials — indeed, even in 1970, its constitution still proclaimed its commitment to the armed overthrow of the capitalist state. Yet both parties had displayed an unerring commitment to electoral alliances, forming broad front organisations for every six-yearly presidential election. Nonetheless, their roots among the working class went deep, and it was these that provided the 36 per cent of the popular vote acquired by Allende in the 1970 elections.

Since Allende obviously did not win a majority of the votes, the victory of his Popular Unity coalition has often been ascribed to divisions within the bourgeoisie.[7] Certainly, their organisations had fallen to bickering and factionalism after the failure of the 'Revolution in Liberty' — the programme for controlled development and reform promised by the Christian Democratic government of Eduardo Frei (1964-70). But an explanation in terms of bourgeois failures ignores the active role of the labouring classes.

The Frei government's failure to enact its promised reforms had set in motion an increasingly combative working-class movement. In 1967, for example, the government's removal of the ban on rural trade unions coincided with the passage of agrarian reform legislation. This measure had then met with the obdurate resistance of the landowning oligarchy, a class that Frei was neither prepared nor willing to confront. The agrarian reform, whose intention was to create a stable class of small farmers, was designed to assuage rural tensions; the result was the very opposite. Those who had hoped to benefit from the land reform, and had voted for Christian Democracy to that purpose, now felt defrauded. The landless peasants who were promised nothing, on the other hand, had already launched a wave of land occupations.

Frei had promised industrial growth, and the promise had attracted the rural unemployed to the cities. Earlier waves of rural migrants had established themselves in the working-class areas, building squatter towns on vacant plots; they had then begun to organise and fight for the right to housing land and for basic facilities.[8] Their organisations were to play an important role in the events of 1972 and 1973.

Both the landless peasants and the squatters lay outside the traditional organisations of the working class and their political leadership. They were therefore open to the political influence of a third section radicalised by the period — the student movement. In 1968-9, a general movement for educational reform had developed in Chile, culminating in a great march on the capital, Santiago, from every corner of the country. But other currents flowed into this movement too. A generation of young revolutionaries had been influenced by the Cuban Revolution of 1959 and by a revolutionary romanticism symbolised by Che Guevara; in Chile that current had found expression in the formation, in 1965, of the Revolutionary Movement of the Left (MIR). And if Frei's reformist experiment had been intended to provide a non-revolutionary alternative for change, its failure had produced a second group of radicalised young reformers: organised in the United Popular Action Movement (MAPU) and the Christian Left,[9] their main energies had been directed to organising the land reform programme. When the Frei government appeared to abandon their commitment to that programme, MAPU joined the UP coalition.

The crisis of the Frei government had not only affected previously unorganised sectors. Within the Socialist Party, a long-standing political division re-asserted itself, in a debate over whether trade-union organisation or parliamentary electioneering should occupy the central place in the party's activities.[10] This old debate did not re-surface by accident, but under the pressure of developments within the working-class movement. Early in 1968, the Chilean trade union federation, the CUT, had called a national strike in protest against Frei's plans for no-strike agreements. The strike's success had fuelled the combativity of the working class: in 1968 and 1969 the workers had faced price increases of around 50 per cent, rising unemployment and an increasingly repressive response from government. Strikes had increased in number from 1,939, involving 230,725 workers, in 1969 to 5,295, involving 316,280 workers, in 1970.

This, then, was the climate in which Allende gained the presidency in 1970. The UP's political programme attempted to reconcile the sometimes conflicting interests of the social forces on whose support the coalition depended. In any event, Allende proposed to enact only those reforms that could be carried out under existing legislation, and which could win the approval of a Congress dominated by the Right. That put severe constraints on what was possible and effectively allowed the right wing to determine the pace of change. Given his resolutely electoralist perspective, Allende would do nothing to alienate the middle-class voters — the much-vaunted 'middle sectors' — who could give him a parliamentary majority. Paradoxically, he could win their vote only to the extent that the government was able to demonstrate its ability to control and restrain working-class activity.

In the economy, UP set out to complete Frei's unfinished programme of growth and modernisation by raising consumption through a general wage increase, thus reactivating much of Chile's unused industrial capacity. In agriculture, Allende undertook to carry through the 1967 Agrarian Reform Act *as it stood*, including its provisions for generous compensation to landowners, coupled with the guarantee that they could keep for their own use the richest 500 acres and the best of the farm machinery.

The central element of the package, however, was the nationalisation without compensation of the US-owned copper mines.[11] Though it had been some years since the US companies had invested anything, the nationalisation gave the Allende government control over Chile's major export industry. On the other hand, while UP's total programme encompassed the nationalisation of the country's key industrial and financial interests, it left the majority of enterprises in private hands.[12] UP envisaged taking into the state sector only 150 out of 3,500 industrial firms, representing 40 per cent of total production, and this figure was later reduced.

There was nothing revolutionary in the UP package, despite assertions in the world's media that Chile had just elected its first 'Marxist' president. In content it differed little from the Frei reform programme, being an orthodox Keynesian plan for reactivating the economy. It contained no challenge to the dominance of private capital; on the contrary, it gave the industrial bourgeoisie a range of guarantees and provided landowners with generous compensation.

The real difference between UP and Frei lay in UP's relationship with the working class. Its major contribution to the Chilean capitalist revival was that it could control the working class and exact working-class support for the programme of economic growth.

Yet even that was not enough to allay bourgeois suspicion. So, as a final proof of his respect for the bourgeois state and his commitment to its survival, and in exchange for the right-wing parties allowing him to assume the presidency in November 1970, Allende put his signature to a 'Statute of Guarantees'.[13] This document promised that the Allende government would respect the state and its structures and leave intact all those instruments which the bourgeoisie had evolved to defend its class interests — the education system, the Church, the mass media and the armed forces. The Statute was kept virtually secret and was never presented to the UP's supporters. Its existence renders cynical and hollow the assertions, by some Communist Party theorists, that UP had 'captured part of power' from which to mount an assault on the remaining institutions of the state. In fact, the Statute was a promise *not* to enact any fundamental transformation of Chilean society.

The UP strategy, therefore, assumed a collaboration between private capital and the state to achieve economic growth. Some banks and insurance companies, as well as the copper mines, would be nationalised; but the government would also offer a range of state subsidies to private capital. The long-term aim was a mixed economy of three sectors — state, private and mixed.

The UP's strategy involved, of course, a parallel collaboration at the political level. When Allende spoke of 'popular power' in his early presidential speeches,[14] he certainly was not referring to any grass roots initiative or any struggle for workers' power. The Statute of Guarantees and Allende's continuing dialogue with the bourgeoisie, coupled with his continuing calls for restraint and self-discipline from the working class, left the political initiative with the bourgeoisie. Such organistions as were formed with government support in the first months of 1971 were essentially instruments for carrying out or winning support for government measures — such as the local supply and distribution committees (JAPs) or the local 'branches' of the UP, the UP commitees. Obviously, Allende's many references to 'popular power' in his first months of government meant an unquestioning acceptance of the decisions of the UP leadership.

Murmurings of discontent

For the first year of the UP government, Allende's credibility remained largely intact. Yet unresolved tensions lay just beneath the surface. For if the election victory had been a response to a rising level of struggle, it also encouraged the idea that gains could only be made through struggle. Many sectors of workers and peasants saw no reason why Allende's arrival in the Presidential Palace should involve their demobilisation. The organisations of landless peasants, for example, encouraged by UP's commitment to agrarian reform, intensified their land seizures. In May 1971 Allende called upon them to stop occupying land and to await the legal process. He also called in the leadership of the MIR, which enjoyed an influence over the peasant and shanty town organisations, and rebuked them for acting outside the framework of law.

At this stage, Allende was willing to discuss the matter; but his and his colleagues' attacks on these and other independent initiatives intensified as the first year wore on. The working-class organisations, on the other hand, generally exhibited more obedience. There were few brushes between organised workers and government in the first half of 1971. For one thing, the parties of UP firmly controlled the trade unions; and, for another, the union members had been the main beneficiaries of the wage rises and new jobs resulting from the re-activation of the economy. In the first year, manual workers' wages rose by 38 per cent, those of white-collar workers by 120 per cent. Unemployment fell below 10 per cent, and GDP rose overall by 8 per cent.[15]

The relative tranquillity of the first months was simply the calm before the storm. The bourgeoisie was only biding its time, healing its own wounds and awaiting the correct moment for a counter-attack. Chile's industrialists had not let 1971 pass them by. They exported as much of their capital as they could and reinvested nothing — government subsidies were in many cases the only funds going into the factories.[16] The rising living standards of workers brought a dramatic rise in consumer demand and consequent shortages, exacerbated by systematic hoarding of goods by the middle classes. The atmosphere of scarcity and insecurity provided the bourgeoisie with the right circumstances in which to mount their first challenge to Allende.

The moment was carefully chosen. In November 1971, Fidel Castro visited Chile. On the second day of his visit, he was greeted by a demonstration, the 'March of the Empty Pots'. Organised by the right-wing parties, hundreds of middle-class women came on to the streets waving empty saucepans to symbolise shortages. The irony was that many of them brought their maids along — presumably to help them carry the pots and pans few of the marching ladies ever used themselves. But behind the protests over consumer shortages lay another and more far-reaching purpose; to mobilise the middle classes, to warn the bourgeoisie on an international scale of the battles to come, and to express bourgeois scepticism as to the UP's ability to contain the working class.

For it was true that, despite UP's pleas and its thinly veiled attacks on strikers and squatters, Allende had not been able to control the working-class movement entirely. Between January and December 1971, the number of strikes reached 1,758 and there had been 1,278 land invasions.[17] The bourgeois parties responded by attacking the government, seeking the impeachment of interior minister Jose Toha, and blocking nationalisation measures in parliament. Outside parliament, they complained of 'Illegal occupations [which were] not only the work of the ultraleft; they [were] also the spontaneous actions of groups of peasants, workers and miners.'[18]

Curiously, Allende and his enemies agreed on this point: that the greatest threat to the continuing dialogue on which his strategy rested was the independent action of the working class itself! UP's Economic Plan for 1971 was discussed at length with the opposition groups and the professional and technocratic organisations; at no stage, however, was it discussed publicly or submitted to the trade unions for approval. It was hardly surprising, therefore, that workers should respond to the growth of the black market, shortages and the renewal of inflation by reactivating their traditional organisations of struggle — trade unions in particular — to protect the gains they had made.

Cracks in the coalition

As UP began its second year in office, the right-wing offensive and the independent working-class response to it provoked a new debate. For while Allende's reaction to these developments was to move to assuage bourgeois fears, this created tensions in UP's relations with its own supporters, and provoked fundamental questions about the so-called 'Chilean Road to Socialism'. Two very different strategies co-existed within UP, and events now demanded a resolution. Should UP support the workers in their struggle to defend their living standards and to stop the bourgeoisie undermining their gains of the previous year, or should it not? And if it did, what political strategy did such support entail?

That was the central question facing the political representatives of UP's constituent organisations when they met in conference at El Arrayan in February 1972, and again at a recall conference at Lo Curro in June. The debate, on UP's future strategy, was centred on the issue labelled as *consolidar o avanzar* — whether to consolidate or advance. The right wing argued the need to halt the reform process, consolidate what had been gained, and seek wider electoral support before going on. Effectively, this would mortgage the 'Chilean Road to Socialism' to the middle-class sectors to whom the right devoted so much attention. The left advocated speeding up the pace of reform, deepening the nationalisation process and taking a lead from actual struggles. The working class, they argued, had shown it was ready to carry the struggle forward: would its political leaders take its lead from the class?

During the whole debate no one argued that any organisation should act outside UP.[19] Always the discussion was about what UP should do, from its position within the state.

The Communist Party and the right wing of the Socialist Party under Allende's leadership argued that the government should go no further in expanding the state sector; it should re-assert its readiness to negotiate with the bourgeoisie by demonstrating in practice that it could control the working class; and it should seek a broad consensus for its policies. Such a compromise, it was hoped, would lead the bourgeoisie to respect the gains already made — even though events had already shown the opposite to be true.

The counter-argument came from MAPU, the Christian Left and the left of the Socialist Party (it was also supported by the MIR, though they were not present at the discussions). The left urged the need to extend the public sector, to re-assert UP's original commitment to nationalise 90 major firms — by government decision that number had been reduced to 43 — and to engage actively in an ideological struggle to win new support.

The left's disagreements with the right were quantitative rather than qualitative. Their 'radicalism by number' never led them to question the *relationship* between the state and private capital, nor the control and direction of the economy as a whole. The whole of the left seemed to agree that 'part of the power' had been conquered; none expressed concern over the other 'parts of power' that Allende had guaranteed to the bourgeoisie. Confused rhetoric was often the order of the day. MAPU called on the government to 'use the state apparatus with a mass style': hardly a clear alternative policy! MAPU's indecisiveness had already been revealed at its own national conference in January 1972: it had given vigorous support to a new joint CUT-UP plan for workers' participation in industry, which in fact offered a *retreat* from nationalisation; and it had joined the rest of UP in condemning the 'ultra-leftism' of the MIR. Were its allegiances with the left, or the right?[20]

To read the discussions and debates that took place in the UP conferences is to gain a growing sense of unreality. The fine and stirring speeches ignored the fact that the future direction of the Chilean political process was being determined outside Congress and well away from the presidential palace at La Moneda. In January, before the El Arrayan conference, Allende had already surrendered to demands that Jose Toha be impeached for insulting the armed forces, and had accepted his resignation. In March, Kennecott — a US copper company whose Chilean subsidiary had been nationalised — called for a worldwide embargo on Chilean copper; and the Christian Democratic Senator Carlos Hamilton set down the first of a series of Congress motions intended to paralyse any further nationalisations. Allende's response to that was so weak that, in April, he felt obliged to make a conciliatory move towards the UP left, opening formal talks with the MIR as a gesture to the left in general — though he did not offer to compromise on his strategic differences with the MIR.

On 12 May the shape of things to come was clearly revealed in an incident in the major industrial city of Concepcion. A right-wing student organisation announced its intention to march through the city. A counter-demonstration was called by a number of left-wing organisations, including the MIR. The Communist mayor then placed a general ban on all marches and called in the riot police against the counter-demonstration. The resulting violence left one MIR supporter dead. The government's response, through its Communist spokesman, Daniel Vergara, was to condemn violence, whether of the left or the right.[21]

Also in May, a national congress of workers in the textile industry rejected workers' participation and instead demanded workers' control of industry and the accountability of all officials. The answer to this came in June, in the announcement of a new UP Cabinet which notably did not include Pedro Vuskovic, a left independent whose public identification with a policy of further nationalisation had made him a favourite target for the right.

In the same month, UP's conference on strategy re-assembled in Lo Curro, where the right wing now secured a victory. One reason was that the left had no clear alternative to offer, even if the left-wing socialists had begun to discuss at Lo Curro some of the demands for a 'Popular Assembly' or 'popular power' emerging from the textile workers' congress.[22] At the same time, Allende resumed talks with the Christian Democrats (they had briefly been suspended a month earlier) and restated his commitment to the pursuit of social peace and the rule of law. What this meant in practice, however, was dramatically revealed at Melipilla, near Santiago, in the course of June 1972.

A number of farms in the area were large enough to be expropriated under the agrarian reform law. But the local judge, Olate, had repeatedly placed legal obstacles in the way of the land redistribution and had consistently collaborated with the local landowners. On 22 June, a demonstration in the town centre led to the arrest of twenty-two leading members of the agricultural workers' organisation. A series of protest demonstrations followed; on the 30th all highways into the town were blocked. On 12 July a mass demonstration marched into central Santiago demanding the release of the twenty-two and the immediate sacking of Judge Olate. The government refused to intervene.[23]

The incidents at Melipilla had a far deeper significance than was at first apparent. In the course of the protests workers from the neighbouring industrial area of Cerrillos joined their rural comrades in the struggle. Cerrillos itself was locked in a series of unresolved industrial disputes: at the end of June, the Perlak and Polycron textile plants, the Las Americas aluminium works and the Cerrillos chicken factory were all on strike. The strikers now joined their brothers and sisters in Melipilla. One agricultural worker said: 'We've people to feed and families to keep. And we've had it up to here' — and his interviewer noted that the rural and urban workers he was speaking to agreed that 'parliament did not represent their interests'. The protestors, while chorusing their support for Allende, complained that the Congress and other state institutions were the main obstacle to carrying out the UP programme.

Yet the joint action of agricultural and industrial workers opened up new and very different possibilities. For out of the joint struggle there emerged a new form of *organisation*, forged in the course of the strikes at Cerrillos and calling itself the 'industrial belt' — the *cordon*. Another *cordon* developed in the Vicuna McKenna area. The Cerrillos *cordon* published a declaration early in July. Its demands for workers' control of production and the replacement of parliament by a workers' assembly went far beyond anything that had been openly discussed by the political parties of the left. Yet at this stage the *cordon* was still described by the radical paper **Chile Hoy** as a committee for maintaining production and implementing government decisions in the economy. Its potential as an alternative base of social and political organisation did not yet enter anyone's head.[24]

The Communist Party and the right wing of the Socialist Party ordered their members to have nothing to do with the *cordones*. All action, they argued, must be coordinated through the official union leadership, the CUT. This reflected the 'consolidationist' line that had emerged triumphant from the Lo Curro conference. For the right, there would be no further encroachments against private capital, no challenges to the state; concessions to the bourgeoisie would, Allende argued, ensure their respect for constitutional procedures.

It was only the workers themselves, it seemed, who realised that the class struggle does not stand still — that the only way to defend what had been won was to intensify the struggle. The alternative was to allow the bourgeoisie to fight to regain what it had lost. Paradoxically, the growing popular support for UP, reflected both in the results of a July by-election at Coquimbo, and in elections for the CUT executive,[25] expressed that realisation among workers. The right wing, however, interpreted that support differently — as representing approval for the UP strategy of class collaboration.

The contradictions of the situation were becoming increasingly visible, as incident after incident brought the government into confrontation with sections of workers, peasants, students or shanty town dwellers. In July, members of an ultra-left group who had carried out a bank raid were caught and tortured by the security police, at whose head was Allende's personal appointee, Contreras. In the mining areas, the government dealt with strikes over local issues by invoking a state of emergency, with the effect that the mining areas were put under direct military control.

On 18 August the police and the military raided the shanty town complex of Lo Hermida, in Santiago.[26] Ostensibly they were looking for other members of an ultra-left guerrilla group; in fact, Lo Hermida was politically a no man's land for UP. Here, as in other slum areas, the MIR enjoyed a dominant political position through front organisations like the Revolutionary Shanty Town Movement (MRP).[27] The police operation met with mass resistance; they retreated and returned the following day with 400 armed men. The assault that followed left one person dead, another fatally wounded, eleven injured and 160 under arrest. Although Allende later offered apologies to Lo Hermida for the raid, the fact was that the government had used the incident to attack the revolutionary left, to warn off all those who were beginning to act outside the constitutional framework, and to reassure the bourgeoisie of the government's determination to guarantee law and order. For the bourgeoisie itself, raids like Lo Hermida were early skirmishes in which it could test the military's muscle and ability to act directly.

For Allende, the central issue was the political authority of UP. While UP undoubtedly retained political hegemony within the working-class movement, the struggle itself posed political questions that could not be answered within the framework of the UP's reformism. If the workers' and peasants' organisations were demobilised because they lay outside UP control, what guarantees could the governent offer in return that the right to protest and demonstration would not be curtailed by the police or threatened by armed right-wing groups? Would Allende take on the factory owners and stop them closing or sabotaging their plants if the workers themselves did not do it? Would Allende lead the workers' side in the class struggle as it intensified, or would he continue to try to play the role of referee?

It was just these questions that would dominate the Popular Assembly at Concepcion at the end of July, when some 3,000 delegates met to discuss the political conjuncture.[28] They represented a wide range of organisations — trade union, popular, student — as well as the organisations of the left. The sole absentee was the Communist Party, which described the Concepcion Assembly, in time-honoured fashion, as 'a manoeuvre by reaction and imperialism, using elements of the ultra-left as a cover'. Allende himself, in a statement issued on 31 July, developed the same idea:

> For the second time in three months Concepcion has been the scene for a divisive action whose effect is to undermine the homogeneity of the Pouplar Unity movement. There is no doubt in my mind that it is a process that serves the interests of the enemies of the revolutionary cause.

In the same speech he defined with absolute clarity his commitment to bourgeois democracy and his opposition to the development of a dual power 'which in other historical situations arose in opposition to a reactionary power structure which had neither social base nor support'. In Chile, he argued, the creation of organs of dual power was an act of 'crass irresponsibility', because the government of Chile represented the interests of the working class as a whole. No sensible revolutionary, he concluded, 'can conceivably ignore the institutional system which governs our society and *which forms part of the government of Popular Unity*. Anyone who suggests otherwise must be considered a counter-revolutionary'.[29]

Within the Assembly itself there were disagreements, especially regarding the relationship with Allende. While MAPU and the Left Socialists believed the Assembly should exert organised pressure on the government to press forward its programme, the MIR called for the elaboration of a revolutionary programme. Yet even the MIR was cautious in its specific conclusions, and at no time called for the formation of a new revolutionary organisation built upon the organisations of struggle represented at the Assembly. Still there was no recognition that the quickening *pace* of the struggle and its generalisation demanded something more than simple support. The logic of events pointed towards the question of the state itself — whose interests did it represent and defend? Yet that question would and could only be posed by a revolutionary leadership prepared to put the issue of power on the agenda.

The incidents at Lo Hermida took on a new, and retrospectively more sinister significance a few weeks later when a state of emergency was again imposed, this time in Bio Bio province where demonstrators moved to defend a pro-government radio station under attack from the right. It was becoming clear that Allende was prepared to use the state against his own supporters, and to call in the army and the police to restore the existing law and the given (bourgeois) order.[30]

Despite their attempts to arrest the process, the class struggle was fast slipping out of the control of Allende and the UP. The bourgeoisie saw his vacillations as a factor in their favour, and openly organised a campaign of political opposition and economic sabotage. On Channel 9 TV, the extreme right-wing priest Father Hasbun had begun to issue calls for military action against Allende at the end of July.

The UP leaders, condemning violence and civil war, were calling on the working class to leave it to the government to respond to the right's mobilisations; yet the government had already shown that far from responding to these threats it simply gave way before them and placed its faith in the police and the military. Thus, at the end of September, when Allende announced a planned Arms Control Law, this was clearly directed at the organisations of workers, and left the army with the task of disarming them. None of these concessions had the effect Allende claimed they would have; on the contrary, each time the workers' leadership declared its unwillingness to fight, the bourgeoisie grew more confident and certain that the working class would offer no response to its attacks.

There was certainly confidence in ruling-class circles, therefore, when in September, Chile's shopkeepers launched a protest strike against price controls and shortages. That confidence was still higher on 11 October, when the lorry owners announced the beginning of an indefinite strike.

They were to get a rude shock — not from Allende and his allies, who continued to deny that a fundamental struggle for power now existed, but from the working class, which took direct control over the struggle and generated a range of new forms of organisation which offered a glimpse of how the struggle for workers' power should be conducted and could be won.

The insurrection of the bourgeoisie

The lorry-owners' strike had been well planned; though it had general approval from the whole of the bourgeosie, the neo-fascist organisation, *Patria y Libertad*, was most directly involved in its actual organisation. Members of this group provided armed guards at the fortified compounds of the edges of all Chile's major cities where the lorrymen took their vehicles on 11 October.

The strike was neither unexpected nor particularly secret. The shopkeepers' strike in September and the well-organised right-wing resistance in Congress to every UP initiative had given clear forewarning. In any case, two left-wing journals had provided detailed information about the strike (its code name was *Plan Septiembre*) a fortnight before it began.[31] If any doubt remained, a mass rally of the right on 10 October in Santiago was notable for its frenzied atmosphere and for the calls, by one platform speaker after another, for mass mobilisation against the government. Indeed one of those speakers was Vogel, a Christian Democrat vice-president of the CUT.

Yet neither Allende nor the UP offered any response at all. In the previous months Allende had resolved each potential crisis by calling on the army to restore order. Yet now, as the lorrymen's strike loomed, it seemed that Allende was deliberately ignoring the Right's preparations, pretending that nothing was happening; it seemed that his fear of independent mass activity was greater than his concern about right-wing opposition to his government.

The impact of the strike might have been expected to be immediate. The absence of road transport could rapidly have halted all supplies — of food, spare parts, raw materials, and especially the distribution of food for the working class. Further, the strike did not take place in isolation. The shopkeepers expressed their support for the lorrymen by closing their shops; the factory owners attempted to stop their machines, by sabotage if necessary. The professional organisations of doctors, lawyers, dentists and others voted to join the strike and suspend all activity, adding to the atmosphere of panic. That indeed was the strategy of the right; to use their economic power — a power that was still largely intact — to create shortages and economic chaos. The assumption was that the resulting panic would either force Allende to resign or, better still, leave him in power to impose the necessary austerity measures, to become completely alienated from UP's mass base, and finally to suffer resounding defeat at the Congressional elections in March 1973.

If that strategy failed, it was entirely thanks to the working class. For the workers the situation was equally clear. The immediate problem was to maintain the transport system, keep the factories open and ensure the supply of food and necessities. Groups of workers took to the streets on the first morning; every available form of transport was commandeered and driven by volunteers. In the factories, vigilance committees were formed to guard against sabotage and production was maintained. In the working-class areas, long patient queues formed outside the stores and supermarkets; either the owners were then persuaded to open them or, if not, the stores were opened and kept open by the local people themselves, who mounted permanent guard. In central Santiago, more than 8,000 people volunteered as drivers, while several of the *cordones* sent groups of people to 're-possess' lorries.[32]

The government's first response was characterically confused, and confusing. Allende called for production to be maintained but then turned immediately to negotiation with the lorrymen. His choice as intermediary — the organisation of municipal bus-owners — proved to be less than reliable: they themselves joined the lorrymen a week later. The general line of UP was to call for discipline, calm and obedience to the official union and political organisations; yet neither the CUT nor UP provided any specific instructions, and indeed the initial call for mass mobilisation in response to the strike was withdrawn two days later.

The problems provoked by the strike, however, demanded immediate resolution. It was hardly surprising that the most vigorous and decisive response came from those areas which had already developed joint working-class organisations. The factories that had been involved in the first *cordones* were able to organise most quickly and take a lead in organising others; Elecmetal in the Vicuna McKenna *cordon*, and the Perlak, Lucchettipasta and Cristalerias Chile factories, part of the Cerrillos-Maipu *cordon*, gave a strong lead. Their demands were radical and sharply defined, echoing the programme first put forward in June: immediate action against the employers, including immediate nationalisation. At the same time, other devices developed by the capitalists demanded — and found — a quick and creative response.

At the Cristalerias Chile glass factory, for example, the management froze the company bank account. The workers responded by evolving a system of direct distribution. As one explained, 'now we sell direct to the co-ops and small businesses and they pay us in cash, so that we can pay wages without having to use the banks at all.'[33]

At the El Melon cement factory, a strike already in progress was immediately brought to an end and its workers returned to work. At the Perlak textile plant, to compensate for the lack of milk from the countryside, the workers organised a high-nutrition soup for their children. The Polycron workforce took their textiles to the working-class areas and sold them direct. Raw materials and finished goods began to be exchanged between factories, but also between workers and peasants.

When the doctors' association announced its support for the strike on 17 October, a joint committee of hospital workers was formed to keep the hospitals running. With a support demonstration going on behind him, one union organiser explained: 'Despite the strike ordered by the Right, the 600,000 people for whom this hospital is responsible will see that we can provide better and more efficient services by working together with the local health committees which include people from the working-class districts.'[34]

The journalists' union meeting that same day was given over to a denunciation of the role of the bourgeois press and calls for new initiatives against the right-wing media. One speaker at the meeting, the journalist Jaime Muñoz, criticised the Statute of Guarantees signed by Allende in 1970, which undertook to respect the existing ownership of the mass media.[35] He contrasted the role of the right-wing media in organising the strike with the response of the workers of two newspapers, **La Mañana** of Talca and **Sur** of Concepcion, who had occupied and taken over their respective offices because their papers were constantly attacking the working-class movement. 'The only statute of guarantees we recognise,' he argued, 'is the statute of guarantees we have given to the working class.'[36]

There had been a tacit agreement among the organisations of the left not to mention the Statute; this was one of the first public references to that crucial inhibiting document. In the aftermath of October, the return of the two expropriated newspapers became a key issue in the debate on the left.

There was a further reason for the rapid growth of autonomous organisations: self-defence. While the majority of the bourgeoisie were content to use their economic power, the extreme right, led by *Patria y Libertad*, organised its own terrorist groups to take the battle on to the streets.[37] These gangs, formed mainly by the young men of the wealthiest families, launched a series of direct physical attacks. On 12 October the officers of both the Socialist and the Communist Parties in Chile's most southerly city, Punta Arenas, were attacked. On the 13th the railway line to Arica, 2,000 miles to the north, was blocked; on the same day, a number of individuals and vehicles were attacked in the major cities of Valparaiso, Concepcion and Viña. The pattern of direct assaults continued through the days that followed.

In the factories, workers resisted the attempts at sabotage by the employers and took direct control over production. At the Sumar textile plant in Santiago, for example, the owner tried to remove parts from the machines, but was stopped by the workers and then thrown out of the factory. For the workers' committees, there could be no question of negotiation — after all, it was the government itself that had made the maintenance of production an absolute priority. One young woman, a 22-year-old worker at Fabrilana, put the question particularly clearly:

I think comrade Allende has been very soft; he says it's because he wants to avoid violence, but I think we should respond with more force, scare them to death. They're trying to take away what we've won.[38]

Workers at Alusa, a packaging plant in the city, echoed this:

Management called out the office workers and they did stop work. But we couldn't let ourselves be part of these manoeuvres. The bosses aren't going to tell us what to do . . . So we opened the stores, took out the raw materials, and just kept on producing — production didn't stop here for a single moment. And we won't stop now or ever. You can see people working with real joy. I think we've realised in these last few days that what we're defending is something more than just a plate of beans.[39]

No one was exempt from the possibility of attack. The workers at the Bata shoe chain, for example, formed defence committees at every one of its 113 outlets:

We've formed self-defence committees at every outlet to repel attacks. We've already had to face a number, particularly [at shops] in upper and middle-class neighbourhoods. But we haven't closed even for one day. We're against this strike and when it comes to the crunch we're not going to give in to anyone. Enough is enough.[40]

A worker from the Ready-Mix concrete plant succinctly summarised the experience:

We've got to thank the fascists for that anyway, for showing us that you can't make a revolution by playing marbles. When there's a problem, we workers have got to be in the front line. We've learned more in these few days than in all the previous two years.[41]

Similar conclusions were drawn elsewhere, particularly in the working-class districts where earlier battles over distribution, housing and so on had thrown up organisations which played a full and vital part in the working-class struggles of October. The JAPs, distribution committees originally formed by the government, became the organising core of a range of local and community organisations — neighbourhood committees, mothers' groups, squatters' associations — which carried the burden of resistance in the communities.[42] Most importantly of all, October brought these community organisations into direct contact with workers and made joint action a reality. The *cordon* now became, as it had promised to become, an organising centre for a number of struggles, coordinating them and providing them with a working-class leadership.

Almost certainly, had the workers not acted immediately, the bourgeoisie would have succeeded in its campaign, the economy would have been paralysed, and Allende would have had to accede to the employers' demands set out in the *Pliego de Chile*, their list of demands. Instead, the workers had requisitioned transport and kept the economy moving. The physical attacks by *Patria y Libertad* had met with organised workers' resistance, whether from district defence committees or the vigilance committees formed in the factories. These were an excellent illustration of the changes that had occurred in the course of struggle, for while they began as committees to oversee production, their function changed during the bosses' strike and they became organs of workers' control over the factories. The JAPs, too, committees set up to monitor distribution, grew into combative rank-and-file organisations, buying and distributing supplies, keeping open shops and supermarkets and defending them from right-wing assaults, and collectivising some of the domestic functions in the poor quarters, particularly the feeding of children in a collective kitchen, the *olla comun*.

There is no doubt that, in the aftermath of October, workers were held back from drawing appropriate political conclusions out of their concrete experience. The generalisation of ideas from specific circumstances does not arise spontaneously; it needs the conscious intervention of revolutionary socialists who can give it a framework, an understanding of past struggles of the working class, within which to grow. In Chile, however, the various political organisations actually inhibited political learning. Nonetheless, the experience of October had given the working class a whole new sense of its collective potential, and that posed serious problems for Allende and UP.

UP's initial call to the working class to act in defence of the government stemmed from the assumption that the workers' organisations would remain 'loyal' to the official leaderships, the CUT and UP itself.[43] But in the event, the working class had taken *independent* action to defend the government, without waiting for instructions. In these circumstances the workers might easily draw the conclusion that revolutionary action was necessary to revolve the crisis in Chile — and no one was more aware of this than Allende himself. After 11 October Allende hesitated and vacillated. But there was little doubt which way, when it came to it, he would turn. He had said it often enough:[44] UP staked its political future on its ability to control the working class and realise its programme for change in collaboration with a majority of the bourgeoisie.

Yet Allende and his colleagues in the political leadership of UP seemed blandly unaware that in October a historical frontier had been crossed, and that the bourgeoisie had long ago lost interest in collaboration. In a sense, the Allende government now became a spectator at the arena of class struggle, trying vainly to reimpose itself on events from the vantage point of the state.

October 1972 offered the most exciting and dramatic evidence of the possibilities of workers' power. Not only did the working class overcome the hesitations of their leadership by acting independently, but in the day-to-day reality of the struggle against the lorrymen and their supporters, old divisions were overcome and a new leadership was forged which was not trammelled by the political compromises or the sectional allegiances of the old trade union leadership. In part, this reflected the arrival on the political stage of groups of workers hitherto excluded from the trade unions or other organisations, workers less affected by the disciplines of party and union membership. Many of the smaller factories lay outside the ambit of CUT influence, for example, because they had fewer than 25 workers. What the *cordones* represented was an alliance between the organised and unorganised workers, the population of the shanty towns, the agricultural workers and some student organisations.

Their political character was less well defined. The CUT claimed they were simply its own base organisations by another name;[45] but the CUT's difficulties in imposing any kind of discipline on the *cordones*, coupled with its frequent attacks on the leaders of the *cordones*, suggested that the relationship was not what they claimed. MAPU, with characteristic ambiguity, described the *cordones* as 'patriotic committees'.[46] The Socialist Party, attempting as ever to reconcile within itself two conflicting political traditions, described them as 'active schools of the masses to discuss problems, exercise constructive criticism, plan solutions and coordinate initiatives.'[47]

As for the MIR, it certainly enjoyed considerable influence among the most marginal sectors of the population through its various front organisations. Yet while the MIR was most overtly critical of the UP's attempt to hamstring and manipulate the *cordones* and other base organisations, and while it employed at times a revolutionary rhetoric, it had no alternative strategy to offer. In the end, the MIR shared with all the other left organisations a fundamentally weak analysis: all acknowledged UP's failure to lead the masses' counter-attack against the bosses, but drew the conclusion that UP should reform itself in the light of their critique — and thus be better prepared to lead the struggle the next time around.

No one on the left saw UP's contradictory postures during October for what they were: the faithful expression of its political perspective. As a result, the left remained disoriented in the face of a new and shocking development.

Faced with a strike by airline pilots, beginning on 31 October, and with the lorrymen's refusal the next day to end their action, Allende decided to invite several generals to join his Cabinet. At the same time, he declared a national state of emergency — thus placing

Chile's government effectively in the hands of the military for the period of the emergency.

The struggle to defeat the bosses' strike had brought the Chilean working class on to the political stage as an independent actor, and for several weeks the day-to-day practice of workers' self-government had been developing in a way that was more and more apparent. The meaning of Allende's decision to turn to the army, there can be no question, was that UP was forcibly removing the historical initiative from the working class, under the guise of restraining the bourgeoisie.

Allende's decision has been justified in retrospect by decribing the situation in Chile at the beginning of November as one of 'near chaos', of 'a breakdown of law and order'.[48] In fact, it was not the breakdown of order which was occurring, but the profound crisis of *an* order. As new forms of organisation and activity evolved among the workers, so their traditional organisations were less and less able to contain them within the boundaries of a pre-established negotiation between capital and labour.

Sadly, this did not mean that the working class was preparing for the seizure of power under revolutionary leadership. For those who regarded themselves as revolutionary socialists were themselves in a complete theoretical mess. They had no coherent position on any of the pressing problems of the hour: the problem of party organisation, the role and nature of the armed forces, or whether they would be correct to split from UP (indeed, this last option was not even *considered* at this stage). They were thus in no position to offer any coherent leadership. When the CUT, in support of Allende, called on the working class to support the armed forces in restoring order, no organised voice was raised in opposition.[49] At this critical moment, the Chilean left proved confused and incapable.

The demand for military intervention came from a Christian Democrat Congressman, Rafael Moreno, but it had first appeared among the list of demands put forward by the Right at the beginning of the bosses' strike. Allende's announcement of the new joint UP-military Cabinet on 3 November was coupled with an address to the workers *thanking them for acting in support of the government* and asking them to return to work and restore the factories to their owners.

Since the lorrymen had returned to work as soon as the armed forces entered the government, it was obvious that the army's main task would consist in policing the workers' return to the factories. Prats, the army commander, stated the position in a studied neutral tone:

> So long as there is a properly constituted state, the armed forces are bound to respect it . . . Obviously the armed forces are the legitimate

instrument which is at the president's disposal to use against anyone who threatens public order . . .[50]

The nature of the threat, however, was to become very clear as the state of emergency began. The strict curfew was employed to control the movements of workers, and the wide powers given to the military were invoked to return the two occupied newspapers in Talca and Concepcion to their original proprietors. The leaders of the Bata defence committees were jailed for over a month. And on 13 November, the minister for the economy announced that 20 out of 28 factories taken over by the workers would be returned to their owners.

It was the distribution system that had perhaps slipped furthest from state control; for that reason it was the area placed under the most direct military control. Air Force General Bachelet was put in charge of DIRINCO, the state distribution agency.

The new Cabinet included, beside the generals, three UP ministers — two from the Communist Party (Millas at the Budget Ministry and Figueroa, head of the CUT, as minister of labour) and one from MAPU (Flores at the Economic Ministry). Since the state of emergency gave actual control to the military, the role of these ministers was not to argue the socialist case in the Cabinet, but rather to argue the case for the military within the working class. Figueroa, for example, argued vigorously with factory workers in Arica that office workers who had gone on strike in support of the lorrymen should be allowed to return to work and should be paid their full salary for the period of the strike, presumably as a gesture of conciliation.

A worker from Ex-Sumar, one of the most militant factories in Santiago, summed up the new situation:

> I think the concessions it has made mean that this government has shifted to the right. It did have another alternative available to it: to seek mass support and implement the programme it originally put forward. But it never really intended to implement it. So the masses have been left on the margins of things, and when they have tried to confront problems, they've been brutally repressed. The right must be celebrating now — you can tell they're cock-a-hoop just by listening to their radio stations.[51]

A government with generals

The Cabinet of UP ministers and generals did not have it all its own way. The situation after November remained confused, and the confidence gained by the workers was not quite that easy to undermine. Figueroa, for example, found that his double authority — as head of the CUT and minister of labour — was not as incontestable as it had once been. The workers at Arica were not convinced by his arguments and were still refusing to work with the office workers on 24 November. When Figueroa tried to persuade the Arica workers to accept the order, they reoccupied the factory and refused to move. In the end the police were brought in to evict them.

The same experience was repeated elsewhere, as workers refused to give up what they had won in October, complaining that such concessions would simply wipe out everything that had been gained and deliver victory to the bourgeoisie on a plate.

The spontaneous and unorganised acts of resistance by the working class, however, were never the object of any attempts at coordination or development. The political leadership of the left, for example, gave no guidance. The extraordinary thing is that *not a single voice* was raised against the presence of the military in the Cabinet. MAPU, for example, described the new Cabinet as 'government and people acting as one',[52] while in the same breath calling for the deepening of 'people's power'.

The Communist Party and the government were as one in their praise for the patriotic dedication of the armed forces, describing the new Cabinet as an indication that the army had been *won away* from the bourgeoisie (history meanwhile kept one of its more savage ironies up its sleeve):

> . . . the presence of the armed forces together with the leaders of the CUT strengthens the government and will allow it finally to carry out the sentence of death on the strike which the workers have already so clamorously rejected.[53]

Most surprising of all was the article by Manuel Cabieses in the MIR's journal **Punto Final**, in which he argued that

> the armed forces do have a patriotic and democratic role to play in conjunction with the people, supporting the workers in their struggle against exploitation . . . That is what should happen, and that is what the working class expects when it sees the armed forces as part of the government.[54]

No professional army has ever helped any working class in the struggle against exploitation, in other words in bringing down the bourgeois state of which it is the central pillar. The writer was guilty of staggering naivete; yet at the same time the MIR was arguing for the maintenance of the *cordones*.

The most consistent note in the declarations and analyses of the left was one of confusion and vacillation. There was an astonishing lack of clarity over how to respond to UP's determination to dismantle the mass organisations of October. Even the most militant statements, such as the speeches of Altamirano, general secretary of the Socialist Party, were directed towards the government, demanding that it act against its own political character, that it be revolutionary and not reformist. Instead of exposing the limits of reformism and tearing the veils from the eyes of those thousands of workers who still had illusions in Allende, Altamirano's rhetoric suggested that UP *could yet be* revolutionary.

Theotonio dos Santos, a regular contributor to **Chile Hoy**, added: 'If they are to conserve the gains that have been made, the government and the workers will have to deepen and extend them, using the existing mechanisms and deepening the roots of popular power.'[55] Even among the most radical voices, though, not one was ready to argue that the political development of the working-class movement beyond October required that it be disengaged from its traditional leadership in UP, that UP had become an obstacle to the qualitative development of the class struggle, and that the only way to ensure what had been won was to move forward. No organisation of the left offered an independent strategy; no one suggested breaking with UP. Only one organisation, and the smallest — the Christian Left — even moved in that direction, refusing to join the new Cabinet and attesting that:

> the advances in working-class consciousness don't seem to have reached their political leaders. The base is far richer than the leadership. The CUT and the *cordones* are far more effective at their level than UP at the political level . . . If the social power [of UP support] were to be organised in a coordinated way at the factory and regional level, and into organs of defence, the situation would move forward and be unstoppable.[56]

Yet the working class itself was demanding such an analysis. On 13 November, 100 delegates from the Santiago *cordones* met at the Cristalerias Chile factory to coordinate resistance to the return of the factories to their former owners. Their initiative found no echo among the left. As the president of the O'Higgins *cordon*, one of the most advanced, complained:

> The left press just ignores us . . . so the *cordones* have to fulfil the function of helping us to know each other better, to understand one another's struggles and to reach some consciousness of our power.[57]

The events of October 1972 brought new groups of workers, many of them previously unorganised, into the very heart of the struggle. It also threw up forms of organisation on which a permanent independent political organisation could have been built. The experience of the *cordones* became the central issue in political debates as 1972 drew to its end. Yet no one drew appropriate organisational conclusions.

Obviously, a working-class seizure of power in November was impossible. Many of the workers were demobilised, others were demoralised and confused; the state of emergency made it difficult even to meet, and the generals were in power. Yet it was equally obvious that the situation had not yet been definitively resolved in favour of either capitalists or workers: there was an air of expectancy everywhere, and both sides were openly discussing future strategies.[58]

In such an environment the immediate task of revolutionary socialists was not organising for the seizure of power, but patient and principled political argument in the working-class movement with those who had led the struggles in practice,[59] coupled with both political organisation and a continuing involvement in the day-to-day struggles of the class wherever it was fighting. But nothing of the kind took place. There was endless debate, much of it was very interesting, but always skirting the key question — the political character of UP.

The first opportunity for all the organisations of the left to discuss the experience of October 1972 came at a public debate organised in Santiago by a left-wing Catholic organisation called Christians for Socialism.[60] The Communist representative, Mireya Bartra, walked out soon after the debate began, denouncing the ultra-left as the main enemy. In reply, Miguel Enriquez, general secretary of the MIR, described the period as 'pre-revolutionary' and called for the creation of 'germs of people's power'. The main issue, he argued (correctly), was the achievement of 'workers' control'; yet in the debates and discussions that followed, it was never made clear by any representative of the MIR how this was to be achieved or organised.

Preparations for battle

The UP continued to have considerable political weight — but it was far from the unquestioned authority it had once been. Its best efforts were not enough to root out the new workers' organisations. It was indeed the actions of the UP government that precipitated their resurgence at the beginning of 1973.

The debate after the bosses' strike provoked a split in MAPU between the left, which kept the party name, and a pro-Allende right wing, which now called itself MAPUOC (Workers and Peasants MAPU) led by Jaime Gazmuri. In January 1973 the minister of the economy, Fernando Flores of MAPU, defied government policy and argued for a price freeze, for stringent controls on speculation and for a guaranteed shopping basket of basic goods at minimum prices. His argument met with an immediate popular response.

On 15 January, in the shanty town of Lo Hermida, 300 families marched on a local supermarket which had closed its doors (claiming shortages of goods) and demanded that it reopen. Immediately, government mediators arrived and tried to disperse the demonstration, but they failed. At two in the morning, the store was opened and local organisations then took charge of distributing goods according to need. The same happened at Nueva La Habana, another shanty town, and at the Barrancas *cordon*.

It was in this climate that Orlando Millas, the minister in charge of the budget and a member of the Communist Party, announced the new Economic Plan. This proposed the return of 123 factories to their original owners, including those belonging to one of the most active opponents of the government, the powerful Yarur family. Further, Millas advocated that just 49 industrial installations should remain in public hands, effectively creating a state capitalist *sector* to act in coordination with private capital.[61] Logically enough, the reopening of political discussions with the Christian Democrats was announced simultaneously. Clearly the plan represented an almost complete concession to bourgeois demands.

The working class reacted with fury. The *cordones* re-awoke and responded immediately. Workers from the Cerrillos-Maipu *cordon* blocked the streets in protest, then led a joint demonstration of all the capital's *cordones* to the city centre. The *cordon* president, Hernan Ortega, declared: 'There will be no compromise, whatever the pressures.'[62] At Textil Bromack, thirteen Communist Party members turned in their party cards in protest. Most significantly of all, the Vicuña McKenna *cordon* began publication of a newspaper for the *cordones* called **Tarea Urgente**. Its first issue carried an enormously significant statement:

> To the workers: the workers of this *cordon* call upon the working class to organise to defend the social property area [meaning the nationalised part of the economy] and the factories that were taken over during the bosses' strike. The law that proposes to hand them back does not reflect the feelings of the majority of workers who are ready to carry the struggle to defend their rights to its ultimate consequences.
>
> Therefore, at its assembly on 28 January, the members of this *cordon* passed the following resolution. 1) That no factory taken over during the bosses' strike should be returned to its owners; 2) That we unanimously reject the so-called 'Millas Plan', which does not represent the real ideas of the working class . . . We must advance without compromises. Not one factory must be returned; many more must be taken over.[63]

In similar vein, the members of the Panamericana Norte Cordon demanded to know:

> How much longer are the people up there going to go on turning the screw the wrong way? It's beginning to get on our nerves, and we're

giving notice that *not one single enterprise will be returned* . . . From now on we will remain in a permanent state of readiness to defend our right to make decisions that shape our own lives.[64]

On 5 February a massive demonstration of workers, squatters, shanty town organisations and community groups assembled in the National Stadium to voice their opposition to the Millas Plan. **Punto Final** reported a banner at the stadium which warned, with a sharp sense of history, 'An unarmed people is a conquered people'. Clearly the class struggle was entering a new phase, and gaining a new intensity.

Yet there was little connection between the rhythm of the class struggle and the preoccupations of the main political parties. The Congressional elections of March 1973 were approaching and these were regarded both by the right and by the parties of UP as a crucial test of the government's capacity to survive. All the organisations of the left agreed that the elections were an absolute priority, including the MIR, which supported candidates of the Socialist Party in parliamentary elections for the first time. In the event the national vote for UP rose to 44 per cent. In the prevailing climate this was a remarkable testimony to the resilience of the working class and proof that sections of the petty bourgeoisie had also been won over.

As far as the Right were concerned, the results represented a serious setback — a failure to undermine UP's electoral support. They now began to discuss alternative strategies for toppling Allende's government. Of the two options presented, the military coup advocated by some sections was set aside in favour of the 'Russian Marshals' strategy argued for by Aylwin, chairman of the Christian Democratic Party, among others.[65] This was an economic 'scorched earth' strategy, aiming to lay waste the economy through disinvestment, hoarding and the conscious mobilisation of international support, creating a state of siege within and without.

If there had been a lull in mass activity during the election period, it now resumed. At the end of March 1973, the generals left the Cabinet and the Millas Plan was abandoned. Allende announced the nationalisation of 45 more enterprises, yet this announcement was followed almost immediately, on 6 April, by a virulent attack on the revolutionary left and on those workers' organisations which had failed to return the factories after the October occupations.[66] In the light of this attack, it was hard to see the incorporation of 45 plants into the state sector as anything other than a symbolic gesture.

However much Allende railed at those who 'provoked' the bourgeoisie, it was he who was blind to the intensity of the class struggle. While he insisted on holding to his original programme of gradual change, and condemned workers' and peasants' organisations for jeopardising it through their precipitate actions, events had already passed him by. The bourgeoisie were openly discussing extra-parliamentary strategies for his overthrow. If Allende and the CUT still insisted that the pace of change was determined in parliament, neither the bourgeoisie nor the working class had any such illusions. The workers were organising themselves for a struggle already under way in the streets, in the factories and on the land. It was not a matter of whether the struggle should be allowed to happen — it was only its outcome that was in question.

The increased vote for UP in the March elections was clearly a demand for action. But if UP did not lead it, then it would take place anyway, outside its control. The UP leadership could not grasp this.

The leadership of the left were certainly discussing the crisis; but their perspective was still limited to demanding that the UP act in new ways.[67] A far more radical solution was required — of the kind that had already been placed on the historical agenda by the working class itself.

The decision to form a Coordinating Committee of *Cordones* was a qualitative leap in the forms of leadership of the workers' struggle. Yet there was no split from the UP. Why? The dominant political current in the leadership of the *cordones* was undoubtedly the left of the Socialist Party; and the party, despite its now characteristic ultra-left rhetoric, was still not prepared to split from UP or openly to challenge the right wing led by Allende. Altamirano, leader of the Socialists and generally regarded as one of the left, saw the development of independent organisations in the class struggle as forms of pressure that could be brought to bear on the battle for the leadership of the party itself. And it was this limited perspective that won over those left socialists who led the *cordones*. Thus the Coordinating Committee, which could so easily have been an embryonic form of working-class power, became instead a political faction inside the Socialist Party.

The other political force in the mass movement was the MIR. The MIR had existed for only eight years, and only since 1969-70 had it addressed itself to organising workers. While it had gained some base among non-unionised workers, its main influence was among the organisations of squatters and in the student movement. While the MIR stood candidates in union elections, and in fact had representatives on the CUT executive, it had no organised presence in the unions. It had remained outside the UP and at times openly critical, but could offer no alternative range of priorities or tasks.

The MIR responded pragmatically to the changing realities of the class struggle, setting a certain priority on its own struggle for political leadership. This came out most clearly in the debate around the *cordones*.

Sometimes, when a number of organisations were involved in the *cordones*, they would form joint organising committees (*comandos comunales*). The MIR laid great stress on these *comandos* as leading organs in the struggle: yet, at the same time, they denounced the *cordones* and echoed the statements of the CUT that they were 'parallel organisations' to the CUT. This was nonsense, of course; they were independent organisations in which the workers had an acknowledged leading role. Paradoxically, despite their commitment to 'working-class hegemony', the MIR seemed uneasy about the leading role played by these working-class organisations in which they occupied no leading positions. Their calls to convert the *cordones* into broad organisations representing equally squatters, distribution organisations, students and others gave the lie to their claim to be Marxist. In practice, their denunciation of the *cordones* specifically denied the central role of the working class in the struggle for state power.

In any case, the MIR's resounding calls were little more than slogans, since they did not lead to any concrete organisational conclusions. Meanwhile, the class struggle itself did not wait. It continued with growing intensity in the weeks after the Congressional elections, as the right escalated its assaults and the government offered no contest. The working-class movement, however, did have its own response to offer.

The challenge of the miners

The copper miners had played a central role in the history of labour in Chile. It was a matter of considerable significance, therefore, when the workers at the world's largest copper mine, El Teniente, went on strike on 19 April.

The strike began quietly; the physical isolation of the miners in a mountainous region of the country meant that the strike's impact on the rest of the movement was not immediate. And the left was not particularly anxious to raise the level of public debate about the strike. For the issue that led to the strike was a vexed one. At the beginning of 1973, UP granted a general wage rise to match the inflation rate. The miners, however, had their own separate agreement, whereby they were guaranteed a cost of living increase and a series of other increments each year. The government refused these increases and the miners struck in response, claiming that the governent had violated their joint agreement. As, indeed, they undoubtedly had.

The strike continued through May and June, though some workers did return to work under intense pressure from all the left organisations, including the MIR, which argued that the whole thing was stirred up by the bourgeoisie and imperialism.[68]

The issues, and the accusations, were familiar enough. The miners were denounced for their 'economism', their defence of their own narrow sectional interests over the interests of the class as a whole. In effect, the left was asking them to sacrifice their hard-won cost of living increases for the 'general good'. The reality, of course, was that the sole beneficiaries of their concessions would be the bourgeoisie — and the government knew that perfectly well. The miners were continuing to produce, but the world market price of copper was falling. Should they be asked to accept the consequences of this decline, as UP urged, or should they conduct themselves like any other group of organised workers defending their living standards?

In any case, the argument that the copper miners were being asked to make sacrifices for the general good, and that the fruit of their selflessness would be socialism, held very little water now. The undoubted gains of the UP's first year had been eaten away in the intervening period by inflation and rising prices, so that the real purchasing power of wages had actually declined by 1973 below the 1971 level. The bourgeoisie, by contrast, was actually benefitting from the situation; or, at the very least, it was cushioned from the worst effects precisely because of UP's willingness to ask the working class to bear the cost.

The Chilean government was not the champion of the workers; it sought to negotiate the price of labour with capital, to use the state as an instrument of *mediation* — against a background of prior guarantees given to the capitalist class. In such a situation, the role of a workers' organisation should have been clear: the defence of its members' living standards — yet none of them saw that as their task. The single-minded orientation of the whole of the left on the internal struggle in UP meant that all rallied to attack the miners for representing a threat to the government.[69] Had their starting point been an assessment of the development of the class struggle, they might have responded differently; instead they denounced the miners' leader Medina as 'a Nazi' and the miners themselves as a 'labour aristocracy'. When, in June, the miners marched to Santiago to demand talks with the government, they were stopped and attacked with water cannon by the *Grupo Movil*, the riot police that Allende had undertaken to disband as soon as he took office back in 1970.

The miners' strike revealed the weaknesses not only of the Chilean left, but also — still more seriously — of the *cordones* themselves. The traditionally best-organised sectors of workers were absent from the national network of *cordones*. Their unions were the core of UP and their discipline the fruit of years of struggle. Since their political leaderships had roundly condemned the *cordones*, many of these sections were persuaded to withdraw from participation; and the CUT worked hard to prevent any direct contact between these workers — overwhelmingly in the public sector of the economy — and the sectors organised in the *cordones*.

The geographical and political isolation of the miners meant that many workers learned of the miners' strike from the right-wing media. The organisations of the bourgeoisie were quick to exploit the contradictions in the UP's position and began to organise collections for the striking miners (an event as rare as it was bizarre). This made the situation even more confusing, but provided the CUT leaders and the parties of UP with the opportunity to 'prove' that the miners' strike was a right-wing plot to undermine the Allende government. It was an insult to the most combative sector of the Chilean working class and an example of the most unprincipled opportunism by both the right and the government. If the right had *used* the strike, it was precisely because the whole of the left had totally failed to understand or respond to the justified discontent of the El Teniente workers.

Elsewhere events were moving faster. At the end of April a CUT demonstration drew tens of thousands into the streets of the capital. As the march passed the offices of the Christian Democratic Party a shot rang out and one worker was killed. A plethora of small local struggles continued. In early May, the 50 workers of a small sawmill in Entre Lagos took over their workplace when their employer announced the mill's closure. When the CUT came along and proposed joint ownership with the old boss, the workers refused:

> We think that with the support of the whole population of Entre Lagos we can break these people who think they can use government money to build factories for the bosses and just leave the workers out of it.[70]

When government representatives tried to achieve the same ends by subterfuge, they were warned not to underestimate the workers. A similar experience was repeated at the JEMO plant and INAPIS Pistons, both in Santiago. When workers took over the SALFA electronic components factory in Arica, the governent cut off the state subsidies it had received while under private ownership.

Perhaps the most dramatic struggle occurred in the coastal town of Constitucion on 10 and 11 May, when the town lived for two days under the undisputed control of mass organisations. The confrontation had begun late in 1972, with the establishment of a squatters' settlement in the town. In January 1973, Constitucion was experiencing the same conflicts over distribution, the return of factories and the lack of adequate housing land as most other Chilean towns. Their response, however, was untypical. On 21 February, the people of the town met in a 'Mass Assembly of the People' to identify the problems that the squatters, peasants and workers shared. Two months later, on 10 April, the Assembly met again, and decided to demand the resignation of the regional governor, who had resisted all their attempts to find solutions and ignored all their demands.[71]

What followed, however, was astonishing. The entire population of the town, some 25,000, simply assumed control. The main highways were barricaded. Health committees and vigilance committees were established to organise health facilities and maintain order. The demand was simple: that the governor be dismissed and replaced by the elected head of the joint workers' commission established at the first mass assembly. For the two days of the occupation the mass assembly remained in permanent session; the shops were kept open and all the bars closed. Late on the 11th, the government conceded the main demand.

The campaign in Constitucion had a limited objective, relatively innocuous in itself. What was significant was the extraordinarily radical *form* the movement took, and the confidence and organisation that it indicated.

This struggle happened in a provincial town with no particular tradition of its own; to that extent it provides a measure of the general level of consciousness among Chilean workers at this stage. It shows, further, that the struggle itself placed the workers in the leadership of the broader mass movement. The divisions, sectional and sectarian, at the top — in UP and the CUT — were increasingly being overcome at the rank-and-file level, as workers organised together to confront specific problems.

Those problems, moreover, were more and more issues of control. As one leader of a *cordon* put it, these were 'tasks of the masses, tasks of government',[72] and they demanded new forms of organisation. Experience was fast superseding the old organisations; the CUT was finding it harder and harder to maintain its authority on the ground, and while UP was still acknowledged in a general sense as the political leadership of the class, its tactical decisions and guidelines were increasingly ignored.

As the final act approached, the Chilean drama seemed to have reached a kind of plateau. On the ground there was intense activity; there were struggles taking place constantly, some of them long and bitter, many of them involving several different sections of workers. Yet there was still no national focus for these struggles. While a number of rank-and-file and local organisations made tentative moves towards united action, the Right already had a national perspective — the overthrow and replacement of Allende — and was openly acting upon it. The left organisations were, it sometimes appeared, locked in an interminable series of debates about unification, yet their focus was always UP itself, rather than the initiatives taken independently by workers.

Allende, for his part, now led a coalition which no longer functioned as a political leadership in any sense — and he largely ignored it as he embarked on one set of discussions after another with the right-wing parties. The talk everywhere was of the impending political crisis — but nobody seemed quite sure what form the crisis would take.

The gulf between UP and the masses was poignantly illustrated early in June, when Popular Unity met for the first time as a single organisation and held its first congress at Santiago's *Teatro Municipal*. None of the party leaders attended, and the discussions and resolutions were pitched at the highest level of abstraction.[74] The Congress's closing declarations of unity reflected only the decision by the Socialist Party delegates not to risk a split. The unity of Popular Unity, in other words, was negative and false, a confession of impotence in the face of the gathering storm outside.

The UP congress had been overtaken by events; much more important were the congresses of workers in each industry which began to meet at the end of May to discuss the possibilities of joint industry-wide organisation. The first three such congresses covered the textile, fishing and forestry industries.

On 19 May at Maipu, peasants conducting a long struggle over land belonging to the family of the assassinated right-wing politician Perez Zujovic called on the workers of Cerrillos for support. The police were sent in by the government to disperse the resulting demonstration. A similar battle at Ñuble at the end of the month yielded more direct concessions from the government, as did the occupation of the local food distribution centre by the peasants.

On 21 May Allende made a very odd speech in which he expressed his approval of the *comandos comunales*; and immediately afterwards the Communist Party gave permission to its members to participate in them. What was odd about Allende's speech was that previously he had consistently attacked these organisations and bracketed them with the *cordones*. Now it seemed he was attempting to make a distinction between them and win some UP influence in the new mass organisations. What made it doubly curious was that the MIR agreed with Allende on this issue, and insisted that a proposal by the Socialists to hold a Congress of Coordinating Committees of *Cordones*[74] should be shelved until a national meeting of *comandos* could be called.

The proposed congress never did take place; yet it was the nearest the left ever came to forming an independent organisation of revolutionaries, an alternative political leadership to the UP. Perhaps Allende's speech added new credence to the illusion that the left could win the leadership of UP; perhaps the internal arguments simply could not be resolved. Whatever the reasons, the step was not taken. So, when events thrust upon the working class for the second time the responsibility for the defence of the class against the bourgeoisie, there was no clear political direction, no organisation which could centralise or direct their struggle towards a revolutionary transformation.

Dual power and the denouement

On 29 June 1973, the tank regiment of Santiago, under the command of Colonel Roberto Souper, took to the streets of the capital and announced the seizure of power. The news reached the EASTON plant, part of the Vicuna McKenna *Cordon*, at nine in the morning.

> At 9.15 we sounded the factory siren and called a general meeting. We agreed that we would all stay in the factory and send out some 'shock troops' to link up with other workplaces and find transport.[75]

A 'joint command' was formed in the *Cordon* Cerrillos and four communiqués were published at two-hourly intervals throughout the day. The first set out the immediate tasks:

> Instructions: No. 1
>
> 1) Take over all the factories.
>
> 2) Organise brigades of 11 comrades, with one leader; the leaders of each brigade, together with the trade union organisers, will take over the organisation of the factory.
>
> 3) Centralise within the factory all vehicles and materials that may be useful for the defence of the factory, the working class and the government.
>
> 4) Every hour on the hour each factory shall sound its siren to indicate that all is well. If help is needed, the siren should be sounded continuously.
>
> 5) Keep permanently tuned to Radio Corporation.
>
> 6) Place a guard on the most visible point in the factory.
>
> 7) Maintain constant communication with surrounding factories and appoint comrades to act as couriers.
>
> 8) Say where the Command will be located and where leading comrades will meet if access is impossible.
>
> 9) Organise assemblies and keep the workers informed.[76]

The experience was repeated throughout the country, with new *cordones* and *comandos* formed within hours of what was now called

'Souper's attempted coup'. In fact, Souper was a maverick, openly associated with *Patria y Libertad* and regarded with considerable suspicion by the army high command (this was not his first attempt at a coup).

Souper's attempted coup was no more than what Prieto calls a 'piece of armed propaganda'.[77] In this it was successful. The leadership of the military opposed only the timing of Souper's action: right-wing circles, which involved most leading military men, had been openly discussing a military coup for some time. As far as those circles were concerned, the response of the working class to Souper's action tipped the balance away from a political solution. In the armed forces, the mass reaction provoked urgent discussion about the need for military intervention.

In a sense, Allende himself had been responsible for the confidence and self-importance of the military. Had he not repeatedly called them in to resolve social conflicts? Had he not agreed to massive (and undisclosed) pay increases for the military just when the working class was being called upon to exercise restraint?[78]

Now, on the morning of 29 June, Allende was once again to display his faith in — and dependence on — the armed forces. While the *cordones* were organising working-class resistance, their president was in discussion with the army commander-in-chief. The UP, in a word, was defenceless and impotent in the face of the mobilisation of the bourgeoisie.

In the days that followed, the MIR, MAPU and the Socialist Party[79] issued stirring calls to the workers to prepare to defend the government, arms in hand. Even Communist Party officials were encouraging industrial workers to use their lathes to make arms, and Allende's speeches were full of veiled threats. The famous picture of Allende practising at a pistol range, which so inflamed the right, dated from this period.

Yet neither this, nor the calls for the building of people's power, meant anything so long as they were associated with a restatement of the old politics and declarations of loyalty to the UP leadership. Not even at this stage, when the working class were at their best organised and most confident, when joint organisation existed across the country, and when the best revolutionaries were in an unequivocal position of leadership, did the left take the road to the seizure of power. For that would have brought them into confrontation with UP itself. So, as in the case of the Cerrillos communiqué, calls for the highest level of independent working-class action contained within them declarations of loyalty to Allende.

For some commentators, that loyalty was a strength, a significant factor in winning the ideological battle inside the army. For the reformists, that was how the battle would be won — by producing a new and progressive army command.[80] In fact, a split in the army could only have occurred if rank-and-file soldiers had acted in class solidarity with their brothers and sisters challenging for power. The generals understood this; Allende did not. The generals understood that the professional army exists as the last line of defence of the bourgeois state; Allende did not. The fond illusion that the army would act out the class struggle on behalf of the workers was not confined to the reformists — in its 30 July issue, **Punto Final**, journal of the MIR, called for a 'joint dicatorship of the people and the armed forces'![81]

Yet a qualitative shift was taking place in the streets and factories; the pace of events was quickening; each day threw up new organs of proletarian order. A new *cordon*, Santiago-Centro, drew together civil servants and slum dwellers. In Barrancas a series of factory takeovers were immediately translated into a new *cordon*, as representatives of each factory met in a joint coordinating committee. When shopkeepers tried to close their stores, they were reopened by local people who then organised direct distribution of goods. When the lorry-owners went on strike again, ostensibly in protest at the plan for a state transport system, the workers commandeered vehicles directly. Hospitals were taken over by committees of their workers.

In some sense, the response to Souper's attempted coup was a re-enactment of October 1972. But there were important differences. First the working class now had several months' experience of self-organisation on which to base their response. Second, the military factor was now central. Third, the Allende government could offer even less in the way of support than in the previous year. In a word, the stakes were higher, and the time shorter. The potential was also far greater.

At El As Clothing, a group of women workers with no previous political history took over the factory. They expressed surprise when their local union leader, who was a Christian Democrat, joined them, and delight when they were invited to join the O'Higgins *Cordon*. As one worker said:

> The CUT's solution is to talk with the bosses and reach an agreement with them, giving them back the factories, that's what it's all about. I was never one for mixing in politics, we never talked very much about the [political] process, but we're all involved now and we know what it means, and all we can say is that this statement is a betrayal of the working class. Perhaps this is a small factory . . . but at bottom what's important here is political and not economic; if we workers want power, we'll never get it by giving back factories, however small they may be.[82]

The conditions of a revolutionary crisis were present; the functions of production, distribution, workers' defence and social services were in the hands of workers' organisations. The bourgeoisie was mobilising for confrontation, while the existing state was impotent to act decisively in a situation it could no longer govern.

Three days after Souper's coup, Allende again declared a State of Emergency; his declaration was neither more nor less than an invitation to the army to resolve the situation in whatever way it thought best. The new Cabinet announced on 4 July did not include a military representative. Allende's assertion that this was 'in order not to compromise the neutrality of the armed forces' did not sound very convincing. On the contrary, it seemed to give them maximum freedom of movement by exempting them from any kind of political control.

The military's first act, as before, was to move against those newspapers and TV stations sympathetic to the workers. One issue of **Punto Final** was removed from the news-stands and the state TV channel was censored; Channel 13, run by the ranting right-wing demagogue Father Hasbun, was allowed to continue its calls for a military coup without interruption.[83] A curfew was imposed, effectively preventing workers from coordinating their activities through the night. And, outside Santiago, reports suggested that the military were already establishing control.

The strength of the military officers was chillingly reinforced when UP supporters in the navy and air force publicly exposed the preparations for a coup that were already being made at a number of key military installations. Their appeal to Allende to act met with the presidential thanks for their loyalty, plus a statement that, under the state of emergency, he would have to leave it to the high command to deal with the matter — as he was sure they would. They did — in their own way. They tried the men at court martial, sentenced them to long jail terms, and tortured them.

Endgame

The final act of the Chilean drama was played out in July and August 1973. The military coup that overthrew the UP government in September, and plunged Chile into a bloodbath, was the *coup de grace*.

In the summer, the secondary issues were cleared away. Now the battle for power remained to be fought. The factories were again taken over — many had still not been returned after October 1972; the distribution centres were placed under direct workers' control; the defence organisations reformed. The working class was prepared for this final phase of the class struggle — but its leaders were not.

Allende, after his hesitation and his unexpected support for the *comandos* in earlier statements, seemed more definite and resolute on 25 July. Again he turned his fire against the *cordones* and the left in general, for driving the country to the edge of civil war. The political character of his speech is both clarified and rendered more despicable by the context in which he made it. The right-wing press was now openly advocating the military overthrow of UP; the second bosses' strike, led again by the lorrymen, was set to begin the following day. Congress was virtually at a standstill, blocked by a string of resolutions to impeach Allende and remove him from the presidency. The economy was paralysed: copper exports fell in value; the bourgeoisie ceased to invest; spare parts and raw materials were increasingly difficult to get; hoarding created shortages. The bourgeoisie was using all its economic weapons. And the assassination of Allende's personal aide, Captain Araya, was ample notice that they were prepared to use real weapons too.

Yet when the Arms Control Law was finally passed at the beginning of August, its purpose was not to provide a legal instrument against those who were peparing a coup, or against the gun-toting ultra-right gangs. It was, on the contrary, the means that permitted the army and the police, under Allende's state of emergency, to carry through pre-emptive strikes against the mass organisations.

This operation was conducted in a coordinated, national and systematic way. On 7 August, reports described the southernmost Chilean city of Punta Arenas as under military occupation, and one worker died. In Cautin and Temuco the property of the peasant organisations was requisitioned and many of their leaders arrested and tortured — **Chile Hoy** actually carried photographs of the torture marks in its issue of 30 August. In each case the operations were possible because the Arms Control Law allowed the imposition of martial law — though it required explicit presidential permission. This was always given.

In the town of San Antonio the state of emergency brought to the fore a man who would become infamous as head of state security after the coup — Manuel Contreras. But in San Antonio he encountered determined resistance from coordinated mass actions. In the *Teatro del Pueblo* in Osorno all the local organisations met under the leadership of the local *cordon* and published a programme for the immediate establishment of control over the town. This programme included further expropriations of factories, support for the struggles of the landless Mapuche Indians, a commitment to reorganise the health service under workers' control, and an invitation to rank-and-file soldiers to desert and join the workers. Here the issue was explicitly set out: it was a challenge to the bourgeois state.

On 3 August Allende announced a new Cabinet of UP ministers and generals. The move was entirely consistent with his action and statements of the previous few days. Allende had conceded and surrendered completely to the idea that the key issue was to defend and sustain the bourgeois state. In this he and the bourgeoisie agreed.

Who then was the enemy? The Communist Party leader, Luis Corvalan, in a tragically famous speech made in Santiago on 8 August,[84] made the issue clear beyond all doubt. He praised the consistent patriotism and loyalty of the armed forces and in the same speech denounced the ultra-left, which he bracketed with the fascist gangs of *Patria y Libertad* as responsible for the violence. In the preceding three days, the army had occupied some of the factories in the *Cordon* Cerrillos, and the navy had forced entry into the Van Buren Hospital in Valparaiso. When Corvalan and Allende attacked the ultra-left, they were directing their venom at the only visible force actively challenging the state — the working class itself.

There can have been few occasions when the organisations of the left have found themselves facing such dramatic and creative possibilities as were offered by the workers' organisations — the *cordones* and *comandos* — in Chile in July and August 1973. The long and patient preparatory work of any revolutionary organisation is directed at just such a moment, but once such a point is reached it allows little time for vacillation or debate. It is a moment to be seized — or it is lost. The Chilean left seemed unequal to the task.

The problem was not just a question of arms — even though, at this critical moment, a disarmed working class would not attract soldiers away from the army's discipline, nor could it resist a confident military. Of course the workers had to be armed; but the central issue was something else. Weapons tip the balance only when they are used in pursuit of a clear political objective, the seizure of power and the overthrow of the state; and when they are used by an organised and coordinated movement led by revolutionaries who understand the nature of the moment.

This is not to say that all that is required is a group of determined revolutionaries waiting in the wings, ready-armed for the right moment. A revolution demands the development of an organisation that can lead the working class, an organisation *implanted in its living struggles* and built around an understanding of the class struggle and its possible outcome.

In the absence of such a political leadership social revolution is impossible; indeed, calls for armed struggle of the kind issued by the MIR or Altamirano, secretary of the Socialist Party, in the early days of

August 1973 were irresponsible in the extreme. At this stage even the Communist Party — in a final piece of opportunism — was calling on the workers to arm themselves. Altamirano's call to rank-and-file soldiers to lay down their arms transferred the responsibility for seizing the revolutionary moment to the individual soldier — when that responsibility belonged clearly to the revolutionary organisations, or those who described themselves as such.

By late August an air of demoralisation had spread through the Chilean working class. The 4 September celebrations of Allende's 1970 election victory were gloomy and depressed — even though half a million people were in the streets. The result of the military coup a week later was a foregone conclusion.

Yet it could have been otherwise. The workers were ready for a struggle and prepared for its consequences; the organs on which a new workers' power could be built were in existence. Yet to the very end, every organisation of the left in Chile directed itself towards the UP, interpreted the high level of mass struggle as a form of pressure *on* the UP, and held back from providing an alternative revolutionary leadership.[85] That failure to lead amounted to abandoning the workers to the savage reprisals of the bourgeoisie, and every organisation of the Chilean left must share the responsibility.

Against that background the much-quoted final speech made on radio by Allende, just before he was killed in the military coup that overthrew him, is not just misguided. His moral outrage, his assertion that 'history would condemn the generals', was an unforgiveable renunciation of his own responsibility and a lie told to posterity.

The events of 1972 and 1973 in Chile gave a glimpse of workers' power, of the capacity of workers to take up the challenges of the class struggle. Tragically, it also showed that at such a moment the enemy of revolution is reformism, the politics of those more committed to the defence of the bourgeois state than to the transformation of the world.

In the aftermath of the disaster in Chile, its real history has been rewritten to protect reformists around the world from the true consequences of the politics of conciliation.[86] The coup that brought an end to the struggles of 1972-3 in Chile was a terrible and savage defeat for the working class; but it was not the result of a world conspiracy nor was it inevitable. There was another possibility on the historical agenda which we cannot allow to be buried. The importance of Chile 1972-73 is its legacy for future struggles.

The coup

On 11 September 1973 a combined military operation, beginning early in the morning, brought down the government of Salvador Allende. The coup was led by Augusto Pinochet, who had been a member of Allende's second military Cabinet, in August. By nine in the morning, tanks surrounded the presidential palace; this was the *last* act of the coup, since the most militant organisations of workers, peasants, students and shanty town dwellers had already been disarmed and destroyed during the state of emergency in effect during the previous weeks.

Rumours of resistance were rife for a few hours; with a final historical irony, the most persistent was that General Prats would lead the army to defend the constitution and stop the coup. In fact General Prats had resigned a week earlier, standing back from the coup he knew to be in preparation. Beyond sporadic individual resistance, there was no fightback. The struggle was already lost, the movement led into proud defeat by its reformist leaders.

As the day wore on, hundreds of people were rounded up and taken to military installations, jails and improvised concentration camps. Thousands were taken to the National Football Stadium and kept there until they were removed to be tortured or murdered. Some, like Victor Jara, the best-known of Chile's folk singers, did not even get that far. His hands were broken when he tried to sing a song of resistance; then he was killed.

The coup was conducted with an extraordinary savagery; thousands were raped, subjected to inhuman torture, starved, abused, murdered. In the following twelve months 30,000 people were killed. They were the best and most courageous leaders of their class, systematically picked off with sophisticated foreign intelligence help. And they were not just killed — they were torn apart, to warn and terrify the next generation. The rest were dealt with arbitrarily, to terrorise the population and give graphic notice that the new regime would give no quarter. That was the significance of the maimed bodies that floated every morning along Santiago's river Mapocho.

For those, like Allende himself, who had always insisted on Chile's deeply entrenched democratic tradition and the 'professionalism' of its armed forces, the brutality and sustained sadism of the coup were inexplicable. Reformists around the world sought an account that would explain the seeming aberration, obscure the mistaken character of their analysis of the army, and cover Popular Unity from the prying eyes of the future. They tried to lay the blame on a CIA conspiracy.[87]

The reality was otherwise. The coup occurred because the rising level of class struggle in Chile came close to threatening the existence of bourgeois society. In this final and decisive moment of the class struggle, the ruling class gives no quarter, whatever its so-called traditions. The Western democracies, after all, are anxious to defend the traditions of 'democracy' to the hilt — if necessary with weapons of horrendous mass destruction. So it was in Chile.

The violence of the Chilean military was not based on personal revenge, but involved the systematic rooting out, from the memory of the working class, of its best and most courageous organisers and leaders. Once they had done that, they could turn Chile into an experimental arena for a monetarist economics unimpeded by an organised working class. Their logic was a logic of capitalism with its gloves off: a minimum standard of living for workers, permanent and structural unemployment, a complete absence of social services, a climate of permanent terror, schools where only jingoism and resignation could be taught.[88]

Yet the reformists warned against organising for the conquest of workers' power, because of the damage they said it would wreak. In their anxiety to save the workers from themselves, the Popular Unity coalition left the working class disarmed and helpless to face the military coup. Today, the struggles of Chilean workers have begun again. It would be a terrible irony if they were not allowed to learn the lessons of their own history.

THREE

PORTUGAL 1974-75
Popular power
Peter Robinson

THE POLITICS we find in our newspapers primarily concern the manoeuvrings of leading parliamentary and establishment figures. Connected to the rest of us only by the occasional cross on a ballot paper, such politics depends on the passivity of the mass of the population. The events of 1974-75 in Portugal show that such passivity is far from inevitable.

For in this small country the attendance on some demonstrations exceeded half a million. In the working-class bars political discussion and argument were intense. Seven-year-old children could tell about the many political parties of the left, their papers, the badges and slogans. What's more, they would explain why they supported a particular party. Workers discussed the situation in France, in England, Argentina and Brazil as if they'd been professors of politics all their lives. Posters advocating armed insurrection were legal. Even the bus tickets had political slogans on them.

The commanders of the state could no longer rely on its army. Tanks rumbled in cobbled streets alongside, and carrying, demonstrating workers. The scale of factory occupations recalled France in 1936 and 1968, Catalonia in 1936 and Turin in 1920. And not only the factories were taken over. Popular clinics and cultural centres mushroomed. In one hospital the workers took over from the nuns, and invited them to come and vote at the mass meetings. Empty houses and apartments were requisitioned; the organisation of tenants and residents was incomparably larger than anything else seen in Europe. On the land workers took over the estates and gave their communes names such as 'Red Star' and 'Dictatorship of the Proletariat'.

We can gain great inspiration from these achievements. But we must also learn from them. For the rulers of Portugal were able to engineer a return to 'normality', to confuse and defuse the revolutionary movement. To understand why and how, it is necessary to begin with a brief survey of the historical background.

The Portuguese monarchy was overthrown in 1910. During the next 16 years there were 45 governments, incessant bombings, assassinations, coups and attempted coups, mutinies, riots, strikes and lock-outs. This period of parliamentary rule was terminated by a coup in 1926. Antonio de Oliveira Salazar was appointed minister of finance in 1928. He built around himself a mass movement, a party and the ideology of the *Estado Novo* (the New State). Within a few years he was to establish a dictatorship — though not, as other dictators did in Germany and Italy, by mobilising a section of the masses, but through a military coup.

Under this regime a handful of private empires were regenerated and flourished. Protected by tariffs and state controls, two giant coroporations emerged; CUF and Champalimaud. CUF grew to control one tenth of Portugal's industry, holding a virtual monopoly of tobacco and a large share in soap, chemicals, textiles, construction and insurance. Champalimaud was involved in tourism and insurance and acquired a virtual monopoly on steel production. These native conglomerates were deliberately fostered against foreign capital. Even Coca-Cola was prohibited. The Salazar regime bred an oligarchy — a few powerful families and their business empires, intertwined with the state bureaucracy and the upper echelons of the armed forces. In the shadow of the oligarchy there was little room for independent capitalists. Political parties, trade unions and strikes were outlawed. Opponents were arbitrarily imprisoned and tortured by the notorious secret police, the PIDE.

By the late 1960s Portugal had three distinctive features.

Firstly, it was the least developed country in Western Europe. It had a large peasantry in the north, landed estates in the south and relatively small, concentrated industrial centres around Lisbon and along the northern coast in the Porto region. Between 1960 and 1970 emigration, a response to underdevelopment, increased five-fold; social provisions were archaic. The population actually declined in the last years of the 1960s.

Secondly Portugal, having acquired the first of the European colonial empires, clung to it long after the others. The African and Far Eastern colonies provided both a source of cheap raw materials and secure, protected markets for Portugal's industrial goods. But by the 1960s anti-colonial uprisings began to weaken the empire. In Africa, freedom struggles began with an urban uprising in Luanda, Angola, in 1961. Guerrilla movements emerged in Guinea in 1963 and Mozambique by 1964.

Thirdly, Europe's oldest dictatorship desperately needed to reorganise and modernise its industry. New developments such as the gigantic shipyard complexes of Lisnave and Setenave were financed in conjunction with foreign capital. In search of cheap labour and a friendly regime, multinationals such as Timex, Plessey, Ford, General Motors, ITT and Philips set up large modern plants, mostly in the Lisbon industrial belt. The urban working class grew along with the shanty towns. Foreign capital provided 52.2 per cent of Portugal's total manufacturing investment in 1968.[1]

But the ramshackle Portuguese empire proved incapable of modernisation without a fundamental political overhaul.

Thanks to the collapse of a British-made deckchair in September 1968, Salazar suffered a stroke and severe brain damage. His withdrawal from politics encouraged attempts to reform the system from above. Salazar's successor, Marcello Caetano, introduced the so-called *primavera*, the 'spring' of liberalisation. Censorship was relaxed. Political prisoners were allowed into exile and some exiles were allowed home. The student movement emerged, encouraged by liberalisation and inspired by the student movements in Europe and the United States. Students who failed their exams could be conscripted into the armed forces, and the movement identified with the anti-colonial struggle in Africa.

In 1968 tightly-controlled elections were held. During the campaign an electoral front of Communists, Catholics and prominent 'left' intellectuals called the CDE — Democratic Electoral Commission — was formed. The CDE was to be an important forum for opposition to the regime.

The 'new spring' meant that the trade unions could run internal elections without first submitting lists of candidates to the secret police (PIDE). Hence in 1969 and 1970 elections took place in five unions. Textile union members chose a student militant as their organiser. By October 1970 there were 20 or so unions with elected leaderships, who convened a semi-legal federation called the Intersindical.

The rise of the student and workers' movements, the drain of the colonial wars and economic crises continued to alarm the regime. By the early 1970s Caetano had returned to traditional conservatism and repression. There was no room for reforms when a war was being fought and nearly half of central budget expenditure went on the armed forces.

But the workers' movement could not simply be pushed back. Caetano had introduced a Law of Collective Contracts which resulted in an annual round of wage negotiations. As a result, in the textile union there was a strike every year between 1970 and 1973. Short-lived spontaneous strikes also took place in a number of other sectors.

Because of fear of repression, strike committees were often not elected or organised. In some cases the workers did not even define their demands. They just said they wanted an increase.

The first major industrial conflict was in 1973, involving the metal workers at TAP, the Portuguese airline. Some of these workers occupied a Boeing 707; two were shot and wounded by the police during the eviction. A workers' committee, one of the first in Portugal for several generations, was formed.

> The police beat up a lot of people. The strike lasted for 15 days. It was a very well organised strike. A *communicado* was produced every day, signed by a 'group of workers' . . . Workers from different parts of the factory met in each other's houses. About 150 were involved with the clandestine organisation of workers inside. The interplay of the clandestine and the legal struggle enabled them to succeed in the strike. Not only did they win their wage demands, they succeeded in releasing those imprisoned, the wounded were compensated and those forcibly dismissed re-instated. [2]

The workers at Lisbon airport were politically influenced by an emerging revolutionary left. By 1972 arguments were developing within the CDE about the use of violence, semi-legal political action, and internal democracy. After a split, between a third and a half of the militants left — 40 or 50 people, providing both the founding members of virtually all the (non-Maoist) revolutionary left groups and the kernel of the Socialist Party — which was founded in 1973.

Both the confidence of the workers' movement as a whole and the development of the revolutionary left were soon to receive a massive boost from events outside the country.

The Armed Forces Movement and the coup

General Antonio de Spinola, with his monocle and swagger stick, had been built up by the press as a war hero. Spinola had fought for Franco in the Spanish civil war and, as an 'observer', alongside the German Nazis on the Russian Front. The general, a former governor of Guinea and director of the Champalimaud group, expressed the growing mood of discontent within the establishment in a book titled **Portugal and the Future**. Published by a subsidiary of CUF, it was in no way a radical text. Both CUF and Champalimaud were pressing for entry into the Common Market, the EEC, as well as for a neo-colonial solution in Africa. Business interests were shifting away from the empire and towards the EEC, and the political strategy favoured in ruling-class circles increasingly reflected this shift.

Caetano wrote in his memoirs:

On 18 February, I received a copy of **Portugal and the Future** with a kind dedication from the author . . . when I closed the book I had understood that the military coup, which I could sense had been coming, was now inevitable.[3]

However, Caetano saw Spinola and his associates as the threat, not the junior officers who were to form the 'Armed Forces Movement', the MFA. He did not yet understand how deeply the interminable colonial wars were undermining the confidence, and ultimately the political loyalty to the regime, of the army's middle ranks.

For there was no prospect of winning the wars. By early 1974 the PAIGC in Guinea was on the verge of victory and FRELIMO — the Front for the Liberation of Mozambique — had opened a new offensive. The number of Portuguese dead, 13,000, was more than Portugal had lost in any conflict since the Napoleonic wars. The army was being blamed for these failures; some officers were ashamed to wear their uniforms in the streets of Lisbon.

Meanwhile a shortage of trained officers led to a decree, in July 1973, enabling conscripted officers with only short service records to be promoted alongside regular officers. Faced with a barrage of hostility, the government published a second decree guaranteeing the security of officers above the rank of captain. This incensed the more junior officers. On Sunday 9 September, amid stringent security precautions, 136 officers, none more senior than captain, met deep in the countryside ostensibly for a 'special farmhouse barbecue'. Thus commenced the first meeting of the Armed Forces Movement (MFA).

The MFA, most of whose members had served in Guinea, now set up an organising committee. On 16 March it was involved in a botched coup attempt, but the regime shrank from harsh measures and transferred most of the leaders to other units, where they continued agitating. By April 1974 the MFA had built a network of 300 supporting officers from all three services, and had drafted its first programme, calling for 'Democracy, Development and De-colonialisation'.

At that time only a few of the officers could have been labelled 'socialist'. There is no evidence of any connections between the MFA and the African freedom fighters, the Communist Party, or the revolutionary left. The MFA wanted a 'democratic, modern, mixed economy' on the Western European pattern, and refused to accept blame for colonial reverses. Such a standpoint was consistent with the class backgrounds of these officers. Yet in the context of authoritarian Portugal, the adoption of demands for 'Democracy, Development and De-colonialisation' was inevitably subversive. It made a clash with the regime inevitable.

On 25 April 1974, at twenty-five minutes past midnight, the

Catholic Radio Renascenca played a song titled *Grandola Vila Morena*. This was the signal for the start of the coup.

Some soldiers had already taken decisive action. The entire engineering regiment, at the fortress of Pontinha on the northern edge of Lisbon, had revolted and occupied its own barracks, led by Otelo de Carvalho. At this time Carvalho's main purpose was to 'reconquer the prestige of the Army and of the Armed Forces'. Earlier photographs show him weeping at Salazar's funeral. But Carvalho was to play an important role in the development of the revolution.

The coup itself succeeded with remarkable ease. A dozen military units were mobilised; the radio and TV stations, the airport and the general military headquarters were taken, all against little resistance. Only four people were killed — shot by terrified police agents. A regime that had lasted nearly 50 years crumbled in less than a day.

> A young peasant soldier standing guard on a Lisbon street corner was asked by a middle-class passer-by what he was doing there; he replied that he had been ordered to keep an eye on insurgent troops. Upon being told, 'but you are the revolutionaries!' he shouted to a colleague: 'Manuel, we are the rebels, *Viva!*'[4]

The MFA leadership was extremely nervous about the consequences of this sudden collapse. The MFA did not intend to govern the country itself, even on a temporary basis. Propelled by a concern for respectability and rank, the co-ordinating committee of the MFA called upon a group of eminent soldiers, headed by General Spinola, to take on the leadership. This Junta in turn set up the first provisional government.

The Carnival

At first, public reaction to the coup was cautious. Many rushed out to stock up with petrol and groceries. Parents kept their children indoors. But soon workers, peasants, women and youngsters went tentatively into the streets to see what was happening. Crowds gathered in the main squares in Lisbon:

> Troops come towards us. What will happen? They raise their fingers in a V (for Victory) sign. The crowd cheer like I've never heard cheers before. I'd heard crowds shout in anger, but this was joy, unmitigated.[5]

The slogan 'The MFA is with the people, the people are with the MFA' soon gained enormous popularity. Red carnations were adopted as the symbol of the revolution; red for the revolution and flowers for peace. They were given to soldiers who stuck them in the barrels of their rifles. By the end of the day the tanks were swarming with joy-riders. Demonstrators attacked the hated secret police, the PIDE, whose agents often escaped lynching only narrowly. About 100 secret police were imprisoned — and 200 political prisoners released — by the crowds. Street and bridge names were changed. The walls flowered with graffiti, slogans and posters, and later with murals. May Day was declared a national holiday. The days between 25 April and May Day became a continuous 'festival of the oppressed'. Even the prostitutes of Lisbon organised: they campaigned to sack the pimps, and offered their services half-price to all ranks below lieutenant.

The coup rapidly released a host of popular energies and aspirations. On 29 April more than 100 families living in the shanty towns occupied a new government housing project on the outskirts of Lisbon. In the next two weeks more than 2,000 houses were occupied around the country. The movement of residents' commissions and shanty dwellers was to emerge, simmer, and resurge, over the next eighteen months.[6]

The MFA was to claim later that *it* was the motor of the revolution. Actually in the days following the coup it was extremely cautious; the real motor was the workers' movement.

On the day of the coup itself only one factory was on strike, the Mague metal works, with two thousand workers. The Mague workers' demand for 6,000 *escudos* (£100) as a monthly minimum wage was immediately conceded by the management, who feared the consequences of being branded as fascists by Portugal's new rulers. The Junta, however, was unhappy about this victory and declared that the new pay deal was an example which should *not* be followed.[7]

After 25 April most workers did go to work, but they spent the day celebrating. Celebrations quickly turned into battles. Managements wanted to restart production, but the workers wanted the 'revolution' to be carried into the workplaces. These spontaneous and therefore uncoordinated disputes were mainly in the new industries such as electronics and the shipyards, and newly expanded parts of older industries, for instance textiles and construction. Both economic and political demands were raised. Wage demands sprouted haphazardly. One participant recalled a meeting early in May, organised by women textile workers:

> There were some seven or eight thousand people there. Everything was completely confused. Somebody shouted should we ask for a rise of 3,000 *escudos*. From across the hall the answer was no . . . 4,000. Then no . . . 5,000 *escudos*.[8]

Workers at the Timex watch factory, predominantly women, went on strike for wage increases and for the purging of six PIDE informers. They sold watches in the streets to bolster their strike funds. On 13 May 1,600 miners at Panasqueira struck for a minimum wage of 6,000 *escudos* a month, free medical care, an annual bonus of a month's wages, one month's holiday and the purging of fascists. Within a week they had won all the demands. On 15 May Lisnave's 8,400 workers occupied their shipyards and went on strike for a 40-hour week and a 7,800-*escudo* (£130) monthly minimum wage.

In May at least 158 workforces were involved in fierce confrontations, including 35 occupations. In four of these, managers were held prisoner.[9]

In the big companies, especially the multinationals, economic demands were accompanied by calls for the purging of all managers with fascist connections.[10] In some places this meant the sacking of them all. This ousting of fascists was known as *saneamento* or 'cleansing'. Very quickly it spread beyond outright collaborators, and came to include anybody who was opposed to the workers. *Saneamento* occurred in more than half the firms which employed more than 500 people, revealing both the weakness of the management and the growing confidence of the workers. *Saneamento* implicitly raised the political question of power in the factory.

At this time in Portugal, 0.4 per cent of all companies, many of them interlinked, held 53 per cent of the capital. Alongside the thousands of small workshops were some of the largest and most modern workplaces in Europe. Even in 1955 86 per cent of industrial production originated from either the Lisbon industrial conurbation or the area between Porto and the coast.[11] Thus the Portuguese industrial working class, which totalled about one million, or four-tenths of the working population,[12] was highly concentrated. So in areas such as Lisbon, where 200,000 workers struck in May, workers could readily learn from and support each other.

Before 25 April clandestine workers' committees existed only briefly, during strikes. After the coup, workers' commissions — often called *ad hoc* commissions — rapidly emerged. But even at proletarian Lisnave, during the May strike of 1974,

> Things were not then properly organised. It was more or less 'you and me, let us do something'. Only later on was there a proper process of elections based upon workplace sections.[13]

By the end of May 1974 workers' commissions, councils and committees had been formed at almost all workplaces in the Lisbon region. It has been estimated that between May and October 4,000 workers' commissions were established, usually by mass meetings, in virtually every workplace. They acted as a unifying force in the extremely common multi-union workplaces.

During May many militants ignored the unions, regarding them as little more than empty shells, remnants of the fascist regime. Sometimes the workers' commissions emerged in conjunction with union committees. Very occasionally, for example in some textile factories, workers belonged to a single union, and the union committee was in effect the workers' commission.

The workers' commissions may have lacked formal organisation, but the high level of struggle forced them to meet and consult frequently. They were highly democratic. The commission at Plessey included 118 workers — all of whom insisted on going to the first meeting with the management.[14]

Workers quickly learnt from, and supported, one another. Inter-factory (*inter-empresa*) meetings were held. One young woman assembly worker from Plesseys, a member of her workers' commission, recalled:

> It was said, why should we be on our own if other people across the road had the same problems. Then we decided to join, and to discuss things in general. Practically all the factories from the Margem SUL [the South Lisbon conurbation] were there. They were a place, a way, for people to meet and discuss. The main purpose of these meetings was to defend the revolution.[15]

In the first weeks of the revolution, the army, including senior officers, was enormously popular. A meeting of women textile workers was interrupted by

> a soldier who was completely pissed out of his mind asking for a whip around for soldiers because he wanted another drink, for himself and his mates.

The chairman of that meeting, a union activist, remembered:

> I told the soldier to piss off. The bloke went. The people in the hall were outraged by my treatment of the soldier. I would have been lynched if I had not explained that I was an officer. I was in civilian clothes. At that time the military could do no wrong — soldiers were looked on as saints.[16]

Such popularity was exploited to the full by the Junta, who were able to use it to persuade several sections of workers to return to work. But such methods were necessarily a stop-gap. The rulers of Portugal had to search for more regular and organised methods of disciplining the workers' movement.

The PCP and the Intersindical

The first step in defusing the workers' movement was to attempt to establish a government of 'national unity', in which the interests of all classes — including the working class — could be said to be represented. Accordingly, in the first Provisional Government, formed on 15 May, the Socialist Party, which at the time had only 200 members and was less than a year old, was given three cabinet ministers. Mario Soares, its leader, convinced a sceptical Spinola that the Communists (PCP) could not 'be excluded from a government of national unity' and would be less dangerous in the government than against it. Thus Alvaro Cunhal, the PCP secretary, became minister without portfolio and Alvino Goncalves from the bank workers' union became minister of labour.

The PCP had a respected tradition of opposition to fascism. It proudly proclaimed that its 247 candidates for the April 1975 elections had served between them 440 years behind bars.[17] Over the years the party had developed a clandestine organisation which had perhaps 5,000 members by 25 April 1974. Thus the PCP was the one party with a substantial base and some influence in the working class. But like other Western Communist Parties, it believed that its task was to build an *all-class* alliance in order to establish a bourgeois-democratic framework, within which it could win positions and extend its influence. This perspective led it to build up the Socialist Party as a prospective 'left' ally. But it also meant the rejection of any idea that a socialist revolution could be achieved in 'backward' Portugal; first the country's industrial base had to be built up. Thus the PCP constantly pointed to the 'crisis of production' and exhorted workers to 'save the national economy'.

The Intersindical union federation had developed since 1970 in order to fight for better wages and conditions and for union recognition. On 25 April it had consisted of 22 unions. Within a few weeks this figure had risen to about 200. The PCP had previously been only one of several groups active in the Intersindical. Now it set out to control the unions, sending its militants to work full time in them at its own expense — the unions were at this stage often too poor to be able to afford to pay wages to their employees. Thus the Intersindical was dramatically transformed into a national trade union umbrella organisation, under the leadership of the PCP.

On 25 May the government was forced to concede a national minimum wage of 3,300 *escudos* a month. Wages rose by 30 per cent on average. Four days later the government sacked about 1,000 company directors who had received patronage from the old regime. The strike wave faltered temporarily and the inter-factory councils (*inter-empresas*) which had sprung up almost disappeared. Committees based on individual factories, however, together with the new residents' commissions in the shanty towns and occupied housing projects, continued to organise.

On 1 June the Intersindical signalled its view that enough wage increases had now been won: it organised an anti-strike demonstration.

The PCP weekly, **Avante**, explained that workers must avoid 'reactionary manoeuvres to promote industrial unrest'. The demonstration was a flop, but it showed how closely the PCP now controlled the Intersindical. Despite this, the strike movement began to revive sharply. The PCP attacked many of these struggles but reserved special venom for those led by workers' commissions, since these threatened to develop as organs of workers' power outside the control of the Intersindical.

The joint role of the PCP and the unions it controlled in attacking strikers was demonstrated particularly clearly in June during the government's first major offensive against the postal workers — a section which it judged to lack economic muscle. On 18 June, faced with a derisory and provocative wage offer, 25,000 postal workers went on strike, led by an elected commission outside the control of the Intersindical. Picket lines were set up, medical and financial aid was organised for the poorest families, and leaflets were produced to explain the strikers' cause to other workers. The PCP and the Intersindical now attacked the strikers for 'attempting to become a privileged group at the expense of the mass of the population'. Abuse was backed up by force; on 19 June the government called in the army.

Faced with this threat a tense meeting of the 260-strong strike committee felt forced to back down in exchange for an increase of only 80-100 *escudos* a month. Understandably bitter, the committee explained what had occurred in a manifesto defending the strike and exposing and attacking the role of the PCP, which had once taken pride in leading militant struggles yet which now abused and sabotaged them.

By contrast the Socialist Party had conspicuously *supported* the strike, stressing its democratic organisation in opposition to the Stalinist PCP. It thus enhanced its reputation as 'left-wing' — a factor which would prove important later.

The dispute was an isolated victory for the Provisional Government; buffeted by the continued militancy and a growing flight of foreign capital from Portugal, it collapsed on 9 July.

The Armed Forces Movement and the September coup

The First Provisional Government had never exerted decisive control over policy. In the period between April and July, effective authority was shared between three centres of power — the Junta, the coordinating committee of the Armed Forces Movement and the Provisional Government itself. Given the enormous prestige of the army and the weakness of the parties which comprised the Provisional

Government, it was probably the *least* powerful of these bodies. But between the top generals of the Junta and the middle-ranking officers of the MFA lay important differences.

The Junta was concerned primarily with maintaining the established political and economic system, with the cohesion of the army under its command and with engineering an 'orderly' transition to a neo-colonial solution in Africa. The MFA, by contrast, included conscripted officers who had no permanent stake in the system. They were hostile to the old political elite which had brought shame on them in the colonial wars. These they wished to end. They were also far more susceptible to the influence of the mass movement.

General Spinola had tried to reconcile the different forces by bringing them together in a Council of State which consisted of equal numbers of representatives from the Junta, the MFA and the powerful civilians appointed by the general himself. But in the colonies the growing strength of the liberation movements and increasing demoralisation in the armed forces necessitated a much more rapid disengagement than Portuguese capital would have liked. At home, equally rapid solutions to the 'problem of labour discipline' were becoming necessary. These aims could only be achieved with the direct participation of the MFA in the business of government.

The new government combination therefore included seven representatives of the MFA officers and was headed by Vasco Goncalves, who was generally regarded as favourably disposed to the PCP. One of its first actions was to initiate a series of strike laws, which legalised wage strikes for the first time, but which banned political stoppages and sympathy strikes. The leftist colouring of the Second Provisional Government reflected the strength of the workers' movement; its aggressive strategy reflected the acuteness of the crisis in which Portuguese capitalism now found itself.

Effective use of the law against workers, however, depended on the loyalty and cohesion of the armed forces, and this was increasingly breaking down. In the period since the coup the strength and militancy of the workers' movement had radicalised important sections of the forces at the disposal of the state. In areas where the movement was particularly strong, sections such as the engineers and the RAL-1 — light artillery regiment in Lisbon — became increasingly sympathetic to strikes and demonstrations. The despised secret police of Salazar and Caetano had been abolished. Widespread disunity and unreliability amongst the remaining forces led on 8 July to the creation of a new force — Continental Operations Command (COPCON) — which, it was hoped, would be able to 'intervene directly in support of the civilian authorities and at their command.' Such hopes were rapidly put to the test in the crisis unleashed by the attempt to enforce the new trade union laws.

These were introduced on 29 August. The workers of the Lisnave shipyard responded by organising an 'illegal' one-day strike and demonstration against the legislation and for longer standing demands for *saneamento*. Their leaflet argued:

> We do not support the government when it comes out with anti-working class laws which undermine the struggles of workers against capitalist exploitation. We shall actively oppose the anti-strike law because it is a great blow to the freedom of the workers.[18]

The demonstration was attacked by the PCP and banned by the government. But would it be physically prevented by COPCON, whose leaders had already expressed support for the laws? More than 5,000 helmeted Lisnave workers marched in serried ranks to the ministry of labour in Lisbon. The shipyards were brought to a standstill. The effect on the rank-and-file soldiers of COPCON was profound, as one of them testified:

> Before lunch the rumour circulated that we were going out and we soon guessed it was to Lisnave . . . We formed up at midday and the commander told us that he'd received a telephone call about a demonstration at Lisnave led by a minority of leftist agitators and that our job was to prevent it taking place. We were armed as we had never been before with G3s and four magazines.
>
> . . . the demonstration began and a human torrent advanced with shouts of 'the soldiers are the sons of the workers', 'tomorrow the soldiers will be workers', and 'the arms of the soldiers must not be turned against the workers.' The commander soon saw that we were not going to follow his orders, so he shut up. Our arms hung down by our side and some comrades were crying. Back at the barracks, the commander wasn't too annoyed but told us that in future we would have to obey orders . . . the following day in the barracks, things were more lively. Before morning assembly many comrades were up and shouting the slogans of the demo: 'the soldiers are the sons of the workers', 'down with capitalist exploitation'.[19]

In a leaflet, the Lisnave workers drew the political conclusion:

> We support the Armed Forces as long as they support the struggles of the oppressed and exploited classes against the exploiting and oppressing classes.[20]

Such highly conditional support was entirely justified, for units of COPCON were still used against workers. Later in September the workers of TAP went on strike. The airport was placed under military control and one of the leading workers, Santos Junor, arrested by COPCON. But COPCON now often spent time listening to the workers and *arbitrating* in disputes — hardly the role of unquestioning servant of the civil power which the regiment's creators had envisaged.

By September industrialists who had welcomed the 25 April coup began to denounce the provisional government in the bitterest terms: they were worried that the troops could no longer be trusted, and longed desperately for 'law and order' to be re-established. Many factory owners and foreign investors were withdrawing entirely from Portugal, and sections of the ruling class now drew the conclusion that the use of armed force was becoming urgently necessary.

Leading industrialists met Spinola and a few of the generals. Spinola called on the 'silent majority' to mobilise a march which was intended to be 300,000 strong. Arms were supplied to fascists who would foster enough disorder so as to give the generals an excuse to intervene, attack the left and re-establish 'order'.

Their calculations omitted to take into account the reaction of the mass of the workers. From 8pm on 27 September, the eve of the projected demonstration, barricades, sometimes armed, were set up on all the major roads into Lisbon. As the gains established by the PCP and Intersindical were under threat they too played a major role in mobilising people. The railway union had instructed its members to refuse to take the special trains to Lisbon and to search scheduled trains for any travelling rightists. The coach drivers' union did the same; only two coachloads of demonstrators left for Lisbon. Soldiers joined the barricades. The demonstration of the 'silent majority' never took place.

On 29 September Spinola resigned as president together with three members of the Junta. Two hundred people were arrested by the MFA; the haul included the multi-millionaire, former officer and member of the Junta Galvao de Melo. The following day the discredited Junta was disbanded and replaced by the MFA-dominated Council of the Revolution. The Third Provisional Government was formed.

The revolutionary left

The failure of September's attempted coup gave a boost to the whole of the left, and encouraged large numbers of people to examine the ideas of all those who opposed the Right. Censorship had been abolished. Workers and soldiers were hungry for ideas. Personnel managers read Trotsky's writings on dual power; Lenin's **State and Revolution** was a best-seller in the shops. But the revolutionary groups did not make it easy for those who were becoming interested in their ideas. Revolutionary newspapers were often boring, full of jargon and remote from workers' experience, expressing their ideas in obscure and sectarian language. Yet a lot were sold. Sellers would go down to the Lisbon Ferry stations with bundles of several hundred papers and return empty handed. The Maoist MRPP paper **Luta Popular** printed 100,000 copies of each issue, though many fewer must have been sold.

The MRPP — 'the Movement to reorganise the Party of the Proletariat' — had been formed in 1970. By 1974 it was the largest and strongest and certainly the noisiest of the Maoist groups. The MRPP constantly condemned the MFA, COPCON, the PCP and the role of the Intersindical. It called the PCP 'social fascists', a phrase used by Stalinists in the early 1930s to condemn social democrats. As far as the MRPP were concerned the PCP were the main enemy.

During the early phase of the revolution, when the government consisted of a partnership of the PCP and the MFA, and when COPCON was frequently sent against striking workers, such extreme sectarian-ism was not a crippling disadvantage — it is significant that the group was strong at Timex and the airport, which had both experienced COPCON intervention. But the MRPP was prepared to align itself with attacks from the right; such influence as it had was often achieved in alliance with the Socialist Party, which had few organised members on the shop-floor and was prepared to make common cause with the MRPP in its battle against the PCP.

When, in the summer of 1975, the reactionaries began burning the offices of the PCP and the rest of the revolutionary left, the MRPP characterised this movement as a 'peasant uprising against social-fascism'. In general the Maoists, while condemning the PCP as 'social fascist' shared the same basic understanding of the struggle. Both the MRPP and the PCP argued that, given Portugal's economic and political backwardness, it was necessary to achieve national independence and democracy through an alliance of classes in which the role of the working class was subordinate. Establishing socialism was out of the question. They rarely stopped to consider that industrial workers formed nearly four-tenths of the working population in Portugal, compared with one-twentieth in the Russia of 1917.

In accordance with these same perspectives many of the other Maoist grouplets amalgamated in December 1974 into the Popular United Democratic Front (UDP), a Popular Front embracing peasants and small businessmen and others who wished to see 'democracy' in Portugal. Portugal itself they saw as an exploited Third World country. The UDP directed its slogans against 'both imperialisms', as if Portu-guese capital had an equivalent relationship with Washington and Moscow, and was hostile to those who wished to move decisively beyond national democratic politics.

The Movement of Left Socialists — MES — had emerged from the electoral front of 1972, bringing with it a number of young militant Catholics. With its open organisation, MES acquired something of a base in the Intersindical, the textile and metal-workers' unions and in the airport (TAP). It often acted as a pressure group on other parties. MES is best understood as a 'centrist' group: it often used revolutionary language in order to attract workers who were breaking from the reformists, but failed to translate its verbal militancy into the practice of building an independent revolutionary party.

Both the 'orthodox' Trotskyist groups — the LCI and the PRT, which were very small — shared this last characteristic. In the case of the PRT, pressure group politics took the even more dangerous form of tailing the Socialist Party, even when the latter was urging that the workers' occupation of the newspaper **Republica** be broken by military force. The LCI was not prepared to go that far;[21] but its basic political approach was not much different. Its flavour is well conveyed by the election campaign of April 1976, in which the LCI demanded 'that the PCP and the Socialist Party assume their responsibilities by forming a government without the representatives of the bourgeoisie.'

The Revolutionary Party of the Proletariat/Revolutionary Brigades (PRP/BR), by contrast, made it clear that the task was not to persuade reformists to shoulder their responsibilities, but the building of an independent revolutionary party committed to the seizure of power by means of armed insurrection. However, guerrilla traditions developed in clandestine operations against the Caetano regime tended to lead the PRP to emphasise the role of an armed few acting in the name of the workers. It tended to shy away from the necessary work of building a mass workers' organisation through work around more humdrum issues and demands. It was, in short, necessary for the PRP, as for other organisations of the revolutionary left, to prove itself in practice.

In the period immediately following the failed coup of September there was a comparative lull in the struggle. From the beginning of January 1975, however, more and more factories were being occupied, and land seizures and school students' strikes multiplied; great opportunities for effective intervention by revolutionary socialists presented themselves.

Rising struggle

On 14 January a gigantic demonstration, perhaps 300,000 strong, was organised by Intersindical in favour of a unified trade union movement — UNICIDADE. The PCP had by now realised that it had made a mistake in ignoring the powerful workers' commissions, which were increasingly open to revolutionary influence, and was trying to gain ground in them. The Socialist Party launched a stinging attack on the UNICIDADE proposals, accusing the PCP of 'sabotaging democracy'. It wished to develop unions outside Intersindical, and so outside PCP control, and split the workers' organisations on religious and political lines. Accordingly the Socialist Party organised a packed mass rally in favour of a less 'monolithic' trade union confederation. In this context that part of the revolutionary left which opposed the campaign against UNICIDADE and supported the Intersindical demonstration was certainly correct.

Further opportunities for revolutionaries presented themselves. On 7 February the inter-factory committee *Inter-empresas* called a demonstration against the growing number of sackings. More than 1,000 workers' representatives from 38 factories, including some revolutionaries, met for a planning meeting. The lead banner was to read 'Unemployment is an inevitable consequence of capitalism. That is why workers want to destroy it and build a new world'. Part of the NATO fleet was anchored at Lisbon at the time and, at the last minute, another slogan was added: 'NATO out, for national independence'.

This demonstration was bitterly attacked by the PCP and banned by one of its most prominent supporters, the civil governor of Lisbon. The trade unions in the south (part of the Intersindical) called it 'an attempt to confuse the democratic forces and to sabotage the construction of democracy'. On television, leading PCP member Octavio Paz urged viewers to give flowers to the marines of the NATO fleet.

All the efforts of the PCP were in vain. After members of the workers' commissions went to see COPCON the MFA raised no objection to the demonstration. Forty thousand people turned out:

> They are in their work clothes, with red helmets. They carry 'without party' banners with names Lisnave, Setenave, Effacec, National Steel. The stewards have walkie-talkies and red arm bands; they are all workers. They form a human chain around the demo . . .
> The demo makes its way to the Ministry of Labour [which was guarded by COPCON units] . . . Those at the front of the march shout: 'Soldiers on our side'. Then occurs a scene that helps you understand Portugal today — the soldiers, with portable machine-guns slung around them, turn to the Ministry of Labour, at the same time they raise their fists, to the great applause of the marchers. With clenched fists, workers and soldiers together shout: 'National independence!' People were crying with joy.[22]

The size and composition of the demonstration made it impossible for the PCP to continue to condemn those who had called it as saboteurs and ultra-left troublemakers. Facing both a breach with the MFA and the growth of workers' organisations outside its control, the PCP was forced to redouble its efforts. *Inter-empresas* had demonstrated that it could not be rubbished or ignored.

However, the *Inter-empresas* depended for its life-blood on generalising the struggle of the workplaces which it represented. In the workers' councils of Russia in 1917, the *soviets*, the lessons of workers' struggle were hammered out, then passed back to the workplaces to inform the next stage of struggle. The *soviets* were a forum in which the workers' parties argued for their ideas, in which these were tested against the needs of the class struggle, and from which a revolutionary leadership could emerge capable of leading the working class in a challenge for state power. The vitality of the *soviets* depended on the interaction between the struggle which had called them forth and the dynamic leadership which they could provide.

The *Inter-empresas* offered this potential. The Portuguese revolutionary left, however, failed to understand this.

The Maoist groups, which were the most influential within the *Inter-empresas*, were at the same time coalescing into the UDP and tended to see it as but another potential part of the UDP. The PRP drifted into a different error. The astonishing achievements of the mass movement had led many people to reject the need for political parties: workers, tenants, agricultural labourers, they said, with the support of the radical soldiers, can defend the revolution without parties. This *apartiderismo*, 'non-partyism', affected large areas of activity — and the revolutionary left went along with it. On mass demonstrations few party banners were to be seen; the left shied away from selling its papers; and there were even instances of MRPP members being thrown off for wearing party badges.

With the *Inter-empresas*, the PRP tended towards 'non-partyism', failing to recognise the vital importance of arguing clear revolutionary politics in this and other organisations of the working class, and the equal importance of testing and questioning the role of the different parties in the struggle. Instead they — and most of the revolutionary left — tended to counterpose the *Inter-empresas* to the unions. The Maoists, with their ingrained hostility to the 'social fascists' of the Intersindical, were especially prone to this.

The result was that the revolutionary left failed to fight systematically for their ideas within the unions as well — and this was especially important, because although the workers' commissions were setting the pace the unions were also taking up bread-and-butter issues. Abstention simply left the field clear for the PCP, which was now regaining lost ground in the factories.

The March conspiracy and the elections

The mass movement of occupations and land seizures continued into February. It is estimated that some 2,500 apartments were occupied in Lisbon alone in a few days at the end of the month.[25] Every new struggle threatened to become a political challenge. As in September 1974, sections of the ruling class saw a military coup as the necessary response. The March conspirators included businessman Miguel Champalimaud (of the conglomerate) and several high-ranking officers who had connections with Spinola. Their first action was to send supposedly reliable troops against one of Lisbon's most radical regiments, RAL-1. On 11 March, paratroopers surrounded the barracks, but could not be persuaded to fire. The RAL-1 soldiers were able to engage them in discussion instead: within hours the paratroopers were explaining: 'We are no fascists — we are your comrades.'

The organisation of military resistance to the coup attempt was led by COPCON; working people responded magnificently. Within hours of the attack barricades were set up along the main roads out of Lisbon and Porto and to the border with Spain, sometimes with the use of expropriated bulldozers, lorries and cement-mixers. Soldiers fraternised openly with workers manning the barricades and some handed over arms. Armed workers searched cars. Strikers at Radio Renascenca went back to work and occupied the radio station — in order 'to defend the revolution'. Many papers printed second editions or special broadsheets, including the workers' committee of the big Lisbon daily **O Seculo**. The Porto section of the union of bank employees commanded its members: 'Close the banks immediately. Don't make any payments. Set up pickets at the doors to check entrances and exits. Watch the telex and the telephones.'

After the failure of the coup, right-wing generals and some company directors were arrested. Spinola and others were whisked off to Spain, as an Intersindical leader put it, 'by the helicopters of reaction'.

Again the successful resistance to the coup gave a considerable boost to the revolutionary left. The PRP, for instance, grew on the basis of organising against possible further right-wing operations, winning new members among army officers, as well as the rank and file. But this again strengthened the tendency to concentrate exclusively on the threat from the right (real or imaginary), and to neglect the less spectacular business of relating to the independent struggles of workers.

The MFA was strengthened by the failed coups. After 11 March it institutionalised its power: at the top was the 'supreme' Council of Revolution, responsible to the MFA Assembly of 240 delegates, in theory from any rank, from the three wings of the armed forces.

Precisely because the Council of the Revolution was so confident, it felt able to honour its commitment to hold 'free elections'.

Behind these successive attempts at a coup lay the strategy of a ruling class concerned to re-establish its control over the Portuguese state machine. Those who had originally backed Spinola against Caetano had had no inkling of the forces that would be released by the 25 April coup. They had wanted merely to replace Caetano with others more willing to modernise Portugal's economic relations with the rest of the world capitalist system. After the failure of 11 March, it became increasingly clear that with the conservative forces in disarray, their strategy of seeking a coup which would establish a paternalist administration was not going to work.

One alternative method of survival for Portuguese capitalism was to seek a strong Western European-type social democracy within a bourgeois parliamentary framework. For some time the United States, through the CIA, had been pumping resources into the bourgeois parties, including the Socialist Party.

The anniversary of the overthrow of the old regime, 25 April, was selected for Portugal's first genuine elections for fifty years. Electioneering was allocated three weeks. Intricate rules were established, including equal TV time for all parties standing, regardless of size. Hence parties to the left of the PCP, which eventually won less than 8 per cent of the vote, had more than 50 per cent of the TV air time given to political parties. Parties were not allowed to flypost on top of one another's posters. It became necessary to carry longer and longer ladders to reach bits of unposted wall. Interest was immense. Of the 6,176,559 enrolled voters, 5,666,696 went to the polls, 91.7 per cent of the electorate.

The real victor of the election was the Socialist Party which obtained 37.8 per cent of the vote. The PCP polled a rather meagre 12.5 per cent, plus 4.1 per cent for its close ally the MDP. Parties of the left won almost 60 per cent of the total: in spite of the 'backwardness' of Portugal, 'socialism' was extremely popular.

The status of the Socialist Party was transformed. From 200 members in April 1974, it had grown to become the leading *parliamentary* party, under the banner of freedom of speech, democracy, and a managed and modern economy. The precise practical meaning of these slogans remained unclear to those who supported them. The experience of reformism in power, commonplace elsewhere, was unknown in Portugal.

The Socialist Party often appeared more left-wing than the PCP. It could afford to tolerate a left wing within its ranks more easily, since it lacked the Communist Party's monolithic structure and discipline. In this respect the lack of an organised presence in the factories was a positive advantage, since it could afford to oppose the unpopular government measures which PCP members were expected to impose. For most of 1974-5 the Socialist Party had little organised base among workers. Its activists were overwhelmingly from the petty bourgeoisie. The very vagueness of its slogans for 'progress', 'democracy' and 'socialism' enabled it to appeal to broad sectors of the population, including the less organised workers who fell outside the influence of the Intersindical and the PCP.

The Socialist Party tended to vacillate according to the balance of class forces, which was natural for a party of this type. In the early stages of the revolution it therefore leaned verbally towards the left. As the crisis deepened, however, it increasingly reflected the despair, rather than the inarticulate hopes, of the unorganised. For the major party of the organised workers, the PCP, was incapable of resolving the mounting conflict on terms favourable to the mass of the population, and no serious alternative was built to its left. Only this twin failure enabled the Socialist Party to develop a substantial base among workers. Many workers came to see the Socialist Party as the party best able to protect the gains they had made since April 1974.[24]

The newly-elected Constituent Assembly was not a supreme body: the president was still appointed by the MFA. The existence of 600 'legitimate' sources of power led to sharp disagreements. Within 24 hours there was chanting on a Socialist Party victory demonstration of 'Down with the MFA'. For the first time there was open conflict between a major political party and the MFA. Over the next six months the Socialist Party relentlessly pursued the interrelated themes of 'power to those elected', 'democracy', and 'freedom of speech'. Behind the phrases of 'pure democracy' the forces opposed to the revolutionary movement increasingly rallied.

Popular Power

The election results were a humiliation for those within the MFA who regarded themselves — certainly not Mario Soares and the Socialist Party — as the 'saviours of the people'. Leftists within the MFA were asking 'Is the Socialist Party merely a face of the bourgeoisie?' and 'Would it help perpetuate the revolution?'

As the Socialist Party gained confidence its differences with the military-dominated government became clearer. In these months after the election *Poder Popular* ('popular power') emerged as the umbrella ideology for the MFA. *Poder Popular* served as a bridge spanning classes, uniting the military with workers, peasants and tenants. In this form it was merely a propagandist slogan of the military.

Now, however, it appeared as a living reality. Every day workers were taking over their factories. Unpublished Ministry of Labour statistics from 1976 — long after the peak of the movement — show that by then 280 firms were under self-management. A further 600 went a stage further and assumed *ownership*, becoming classed as co-operatives.

The take-overs were usually of small firms — the co-operatives averaged 45 employees while self-managed firms averaged 61. Many had been abandoned by their former owners, and many would have gone to the wall in any programme of capitalist modernisation.[25] Often, in the largest and most militant enterprises the workers decided *not* to take over completely. For example the workers' commission at the headquarters of the construction firm Edifer took over the board-room (and kept the drinks cabinet as a memento) but decided not to kick management off the site. When asked why, they said: 'It is better we can see what they are doing.' A militant from the Setenave ship-yard put it this way:

> Even at Setenave we don't have workers' control. How can we if we don't control the banks? Our attitude is that we want to know everything . . . We want to control decisions but we do not take responsibility. We don't believe we can have workers' control alone.[26]

In the case of the larger enterprises the action of workers forced the nationalisation of the firm or the industry. The first act of the Council of Revolution, after 11 March, was to nationalise the banks and insurance companies where these were not foreign-owned. By now nearly 60 per cent of the economy was in the public sector.

The take-over in Lisbon of Radio Renascenca, the former Catholic radio station, became particularly well known. The broadcasters hung a live microphone in the street so that whenever there was a demonstration passing by, or a deputation outside, there could be a live broadcast of street politics.[27]

After the failure of the March coup, land occupations increased dramatically. Landworkers in the Alentejo region were in the process of occupying 200,000 hectares. The importance of the landworkers' struggles cannot be over-emphasised. For the first time in living memory the drift of workers from the land was reversed.

Agricultural co-operatives were set up, often named after political events and characters; for example the *Soldado Luis* co-operative was named after the soldier killed on 11 March at RAL-1 barracks. This large estate was owned by a count who mainly used it for shooting. One hectare of rice was grown — for the water fowl. Most labour was casual. Very little money was invested in the estate, except in the shooting lodge.

Now the workers organised regular meetings and elected a small committee to run the place. Most impressive of the changes was the transformation of the traditional peasant women. Often illiterate, dressed in black from head to foot, they did much of the backbreaking labour. Now they not only ensured that they were paid regular wages and at almost the same rate as men, but also played an active part in the management of the co-operative. The hectarage of rice was extended and the number of cattle increased. Tractors were borrowed, with the help of agrarian reform organisations.

The shooting lodge was converted into a cheese factory. The cheeses, made from sheep's milk, were supplied to factories in the south of Lisbon who would provide trucks to help with transportation. Factory workers, students and the unemployed also helped the co-operative at harvest times.

These take-overs, and those of houses and apartments in the cities drew many people into self-organisation who would otherwise be excluded since they didn't work in factories. This was a massive movement. Unemployed workers helped in the countryside. Children taught adults to read. Popular clinics and cultural centres flourished. People's tribunals were established. A golf course in the Algarve declared that it was now open to all — except the members.

The growing radicalisation affected sections of the army and threatened the unity of the MFA, which now increasingly oscillated between the claims of 'discipline' and those of Popular Power. Some talked of refusing to hand over power; others of a benevolent dictatorship. Various schemes were hatched to try to contain the contradictions. The most radical was the attempt to build a national network of 'revolutionary councils of soldiers, sailors and workers' — the CRTSMs, first conceived by the PRP but now also backed by elements of COPCON, including its commander Otelo de Carvalho.

Meetings were held to elect local CRTSM committees in factories and barracks. Only in the Lisnave and Setenave shipyards was the project approved by general assemblies of workers. In both the PRP had active cells of at least 25 militants. Each workers' assembly was addressed by a member of the MFA, Sobral Costa, and a speaker for the CRTSM.

Those who set up the CRTSMs saw the workers' commissions as being merely economic. This was not so: many workers' commissions had organised political demonstrations, occupations, strikes and other actions. But the CRTSMs drew an artificial distinction between their own 'political' role and the 'economic' concerns of the workers' commissions — and this led them to abstain from taking up 'bread and butter' issues in the workplaces.

This had two results. Firstly it prevented the CRTSMs from

sinking deep roots in the workplaces. Secondly it gave credence to PCP arguments that the CRTSMs were divisive, that they were trying to take over the political role of the workers' commissions. The leaders of the CRTSMs not only tended to separate politics from economics, but to separate politics from parties. On a CRTSM demonstration on 17 June, two of the slogans were 'We are the first Soviet of revolutionary Portugal' and 'For a revolutionary government without political parties'. This disdain for party politics neatly dovetailed with both the military tradition of the MFA and its role in reflecting and mediating the different class pressures within the popular movement.

On 8 July the General Assembly of the MFA narrowly approved 'guidelines for the alliance between the people and the MFA — the MFA/POVO pact. Its aim was to build up the popular assemblies as a parallel authority to the state and parliamentary system. The organisations of popular power, the residents' and workers' commissions, the soldiers' committees and other local organisations would integrate into a pyramid under the protection of the MFA.

In the movement to build soldiers' committees, the Pontinha assembly was cited as a living example. The Pontinha regiment of engineers had been the command headquarters for the 25 April coup. Most of the soldiers were trained mechanics and workers by background. Their regimental assembly became a model for other units. The soldiers and officers formed direct links with the local population, building roads and bridges with military equipment. After the attempted coup of 11 March, meetings between workers and soldiers became far more organised. The first joint assembly was held just before the MFA/POVO pact, with some 17 factories and 30 local tenants' associations present. At its peak the assembly had some 200 delegates from its constituent associations.[28]

There was much talk of assemblies — **Republica** mentions at least 38, and many planning meetings for others. Few in fact got off the ground. Usually the more stable were those that in effect assumed the functions of local government. The assemblies were dominated by representatives from residents' commissions, who swamped those from workplaces. In general the weakness of the popular assemblies was that they attempted to bridge classes, between 'the people' who lived in a particular area or between soldiers and officers in a particular regiment, and that they were set up from above as an initiative of the left in the MFA and not from below as a response to the class struggle.

But some forms of 'popular power' posed rather than concealed the question of class power and control. The struggles at the newspaper **Republica**, owned by prominent Socialist Party member Paul Rego, and at the Catholic Radio Renascenca are examples. In May 1975, the workforce took over **Republica** to establish its political independence, as their statement indicated:

> **Republica** will not henceforth belong to any party. All the progressive parties will be given identical treatment, depending only on the importance of events.[29]

In response the Socialist Party tried to characterise the take-over as a Communist attempt to muzzle the paper. Actually the workers were also critical of the PCP; almost all the Lisbon papers were to the left of both reformist parties, due to pressure from their politicised workers. There were certainly widespread 'non-partyist' sentiments amongst **Republica** workers, but their action polarised the supporters of 'free speech' and those of 'working class control'. As the **Republica** manifesto proclaimed:

> We declare to all workers that we struggle to ensure working-class control over information . . . We are only 150 workers but in a sense we are representatives of our class, of millions like us. What is at stake is political power and knowing in whose hands it is.[30]

This realistic appraisal was understood by the government too. It attempted to use COPCON to restore the paper to its legal owner, but when it became clear that this would lead to the dismissal of the workers' committee, COPCON refused to cooperate, and gave back the keys to the workers. The continued failure of the government to ensure the return of **Republica**, and of Radio Renascenca — where mass demonstrations forced the MFA to veto a government decision to return the station to the Church and to allow the workers to continue in control — led to the resignation of Soares and the Socialist Party from the government, and the formation of yet another — the Fifth — Provisional Government.

Reaction and resistance

Outside Lisbon the forces of reaction were gaining in strength. Western capitalist governments were insisting more and more urgently that Portugal 'put its house in order'. The retreat from Portugal's colonies of Angola, Mozambique and Guinea-Bissau meant that half a million bitterly disillusioned refugees had to be resettled in Portugal itself. They went mainly to the traditionally conservative central and northern regions. The north in particular was being left behind by the radicalisation that was sweeping other parts of the country. There were several reasons for this.

Firstly, local government in many northern towns had been taken over by the Communist Party, whose focus on extending its influence within the state machine did little to raise the consciousness or morale of the mass of the population. Secondly, land reform had far less impact in the north. In contrast with the south, where the land was worked by wage labourers on large estates, most farms in the north were extremely small. The proposed land reform, limited to holdings of over 300 hectares or 50 hectares of irrigated land, scarcely touched them. The new minimum wage law did not apply to agricultural workers.

Peasants who rented their land now had to be given *18 years'* notice before eviction — but they were not given the right to own the land. Nor were they given any relief from their enormous burden of debts; the banks were nationalised — but the agricultural credit institutions were left untouched.[31] Meanwhile fertiliser prices had doubled. The endless media talk of a new life in Portugal contrasted starkly with the continuing grind of existence in the backward regions.

The failure of agricultural policy played into the hands of the reactionary forces, especially the Catholic Church. The Archbishop of Braga urged action against 'the Communist Anti-Christ': 'We are called upon to fight for God or against Him. To draw back would be betrayal. And betrayal would be death!'[32] This same archbishop regularly supplied funds to shadowy far right organisations,[33] which in the summer of 1975 were directly responsible for burning 60 offices of the PCP and the revolutionary left.

However, the political context within which the extreme right felt able to start operating openly was provided by the Socialist Party, which in the wake of its resignation from the government unleashed a virulently anti-Communist campaign veiled with democratic rhetoric. Right-wing violence in the provinces sharpened, in its turn, the political conflict in the capital. For the 'moderates' in the MFA urgently needed to win back the Socialist Party and the PPD, their former partners in government. On 9 August, Major Melo Antunes and nine other members of the Supreme Revolutionary Council issued an open letter which became known as the 'Document of the Nine'. The letter began with a significant appraisal of the period: 'It is a time of great decisions, a time to end ambiguities.' It went on to spell out which direction those decisions should take:

> From day to day an open rift is appearing between a very small minority social group (part of the proletarian zone of Lisbon and the south), who support a certain revolutionary project, and practically the whole of the rest of the country, who are reacting violently to the changes that a certain revolutionary minority is trying to impose without thought for the complex reality of the Portuguese people's historical social and cultural life.[34]

Antunes and most of his co-signatories were removed from the Supreme Revolutionary Council, but their document was symptomatic of the weariness and impatience of sizeable sections of the officer corps. It became a rallying call for moderates everywhere. The focus of Antunes' campaign was the Fifth Provisional Government, which was strongly influenced by the PCP and was therefore widely seen as the most left-wing. But the new government was also criticised from the left: a demonstration in favour of Popular Power on 20 August drew 100,000 people, including a large number of soldiers, and the support of more than 200 workers' and neighbourhood committees.[35]

The growing isolation of the government and of the PCP led the latter to initiate a 'popular united front' with six left groups, which included MES, LCI and the PRP. O Seculo, a Communist Party daily paper, produced a special midday edition on 25 August to greet the front as 'an historic occasion', and another enormous demonstration was held on the 27th. The Popular United Front must have caused some bewilderment among the PCP rank and file, whose leaders had only recently been stressing the 'battle for production'. Their confusion was quickly resolved: within 24 hours of the demonstration the PCP withdrew from the front and called for a reconciliation with the Socialist Party and the formation of a coalition government.

'Soldiers united will win'

The authors of the 'Document of the Nine' were particularly worried by lack of discipline within the army:

> We see a progressive decomposition of state structures. Everywhere wildcat and anarchistic forms of the exercise of power have taken over little by little even reaching as far as the armed forces.[36]

The growing strength of the right in the north led among career officers to a renewed confidence and determination to reimpose 'discipline'. But it also led to a counter-reaction by the rank-and-file soldiers of the region. Many of the soldiers involved were from northern peasant stock, which, unlike the landworkers in the south, had no tradition of struggle.

In September half a dozen revolutionary soldiers, including members of the LCI, PRP and MES, met secretly in a forest and drew up a leaflet protesting against poor conditions. Thus began *Soldados Unidos Vencerao* ('Soldiers United will Win'), the first autonomous rank-and-file soldiers' organisation in Portugal. SUV called a demonstration in the northern city of Porto on 10 September:

> As soldiers aren't allowed to sing in public we started whistling. However by the end everybody ends up singing . . . singing the *Internationale*. The number of people on the demonstration grew in front of our very own eyes.[37]

It was estimated that around 30,000 workers marched behind a contingent of 1,500 soldiers that day.[38]

SUV began to reveal to the soldiers the conservatism of their officers, which had been obscured by the prestige of the MFA.

> The day after the SUV demonstration was the anniversary of [the military coup in] Chile and we wanted to have a minute's silence. The officers said no. We put bullets in our guns — and held our minute's silence.[39]

The soldiers began to advance demands which faced up to inequalities between them and the officers. They began to agitate for pay increases and free transport. A single trip to see their family was enough to wipe out almost a month's pay for many soldiers.

> In the general headquarters of Porto there were three separate mess halls, one for soldiers, one for NCOs, and one for officers. Three days after the Porto demonstration, some soldiers calmly walked in and sat down to eat in the officers' mess. The next day all the soldiers occupied the officers' mess. Since that day there has been a struggle to eliminate the separate mess halls and unify them.[40]

Within weeks SUV had a national organisation, much to the consternation of both the new Sixth Provisional Government and the MFA's Council of Revolution. On 25 September SUV held a demonstration in Lisbon, in support of the Lisbon soldiers' and workers' councils and the workers' commissions. The 100,000 demonstrators included members of the PCP. About 4,000 demonstrators requisitioned buses, and freed soldiers who had been imprisoned 15 miles away when SUV leaflets were discovered in their lockers.

SUV was the first organisation to take up rank-and-file, bread and butter demands in the armed forces. This is what gave it its strength and made it independent of the MFA. It was critical of the networks of soldiers' and officers' assemblies set up by supporters of the MFA in the majority of barracks. These had only 50 per cent representation from rank-and-file soldiers. There is no doubt that SUV played an important part in arousing the class struggle in the army. But the struggle of the rank-and-file soldiers was interlinked with, and conditioned by, the general class struggle. However great the radicalisation of individual soldiers or units, the armed forces remained an instrument of bourgeois state power. The control of the bourgeoisie over the state machine was shaky, but this could only be a temporary state of affairs. Ultimately the development of the class struggle in the army depended on whether the workers' movement could offer an alternative authority to that of the bourgeois state, a potential workers' state. Unfortunately this was not understood even by the best of the Portuguese revolutionaries, who continued to overstress the *independent* role of the struggle in the army.

The crisis intensifies

The resurgence of the right in summer 1975 led to renewed fears of a coup. In Portugal, two such attempts had already been made. Many on the left began to warn that the vicious military coup in Chile two years previously might be repeated in Portugal. Thus Otelo de Carvalho, commander of COPCON:

> What worries me is the possible 'Chileanisation' of Portugal . . . they are building machines to kill; machines for repression. With them they can set off a new Chile. I am haunted by that fear.[41]

The neo-fascists were not in fact a real contender for power. The previous right-wing authoritarian regime had proved a problem for the Portuguese ruling class, which was why it had been removed. Nor was the example of Chile as inspiring to multinational big business and the American CIA as the left liked to imagine. Since the coup of September 1973 the Chilean economy had faced continuing crises. Both the NATO powers and the Portuguese ruling class far preferred to build a 'stable' bourgeois parliamentary system if at all possible.

The Sixth Provisional Government took office on 19 September. Again all the major parties were represented, but the Socialist Party and the 'Group of Nine' had gained at the expense of the PCP. This was to be the government until the next round of elections, in April 1976. But continuity is not the same as stability.

The government had failed to exert control over whole sections of society. The mass movement was still very strong. Land occupations accelerated towards the end of September; within little more than one month three times as much land was occupied as had been in the previous year and a half. In the towns and cities, many workplaces were still under workers' control.

The ideological control of the media had still not been re-established. The unresolved struggle over Radio Renascenca epitomised the continued weakness of the government, and on 29 September prime minister Pinheiro de Azevedo ordered COPCON to occupy it. After a demonstration of workers COPCON commander Otelo de Carvalho, in tears, ordered his troops to withdraw again. Within six hours the radio station was occupied by the commandos under Colonel Jaime Neves. An enormous demonstration on the evening of 16 October then forced the commandos to withdraw and the radio started transmitting again.

The government was almost powerless. Their only resort was terrorism: on 7 November its saboteurs, under protective cover of the supposedly loyal 'and backward' paratroopers, blew the station up.

The paras thought they were providing protection and that 'the orders came from the left'.

While the mass movement had involved huge numbers of people, and there was still enormous potential, the weaknesses were becoming ever more apparent. Political consciousness was inevitably uneven and frequently contradictory:

> More than once I'd visit a factory which the workers were running. They would be telling me about the evils of capitalism, how well workers would run things, the need to take state power sooner or later . . . then they would readily slide into 'and now the most important thing is the battle for production'.

The absence of a visible and viable alternative, a struggle for workers' power over society as a whole, led to demoralisation and passivity, to a renewed tendency for workers to allow the still dominant reformist organisations to 'do it for them'. The Communist and Socialist Parties increasingly won support from workers looking for safer and easier solutions.

In Lisbon militants in the factories were turning to a network of workers' committees built by the PCP. The inaugural conference of *Cintura Industria de Lisboa* (CIL) was held on 8 November 1975, with delegates from 124 workers' commissions and total attendance of 400 people. Most of the major workplaces were delegated. Several unions, including the Intersindical, sent observers. On paper this was the most powerful conference yet of workers' committees. Many non-aligned militants attended but the agenda and discussion was dominated by the PCP.

The CIL attempted to set up a co-ordinating framework for the popular assemblies. It also launched a gigantic demonstration on 16 November against the threat from the right; possibly 300,000 people supported this.

The PCP militants who built the CIL were certainly to the left of their own party, whose toleration of this initiative was part of an overall shift to the left designed to preserve militant support. But the revolutionary left had no tactics for intervening inside the conference. The PRP and UDP decided not to make an intervention on the grounds that the conference was dominated by the PCP. The PRP wasn't willing to fight for what were dismissed as reformist demands. The intervention by MES made no impact.

In contrast, only 30 miles to the south in Setubal the Committee of Struggle showed what could be done. Here the revolutionary left set the pace; while the PCP were sufficiently flexible (and isolated) to feel that they *had* to be involved.

Setubal, with a population of 78,000 in 1976, was Portugal's third largest city. Its rapid growth in the late 1960s and early 1970s was due to new industries, especially the Setenave shipyards. Setubal was an important working-class centre, where housing and social amenities were noticeably lacking. The Setubal Committee of Struggle, unlike the popular assemblies, was formed from below in reaction to the attempt of the Sixth Provisional Governent to close down Radio Renascenca. Five hundred people attended its first meeting. It was no accident that it saw itself as a committee of struggle, and not as a popular assembly.[42]

The committee showed that practicality was the way to win mass support. Thus at one meeting, in mid-October, there were several members of the workers' commission from the local paper **Setubal-Ense**, who reported how the proprietor had threatened to sack three journalists. It was agreed that the paper be occupied by the workers and the committee would support them.

The Setubal Committee of Struggle shows that even at the end of November 1975 the workers' movement was by no means exhausted — given a visible way forward and a positive lead. The building workers' strike in November is another illustration. Hitherto construction workers had not been an active sector of the working class. Many were peasants who had migrated to towns for work; some were blacks from the Cape Verde islands. In mid-October representatives of 32 building workers' commissions met and formulated a demand for a national wages structure and one union for the industry. A national strike and march was organised. The climax was an impressive demonstration outside the Constituent Assembly. The workers erected barricades, blocking the streets with tractors, cement-mixers and trucks, armed themselves with pick-axes and clubs, and held the Constituent Assembly hostage.

Prime minister Azevedo asked the commandos to come and rescue them. They refused. He then requested a helicopter to rescue just a few of them. The Military Police overheard the request, alerted the building workers and the helicopter was prevented from landing. After 36 hours the prime minister conceded all the building workers' demands, to take effect from 27 November.

The victory of the construction workers and Azevedo's humiliation appeared to halt the government offensive in its tracks. On 20 November it declared that it would do nothing 'political', but merely act in an administrative capacity.

25 November

Behind the scenes, preparations were now being made for a decisive move against radical sections of the troops. From October onwards the right in the army had been consolidating its position. It outmanoeuvred an SUV occupation in the north; then sent home three captains and 49 airmen after SUV disturbances at Beja in the central region. With the granting of independence to Angola there was less need for conscripts; several thousand were demobbed.

On 18 November Soares of the Socialist Party met with right-wing senior MFA officers to discuss how to re-establish 'discipline' throughout Portugal. An operations centre was quietly set up under the command of Colonel Ramalho Eanes. This consisted of picked troops, including the commandos' leader Colonel Jaime Neves. This was not intended to move into action immediately but to wait for a favourable opportunity.

Events in the army were coming to a head. The paratroopers who had been used in the destruction of Radio Renascenca had learned from the harsh criticism directed at them by workers and by soldiers from other units through the pages of the Lisbon press. They now rebelled against their officers.

Left- and right-wing military intrigues had been on the increase for some time; rumours of impending coups were endemic. In Barreiro, across the Tagus estuary from Lisbon, the voluntary firemen would sound the firebells at any sign of an attempted military takeover; the local people were woken several times by false alarms. While the memory of Chile meant people feared the right, it also meant they wanted no part in left-wing military adventures.

On the evening of 24 November Otelo de Carvalho was removed from command of the Lisbon military region and replaced by Vasco Lourenco. In the early hours of the following morning officers opposed to this ruling urged Otelo to defy it. He declined and went home to bed. In his absence an *ad hoc* grouping of officers decided that the military administration school would take over the radio; the military police would protect the TV; and RALIS (formerly RAL-1) would guard the motorway leading north out of the city.

By morning paratroopers at five bases had occupied their barracks, demanding the dismissal of their own commanders and that they be placed under the command of Otelo and COPCON. Otelo's response was to consult his fellow officers and the president at the presidential palace. Here he was forcibly detained. On the pretext that the measures these soldiers had taken in defence of Otelo were 'insurrectionary', the government now felt able to declare a state of emergency and to send in the specially picked group of commandos.

The officers must have been surprised at the ease with which they succeeded. They were not sure that the commandos, only 200 in number, would leave the barracks — let alone fight. Once on the road, however, the confidence of the force grew. It paraded past the Military Police barracks in the afternoon of the 25th, and proceeded to one of the paratroops barracks. After ordering the firing of a few warning shots, Neves used a megaphone to demand the paras' surrender. Isolated in the barracks, they did so.

The operations force then returned to take on the Military Police in the early hours of the 26th. Several soldiers were killed before the Military Police too surrendered. Now, one by one, all the rebel units collapsed.

No one seemed able to give a clear lead how to respond to these new developments. For example, just before midnight on the 25th, several hundred working-class people gathered on one of the approach roads leading to the Military Police barracks. There was a discussion with a bus driver. Should they turn his bus over? It would help make a good barricade. On the other hand perhaps the soldiers inside the barracks wanted to take to the roads. Nobody seemed to know. Nothing was done.

The previous day, the Lisbon ferries and many factories had emergency meetings and stoppages lasting two hours in order to discuss the threat from the right. But on the 25th the vast majority of the factories did nothing. A notable exception was the building workers, some of whom, using their two-way portable radios, commandeered enormous earth-movers and concrete-mixers to try to block the advance of the commandos.

The left groups confined their attention to military matters. It was noted with regret, for example, that the workers at the Lisnave shipyard had only 60 guns. None called for strikes and occupations — though such action by a powerful group of workers such as Lisnave would have given a lead to other workers and to the waverers in the armed forces.

In August the PCP had turned left in order to retain its militant support and to buttress its position within the unstable Sixth Provisional Government. On 24 November it called a two-hour general strike against the threat from the right, with limited success. The NCOs and officers who organised the resistance to the removal of Carvalho were encouraged by the PCP. But on the afternoon of 25 November the PCP sharply altered tack: now its argument was that the gains o 25 April should not be sacrificed for a few 'ultra-leftists' and their 'lunatic' actions.

It is clear in retrospect that the events of 25 November marked a decisive turning point. There was no bloodbath like that in Chile, but after 25 November the scale of working-class struggle never achieved the same heights. The ruling class, despite some nasty moments, was never again reduced to the paralysis of much of 1974 and 1975. One precondition for this success was the reimposition of discipline on the state machine. This was achieved on and just after 25 November.

Before this, radicalism in the army could feed into the workers' struggle, inspiring it with extra confidence — such as that displayed by the construction workers in mid-November. The events of 25 November did not abolish the struggle, but they did alter the terms on which it was fought. There was a widespread realisation that successful action would be more difficult now that the opposing forces had regained their cohesion. The appeals to caution made by the PCP and the Socialist Party became more attractive.

The purge of the radical soldiers and officers on 25 November was planned and carried out by 'moderate' generals and officers in the MFA, but the Socialist Party provided the ideological backcloth against which the moderates could operate. The Socialist Party publicly welcomed their actions.

By far the largest and most influential organisation capable of mounting resistance was the Communist Party. It had been the major force behind the massive anti-government demonstration of 16 November; it had launched a two-hour general strike on the 24th. The PCP's general policy from August right up to the afternoon of the 25th was designed to buttress its position in the Sixth Provisional Government, which was coming under increasing pressure from the right. By partial mobilisations of its supporters, it hoped to achieve two ends: first to convince the bourgeoisie that it was an indispensable part of the government alliance; second to hold on to its militants, who were beginning to be influenced by the far left. But this second aim was *subordinate* to the first. The position of trusted partner in government cannot be attained only by displays of the ability to mobilise; these must be complemented by proof of loyalty, by proof that the PCP could control and demobilise this militancy.

Oscillations, therefore, were inevitable in the strategy of the PCP. Its supporters, however, were not aware of this. When the removal of Carvalho was announced, those officers under its influence, motivated by an entirely justified and urgent desire to defend the radicals in the army, set about organising resistance. There is no doubt that the form this took enabled it to be presented as an attempted coup — though there is no evidence that it was intended as such. But the PCP itself sold its radical army supporters in the army, and a great many others, in exchange for a continued stake in the government.

What was the role of the revolutionary left in the events of 25 November? *All* the different groupings, having expected the blow to come from the extreme right as it did in Chile, were taken completely unawares by events; none was involved in instigating the military response; none organised any industrial response. To their credit, however, all except the right-wing Maoists understood that the paratroopers had to be supported. After their betrayal by the PCP, the radical soldiers and their friends on the revolutionary left were completely isolated, amidst a barrage of lies orchestrated by the government, backed by the PCP, to the effect that the attempt to prevent the purge of Carvalho represented a bid for state power.[43]

Now the PRP *had* for some weeks been issuing propaganda which gave the impression that this *was* a short-term prospect. This mistake did not directly influence the main course of events: the role of the PRP in the organisation of military resistance was negligible. But it did make the organisation particularly vulnerable to the *charge* of 'putschism', and reveal to its now isolated supporters how demoralisingly wide was the gulf which still lay between reality and the achievement of workers' power.

Lessons of the Portuguese Revolution

On 25 April 1974 there had been no mass working-class organisations of any kind. The almost complete absence of the constraining influence of a trade union bureaucracy, the unattractiveness of an interminable period of waiting to a working class which had been crushed down for decades, compared with the suddenly limitless prospects for action and for struggle, gave those who sought to build a revolutionary alternative great opportunities. Even Soares talked in terms of revolutionary struggle, though of course only in order to harness it to his own objectives.

But the vacuum left by the removal of Caetano was not entirely positive. The long absence of a framework within which reformist politicians could manoeuvre also enabled them to pose more effectively as the champions of workers' interests; the experience to prove otherwise was missing. This did not guarantee in advance that the Socialist Party and the PCP would achieve their objectives, but it did mean that as the mass movement began to grow, even militant workers would remember the reformists not as architects of betrayal, but as prominent anti-fascist fighters, as fellow sufferers under the old regime.

To show that the way to socialism was through revolution required a consistent intervention in every area of the mass movement, but most especially in its core, the struggle of the working class, not only to 'expose' the reformist leaders in their conduct of 'high politics' but to build an organisation which could link together the innumerable struggles and demonstrate in practice that their success depended on revolutionary organisation. There were certainly opportunities to do this, and the revolutionary organisations did at time influence events. 'Soldiers united will win', *Inter-empresas* and the Setubal Committee of Struggle, for example, were organisations which owed much to the initiative of revolutionaries. Through them, some individual militants were won to the belief that society could be changed only by means of insurrection.

But what of the essential precondition for socialist revolution, that far broader layers both support and understand the need for it, that the revolutionaries have to win hegemony in the working class as a whole?

To this difficult task, the small groups of revolutionaries brought political traditions which had been shaped firstly by their experience of trying to work in the ruthless environment of Caetano's Portugal, and, second, by how they defined themselves in relation to other movements internationally. A tendency towards 'Third-Worldism', and to seek armed short-cuts was prevalent. Much the largest group-ings identified themselves with Maoism, combining a virulent hatred of the 'social fascist' PCP with an identical 'stages' theory. Others aligned themselves with one or another faction of the 'orthodox' Trotskyists of the Fourth International. Many of the groupings underwent considerable evolution in this turbulent period.

The International Socialists in Britain, forerunners of the SWP, opened discussions with the PRP, in the belief that fraternal criticism, practical support and the PRP's own experience would enable it to provide effective leadership in the struggle; it was impossible, given the urgency involved in any revolutionary upsurge, to wait for the possible emergence of an organisation which agreed more closely with its own politics. The PRP was clear that society could not be reformed, that it was necessary to smash the capitalist state. It shared neither the 'stages' and 'social fascism' theories of the Maoists, nor the persistent tendency of the orthodox Trotskyists to put demands on the reformists in such a way as to suggest that they were capable of revolutionary action.

But the PRP was unable to overcome some of the more negative features derived from its clandestine work under the Caetano regime. A certain 'guerrillaism' blended easily with the notion that the struggle in the military was the main focus for revolutionaries.

Certainly the origins of the Portuguese revolution as a revolt within the state machine made sections of the military far more susceptible to the influence of the mass movement outside it than has frequently been the case in revolutionary movements, where the fracturing of the army has occurred late, as a culmination of the social and political crisis. At such points the key question is whether the workers' movement has developed to such an extent that it presents rank-and-file soldiers with a potential alternative authority — that of a workers' state.

The class struggle within the Portuguese army had enormous potential, but its development beyond a certain point was impossible unless the workers' movement itself was close to settling accounts with the bourgeoisie. The radical officers could not substitute even for the soldiers, let alone for the working class. As a member of the Group of Nine, Pezarat Correia, later remarked:

> I would like to see radical political change in Portuguese society, but I don't think the military make good revolutionaries. The officers belong to the bourgeois class and although they may have made a stand, as the MFA did, they are not the true revolutionary class. They end up facing internal contradictions . . . I think that my own position shows up these contradictions. Because of my military training I am concerned about order and discipline, but because of my social conscience I would like to see certain changes made with order and discipline. Is this possible?[44]

The decisive question, then, was the development of the working-class movement itself. Many on the left were inclined to underestimate the scale of the influence of the Communist Party in the working class and to overestimate the extent to which the struggle would *automatically* break its grip. This perspective led the revolutionary left towards 'non-partyism', towards concentrating those resources it did deploy outside the armed forces on the building of workers' organisations as sufficient in themselves — rather than struggling for influence within them, and within *all* the mass workers' organisations.

Thousands of workers, disgusted with the antics of the Communist Party, *were* looking for a practical altnerative, but they saw only Mario Soares and the Socialist Party. Consistent and hard practical work around day-to-day bread-and-butter demands could have laid a firm basis for a real alternative. Instead the PRP argued, referring to Cuba, that working-class support could be built further *after* the insurrection and the seizure of power.

In Portugal in 1974-5 there was enormous potential for building a mass working-class revolutionary party. Very large numbers of workers were open to revolutionary ideas, especially when it became clear that some of the professed friends of the revolution — such as Spinola — were in fact its most implacable enemies. Such experience gave rise to widespread questioning, a much more critical spirit among many workers than had existed in the heady days of April and May 1974, when a mood of indiscriminate fraternity to all but the fascists themselves prevailed.

It was the failure of the revolutionary left rather than any inherent attraction of reformist solutions which allowed the Socialist and Communist Parties to play the role which they did.

The reciprocity of the roles of the Socialist and Communist Parties needs stressing. In most of the period up to the late summer of 1975, it was the PCP which played the central role of dampening down strikes and waging the 'battle for production', leaving the Socialist Party in the happy position of being able to combine 'responsibility' in the regions where the struggle was weak with occasional declarations of opportunistic radicalism in areas where it was advanced. This was a bonus, enabling the party to make the most of its social-democratic structure, to recruit workers and give a revolutionary gloss to its activities. This fooled a good many would-be Trotskyists who saw the Socialist Party as representing a democratic vanguard against the Stalinist tendencies of the MFA and the PCP, and gave rise to talk to the effect that the party was in some way unique as Socialist Parties went.

The Socialist Party's uniqueness is actually most clearly dispelled by its behaviour in the summer of 1975 when its verbally strident anti-Communist campaign, which in the name of democracy sought to restore the media to the stockholders, and the radical soldiers to their place, resulted in a series of vicious reactionary assaults on the offices both of the Communist Party and the revolutionary left. The party was careful not to associate itself directly with this, though it has been shown that many of its right wing were involved.

The objective truth, however, is that the Socialist Party gave reaction a political lead. Parties of its kind have often prepared the ground for extreme reaction. In 1919 the German Social Democratic Party went even further, organising on its own responsibility the crushing of the revolutionary movement in the name of democracy. In Portugal any serious attempt to roll back the gains of the mass movement had to involve an attack on the best organised sections of workers and on the radical officers. The willingness of the Socialist Party to take on this role was circumscribed only by the existence of other forces willing to take on the dirtiest aspects of the work.

The course of the struggle also imposed some peculiarities on the development of the PCP. Well-publicised arguments were rehearsed between its spokesmen and those of the Spanish and Italian Communist Parties. All three were concerned with achieving a partnership in their respective national capitalisms. But the Portuguese party had to pursue this aim in very different circumstances.

In the first place the PCP could not rely on a large and loyal membership schooled over many years in the mysteries of the special nature of its particular parliamentary road to socialism, ideas which

Communist Parties had long ago successfully inculcated elsewhere. The newness and the considerable militancy of the PCP's membership must have led to some hard and awkward arguments about the necessity for the battle for production. It certainly led to an internal differentiation, once unknown in Stalinist parties accustomed to monolithic discipline, with the formation of three groupings within the PCP leadership.

But above all the PCP had to deal with sustained pressure from the strong and expectant workers' movement which it was trying desperately to control. By the late summer of 1975 the pressure for militant action was threatening seriously to undermine its base. This is part of the explanation for its abrupt left turn at this time. A further peculiarity of the context in which the PCP was operating was the central role of the MFA. Accommodation with social democracy, so important in most other countries, was eclipsed by a sharp battle for influence in the business end of the state machine. The refusal of the PCP to bow to Socialist Party hegemony after the latter secured more votes in the elections for the Constituent Assembly — unthinkable for Communist Parties elsewhere in Western Europe — illustrates this.

Both the reformist parties, then, were forced to behave in ways which were in some respects different from the general experience of Western Europe. But in all the main essentials they remained reformist parties, committed to the continuance of capitalist society in the same basic form and prepared therefore to act in direct opposition to the interests of their working-class supporters. By means of a division of labour in this task they were able to extricate the Portuguese ruling class from what had been a traumatic experience.

In the years since 1975, capitalism has reimposed its control over the Portuguese working class. This process has not always been smooth, but by and large the working class no longer held the centre stage. One lesson of the Portuguese Revolution is that such passivity is never inevitable: the massive changes in political consciousness and organisation in 1974 and 1975 attest to the power and creative potential of the working class. The second lesson, however, is that without an organised revolutionary party — able to pose clearly the question of state power and focus the creativity of the working class towards its solution — then socialism is not on the agenda.

FOUR

IRAN 1979

Long live the Revolution! ... Long live Islam?
Maryam Poya

THE VICTORY of the revolution in Iran in February 1979 was the outcome of years of struggle by workers, peasants, women and national minorities against the repressive regime of the Shah. These struggles ranged from peaceful demonstrations to armed confrontations, from sit-ins to sabotage, from small gatherings to mass demonstrations of millions. In the end the oil workers' strike in 1978, and the general strike that followed it, played the crucial role in bringing the Shah's regime to its end.

It is, however, one thing for a popular revolution to smash a hated and oppressive regime, and quite another for the popular movement to succeed in creating a new political and social system conforming to its needs. Tragically, the eventual outcome of the Iranian revolution was the imposition on the population of a new form of repression, now flying the flag of the 'Islamic Republic'. The events in Iran revealed simultaneously both the immense potential power of the working class, and the desperate consequences of a workers' revolutionary movement that lacks adequate socialist organisation.

The forces which were to overthrow the Shah were the product of capitalism's uneven development in twentieth-century Iran. If imperialism is the international expression of capital's historic mission to develop the productive forces, the process is by its nature uneven and contradictory. In Iran, the form of development was one that strengthened the role of the state. The Iranian state has been the key agent for the accumulation of capital.

From the middle of the nineteenth century, Iran's peasant economy began to be incorporated systematically but unevenly into the world capitalist economy. In this period the Shah, members of the royal family, government officials, tribal leaders and prominent members of the Islamic clergy controlled between them 55 per cent of all Iran's cultivated land, though they constituted only 25 per cent of all landowners. Central government was weak; the holders of large landed properties exercised considerable political power, and carried out most governmental functions. Further capitalist development required a change in the state form: a more centralised state was required that could provide the conditions for capital accumulation for Iran's ruling classes in alliance with international capital.[1]

The Constitutional Revolution of 1905-6 broke out as a protest against the weakness of the Shah and the domination of Iran's economic resources by Britain and Russia. The Majlis, Iran's first National Assembly, met in 1906. It abolished the traditional land assignment and established a modern tax system, taking away from the landlords and the clergy their governmental functions. But the heart of the new central power passed to the monarchy, the Shahs.[2]

Throughout the twentieth century, Iranian development has been tied to oil. Initially, most of the swelling mass of oil profits passed to Western capitalist companies, above all the Anglo-Persian Oil Company (APOC), founded by the British engineer William D'Arcy in 1909. Up to 1951, when Iranian oil was nationalised, APOC produced £700-£800 million for Britain, while Iran received no more than £105 million.[3] Little of the company's wealth flowed to its workers, whose wages remained sufficient only to secure the barest necessities of existence. The company dealt ruthlessly with strikes and other opposition, using its own police force.

Iran was a client state of British imperialism. From 1921 until the Second World War the government of Reza Shah brutally suppressed all the movements of trade unionists, of national minorities and of all oppositional groups whether communists, liberal nationalists or the Muslim clergy. At the same time, the regime promoted an extensive development of the infrastructure of roads, ports and railways, in support of the oil industry. Numbers of modern industrial plants were developed, along with a working class. The Shah confiscated land from the large landowners and himself became the largest national landlord.[4]

During the Second World War, in the face of the pro-German policy of Reza Shah, Britain and Russia invaded Iran to keep it 'safe'. They forced Reza Shah to abdicate in favour of his more reliable teenage son, Mohammed Reza. The new Shah continued to pursue economic development. But after the war nationalist sentiment against the foreign domination of the oil industry expanded. In 1947 the nationalist leader, Dr Mohammed Mossadegh, and his followers set up the National Front, which won power in 1951 and nationalised the Iranian oil industry. The international oil companies responded by organising a boycott of Iranian oil.

Over the next two years, workers' strikes and demonstrations pressed for further economic and political changes. The pro-Russian

Tudeh Party, in alliance with the National Front, worked to defuse the revolutionary mood among the workers. In August 1953, the Shah's Imperial Guards attempted a coup, but were defeated by loyal army officers and soldiers. Faced with popular demonstrations demanding a complete clean-out of Iranian politics, however, Mossadeq called on the army to clear the streets and restore law and order.

The very forces that might have saved the Mossadeq government were thus demobilised. Within days it was overthrown by a second coup engineered by the American CIA with the help of British Intelligence. The oil companies again won access to Iranian supplies, but the British monopoly was now broken. A consortium of international companies struck a new deal with the revived Shah: the Iranian state's share of the oil revenues rose from 16 per cent to 50 per cent; 40 per cent of the consortium's share went to five US companies, 40 per cent to British Petroleum, and the rest to several smaller companies.

With considerable American guidance and assistance, a new military dictatorship under the Shah was developed between 1953 and 1973. Central to the operation was the creation in 1957 of SAVAK, Iran's notorious secret police.

The Shah's oil revenues rose by more than twelve times over the decade from the early 1950s. To these oil revenues were added $500 million in military aid sent by the United States between 1953 and 1963. This enabled the Shah to expand his armed forces from 120,000 to over 200,000 men and to lift his military budget from $80 million in 1953 to nearly $183 million ten years later.

Little of the regime's hugely increased wealth had flowed to benefit the people. In 1960, 87 per cent of Iran's villages were without a school; only one per cent had any kind of medical facility; 80 per cent of the population was illiterate. Prices had risen steeply, while the Shah was spending between 40 per cent and 50 per cent of his budget on the military.

The early 1960s, however, brought a serious economic crisis. Heavy overseas borrowing had depleted the foreign reserves, obliging the Iranian government to seek emergency aid from both the International Monetary Fund and the American government. The economic crisis was magnified by an upsurge of popular opposition. The strike rate in industry went up sharply: there had been no more than three major strikes in the years 1955-57, but over the next four years the number jumped to over twenty. Some strikes ended in bloody confrontations between workers and the army. And resistance was spreading to other sectors. In 1962 there were mass student demonstrations and university occupations. Hundreds were injured, and numbers killed, when the Shah's troops stormed Tehran University. In June 1963, after several days of street fighting in the capital city, the Shah ordered his troops to 'shoot to kill'. Thousands of people were slaughtered.

In the face of this crisis, the Shah's government launched a major programme of reform-from-above, the 'White Revolution of the Shah and People'. The 'White Revolution' transformed Iran. Its key objective was to provide a stable social, economic and political basis for the regime. The means chosen was the promotion of two important social groups who would have an interest in the Shah's stability: medium-sized capitalist farmers in the rural areas, and a vastly expanded state-employed petit-bourgeoisie in the cities. This effort was accompanied by a re-casting of the state apparatus to develop an infra-structure of health and education services. Gestures were made in the direction of political and cultural 'modernisation': women were given the vote to the Iranian parliament, profit-sharing for industrial workers was introduced, rural courts of justice were reformed.[5]

Those who lost out were the traditional middle classes of the bazaar. Their position had been constantly threatened by the pattern of capitalist development of Iran, whether by the state or by international capital; they wanted the return of religious power and tradition, and were to remain in opposition to the state until their representatives, the Islamic clergy, came to power in 1979. Under the 'White Revolution' the regime made less effort to conciliate the traditionalist clergy, whose opposition now grew.

In the countryside, large pre-capitalist land-holdings were broken up; capitalist relations of production were given a major impulse through the introduction of monetary rents, loans and debts. Rich peasants were provided with capital so that they might become capitalist farmers, employ wage labour and produce for the national market. In this way land reform broke the power of the large-scale landowners and created a new layer of land-owning farmers.

The Iranian countryside was differentiated along new class lines. At the top, the remnants of the old land-owners, enriched by land-reform compensation, developed their smaller but still significant holdings; beside them purely capitalist operators ran 'industrial farms' and numbers of richer peasants became medium-sized capitalist farmers. Below them were sizeable numbers of small-holding peasants, hanging on to their plots and producing little more than was needed to feed their own families. This group dreamt of becoming successful farmers, and had nightmares about being forced further downwards. For below them again was a swelling class of 'poor peasants', in reality of landless wage labourers. The land reform failed to improve food production or to abolish rural poverty. Agricultural production from the early 1960s onwards rose by at most 2½ or 3 per cent a year, well below the rate of population increase. As a result, food imports rose considerably: by 1977 they were running at $2.6 billions, paid for out of oil revenues.[6]

In the 1970s about a million of these landless wage labourers migrated to the cities, in search of the 'great civilisation' their radios had told them was being built there. Yet once in the cities, most of them could find no regular work. Would-be proletarians, they drifted back and forth between casual work and unemployment. Living in slums and shanty towns, the great majority of them experienced a profound sense of rootlessness and alienation. They lacked a material base that could enable them to relate positively to the urban world, and were thus unable to throw off their past with its roots in the 'idiocy of rural life'.

The onset of the 'White Revolution' was accompanied by a quite rapid economic expansion, from the mid-1960s onwards. The state's role in capital formation became ever more important, at the same time that it spent massive funds on the military and the state bureaucracy as a means to hold society together.

In the early 1970s, Iran joined the Organisation of Petroleum Exporting Countries (OPEC) which gave it, along with other oil-producers, a degree of power over the oil industry. When, from 1973, OPEC raised the price of oil by five times, Iranian oil revenues multiplied accordingly. In 1963-4 they had been $555 millions; in 1975-6 they amounted to nearly $20 billion.

This vast increase in oil revenues fuelled a further expansion of Iranian industry, and further strengthened the position of the Shah's state. Industrial production, at the height of the oil-boom, accounted for 15 per cent of Iran's Gross Domestic Product, and for 20 per cent of total employment. The main areas of development were textiles, construction, steel, petrochemicals and plastics, vehicles, mining (copper and aluminium), food processing and modern consumer goods assembly.

Three main forces acted as agents of capital accumulation within Iran: the state, Iranian private capital, and foreign capital. As an illustration of the relative weight of these three forces, the Plan for 1973-78 projected state investment at $46.2 billion, private local capital at $23.4 billion, and foreign capital at $2.8 billion.[7]

The Iranian state, as the recipient of the oil revenues, had always been the main instigator of industrial growth. It was itself a major investor in industry. In 1975 a full 60 per cent of all industrial investment came from government sources. Secondly, the state also provided funds for the private sector throughout the financial institutions. By this means, the government promoted a significant development of an indigenous Iranian bourgeoisie which, while participating in the fruits of industrialisation, remained dependent on state funds and thus subservient to state policies. Thirdly, Iran attracted foreign investment. By the mid-1970s more than 200 foreign firms were investing in Iran. Initially the Americans, with 43 companies investing in 1974, were the largest group, but in the wake of the oil boom Japanese capital overtook the USA. In 1975-76 Japan accounted for 43 per cent of all foreign investment, much of this going into capital-intensive petro-chemical projects.[8]

Iranian and foreign investors alike benefitted substantially from rapid industrial growth. Iran's exports of manufactured goods and its imports of industrial equipment both increased. The rising consumption of the professional middle classes and to a degree of the working class expanded the domestic market, providing a basis for growth for the indigenous Iranian bourgeoisie.

Both the growth of industry and the expansion of the state's civil apparatus promoted the growth of a modern professional middle class. The state bureaucracy grew to 304,000 civil servants.[9] And, more significantly, there was a substantial growth in the numbers of workers in manufacturing and construction. By the time of the revolution in 1979, it was estimated that there were some two and a half million workers in manufacturing industry (though only 30 per cent worked in modern industrial units of any size), while the service industries (the civil service, education and health, communications, electricity and gas supplies) employed another three million.[10] Most of the large-scale enterprises were in the public sector. The growth of industry increased the bargaining power of skilled workers especially; they were able to use labour-market shortages to push up their wages by 30 to 50 per cent a year.[11] The modern working class had become a decisive force in Iranian society.

The modernisation of the economy, however, was accompanied by a strengthening of the state's repressive machinery. The oil revenues were used to finance not just industrial development but also the Shah's expanded dictatorship. Political opposition was brutally suppressed, and domestic consumption was subordinated to high profits and a high rate of exploitation.

The Shah used his massive oil revenues for more than simply industrialisation. They also strengthened his iron grip over Iranian society. Iran in the 1970s became the world's largest importer of armaments, at the same time that the state's client relationship with the USA was further developed. In 1973 Tehran became the Middle East headquarters of the CIA. The number of American 'military advisers' reached 24,000, and was projected to rise by 1980 to some 60,000.

The Shah's already extensive repressive apparatus was built up further. SAVAK, the notorious Iranian secret police, grew to a total of over 5,300 full-time agents with a larger but unknown number of part-time paid informers. In 1975, the existing political parties were dissolved as the Shah announced a one-party political system, centred on his newly-formed 'Resurgence Party'. In the workplaces, only state-run 'Syndicates' supervised by SAVAK were permitted; in most major factories SAVAK officials had their own offices.

The state was fiercely repressive. All political challenges to the Shah's dictatorship were dealt with by the most brutal methods: murder and torture were everyday weapons of the state. The Shah's highly authoritarian regime allowed no room for the growth of political democracy or for any degree of trade-union freedom.

This political regime reflected the highly uneven character of Iranian development. On the one hand the state was pressing forward the technological modernisation of economic life, a process which implied raising the cultural level and overall productivity of the working population. On the other hand, this modernisation programme co-existed with older forms of labour exploitation, based on long hours and the depression of popular living standards.

Rapid economic growth produced sharp economic and political tensions. The sudden increase in oil revenues had inflated people's expectations. The gap widened between what the regime promised, claimed and achieved and what the public expected, obtained and considered feasible. Although economic development did permit great forward strides to be made in the field of public welfare, Iran still had one of the worst health and education services in the whole of the Middle East. The regime's economic and social programme did not benefit all classes equally. Not only class but also regional inequalities widened, fuelling the demands of Iran's national minorities.

Working-class activity began to revive. The number of strikes rose from a mere handful in 1971-3 to as many as 20 or 30 a year by 1975. None of the strikes was permitted to last any length of time: either the regime immediately met the workers' demands, or they quickly suppressed the strikes by force. The strikes in the key oil industry were mostly short and successful: here at least, despite the repression, workers' confidence in strike organisation could grow a little.

Despite the industrialisation, the role of oil in the economy was larger than at any time in the past. Thus the fall-off in world demand for oil from the end of 1975 was quickly reflected within Iran. A drop in oil revenues, coupled with the high rate of international and domestic inflation, led to cash-flow problems. In order to continue with its industrialisation plans Iran had to borrow massively from the international banks. Rapidly Iran's image altered. What had seemed a country enjoying spectacularly successful modernisation now appeared increasingly as a country unable to feed large parts of its population, in massive debt to international banks, with falling oil revenues and even more rapidly falling oil reserves.

In the face of growing crisis, Iran's ruling class launched on an orgy of corruption and speculation, making and spending quick profits and salting money away in foreign banks in anticipation of the crash they sensed was coming. Property speculation and generalised hoarding of commodities contributed to an inflation rate of nearly 40 per cent a year. In 1975, the government imposed strict price controls. SAVAK and the Shah's Resurgence Party organised 10,000 inspectors, despatching them to harass small traders and shop-keepers; 8,000 small businessmen were arrested, fined and banned as 'profiteers, cheaters and hoarders' in the name of an 'anti-inflation war'.

Workers found their rents were now consuming a quarter of their earnings. Cheap food disappeared from the market. Industrial production began to fall back, and urban unemployment reached 15 per cent — with no unemployment benefit available to soften the hardship. The regime responded by intensifying the cult of the Shah and praise for his 'White Revolution'. The official media portrayed Iran as 'the great civilisation' and 'the seventh great power of the world'.[12]

The Iranian Opposition

The 'White Revolution' failed in its most important aim: it never won the Shah an adequate social basis for his regime. A variety of social forces remained in active opposition.

Firstly, and crucially, the working class: industrialisation has expanded its forces in Iran very considerably during the twentieth century, while leaving it profoundly dissatisfied. Iranian workers have participated centrally in every major movement of resistance: in 1905-6, in the 1920s, in the 1940s and 1950s and in the 1960s as well as in the 1970s.

Secondly, the national minorities: Kurds, Azaris, Arabs, Baluchis, Qashquaia and Torkmans between them constitute one third of the population of Iran. All are non-Persian. Living mainly in the countryside, the various national minorities have been regularly repressed by each ruling regime in Iran. Their linguistic, cultural and national rights have been denied. Each of these groups has a long tradition of fighting the central state for their political and cultural autonomy, as well as for economic demands.

Thirdly, intersecting with the national minorities, various religious minorities. Iran has a non-Muslim minority. The majority Muslim population is itself divided into a Shi'ite majority and a Sunni minority, consisting of the Kurds, Torkmans, Arabs and Baluchis. The non-Muslim population is made up of Armenians, Assyrians, Jews, Zoroastrians (remnants of the ancient religion of Iran) and Baha'is. The religious minorities, including in particular the Sunni Muslims, have always suffered a double oppression by the state. Baha'is in particular have been persecuted by the state since 1844 when they split from Islam. According to Shi'ite Islam, the Baha'i faith is the only one that cannot be recognised. Its followers are condemned to death.

Fourthly, the mullahs and the bazaar. Capitalist development in Iran has reduced the power of the clergy. Various developments have undermined the clergy's role in education and law: the Constitutional Revolution of 1905-6, the Shahs' modernisation drives and the growth since the 1920s of a centralised and powerful state, promoting secular courts and modern schools. The land reform of the 1960s was a major blow to the mullahs, for they lost the religiously endowed lands which were a major source of both their income and their independence from the state. Simultaneously, the rise of commercial and financial institutions such as large supermarkets and banks threatened the class interests of the numerous small traders and merchants of the bazaar. This class continued to provide vital economic and political support to the mullahs, especially by paying *zakat* (religious taxes). Their joint resentment and opposition to the Shah grew with every strengthening of the capitalist state.

Fifthly, students and intellectuals concerned to enhance freedom of cultural, religious and political expression: these have provided the leadership of many of the political oppositions during this century, including the 1905-6 nationalist movement, the communist movement of the 1920s, the nationalist and communist movements of the 1940s and 1950s, and the 1960s student movement. Their social composition reflects a mixture of the traditional and the modern professional middle classes.

A mixture of state repression and political failures over the previous decades produced a situation, by the 1970s, in which two political forces dominated the opposition to the Shah's regime: the guerrilla movements and the Islamic clergy.

From around 1970, two guerrilla organisations developed within Iran: the Mojahedin and the Fedayeen. Both had their origins in the student struggles of the early 1960s, but their political roots lay further back, in the nationalist and communist movements of the

1940s and 1950s. In that period opposition to the Shah was focussed firstly on a loose 'National Front' representing two divergent social forces: the traditional middle class, based on the 'bazaar' and inspired by the Islamic way of life and Islamic laws, and a modern professional middle class whose intellectual representatives considered religion to be a private matter. The professional middle class grew in size and importance under the Shah's modernisation drive; economic development involved the expansion of new occupations and with them the attractive power of new concepts and aspirations. This class was partly integrated into the state apparatus during industrialisation. Its opposition to the Shah tended to be secular and nationalistic. There was much less room for the traditional middle class of the bazaar, however, within Iranian capitalist development. They disliked intensely the material and cultural effects of 'modernisation', and desired the re-shaping of the state to restore religious power and traditionalist values.

To the left of the National Front stood the Tudeh Party, formed after the Anglo-Russian take-over in 1941 by a group of 53 intellectuals under Russian protection and encouragement.[13] This party, from the beginning, took 'popular front' tactics for granted, regularly subordinating the specific interests of workers to their supposedly 'progressive' allies in the middle classes. The Tudeh Party, despite the growth of working-class activity, argued consistently that Iran was not ready for socialist revolution.

Until 1945 Tudeh Party trade-union leaders opposed militant action by workers for fear of damage to the war effort. The party's degree of surbordination to Moscow was revealed at the end of the war, when it supported Russian imperialist claims on Iranian oil. This stance completely alienated the Tudeh Party from the nationalists, who wanted both the English and the Russians out of the country. In 1946 the Tudeh Party — at that stage represented in the government — helped to demobilise a general strike of oil workers at the Abadan oil terminal. Shortly afterwards, they were nonetheless thrown out of the government, and — like the Communist Parties of Western Europe — swung left and supported the National Front demand for oil nationalisation.

Both the National Front and the Tudeh Party were suppressed in the wake of the 1953 *coup d'état*, an event for whose success they were, as we saw earlier, partly responsible.

Both of the guerrilla movements of the 1970s reflected the impatience of a section of the young radical intelligentsia with the failures of the traditional methods of the old opposition parties in Iran. The Mojahedin and the Fedayeen were both inspired partly by the apparent successes of Mao, Castro and Ho Chi Minh and the ideas and practice of Palestinian and Latin American guerrilla groups. The Mojahedin emerged out of the religious wing of the National Front, while the predominantly secular Fedayeen grew out of a split from the Tudeh Party, drawing its forces also from the left wing of the National Front.

Both movements shared a common conviction that armed struggle was the prime means by which the masses could be activated. However, the politics of both the Mojahedin and the Fedayeen also reflected those of the previous Iranian oppositions. Both organisations had inherited elements of conservatism from their respective predecessors, the National Front and the Tudeh Party. The Mojahedin had illusions in Muslim nationalism and the Fedayeen in Russian Communism.

The guerrilla movements were the regime's most active opponents, and their bravery was immense. They carried out a series of successful armed operations against banks, police informers, millionaire industrialists, foreign embassies and police and military buildings. But by 1975, the regime had succeeded in hunting down many of their members, practically defeating their two movements.

The guerrilla organisations' key weakness was that they operated in isolation from any mass movement. Neither the Mojahedin nor the Fedayeen saw any need to engage themselves in the specific struggles of industrial workers in the towns. They saw the mass movement as 'dormant and in a general state of inactivity' and saw themselves, by contrast, as 'a vanguard that would revive the mass movement through struggle'. For both workers and peasants in Iran, it was impossible to identify with the middle-class intellectuals of the guerrilla organisations. As for the guerrillas' strategies, they amounted to a vote of no confidence in the working class. Neither the Mojahedin nor the Fedayeen ever argued seriously that the workers of Iran should themselves struggle for power, for their own class rule. Though both organisations regularly applauded each round of working-class resistance for its heroism, neither made any serious attempt to gauge the real material forces at work in Iran. Their guerrilla strategy involved placing the whole emphasis on the heroic actions of a brave minority, rather than on the perhaps less glamorous but essential work of propaganda and agitation among the broad layers of the urban and rural masses.

The tragedy of guerrilla politics in Iran is that the militants thereby cut themselves off from the day-to-day struggles and problems of the mass of the Iranian population, leaving the political field open to the other major opposition force, the Islamic clergy. It was the clergy who took the leading part in calling for protests against the regime and its brutality. Relatively protected from arrest by their religious positions, the Islamic clergy commanded a sort of national network beyond the immediate reach of the secret police. The left's weakness made the clergy appear great.

The social basis of the clergy is to be found above all in the traditional middle classes of the bazaar. They expressed that class's resentment at its exclusion from the state capitalist development pattern under the Shahs. The development of capitalism in Iran was severely undermining the clergy's political role. They organised opposition, on traditionalist religious lines, to the evils of 'Westernisation'.

At this stage, in the 1960s, the mosques' influence among factory workers and white-collar employees was still small. But for the large masses of the urban poor who had been driven from the countryside by the land reform, the mosques provided a rallying centre. While the populations of the slums and shanty-towns were largely ignored by the guerrilla organisations, the religion of the mosque offered them a sense of community.

Not surprisingly, therefore, all the popular struggles against the Shah's regime were invested with religious meaning. In the mass movement that developed against the Shah in the later 1970s, the religious leaders' vision of utopia developed a vast popular appeal. The Islamic clergy offered the dream that 'everything will be better' once the Shah was overthrown and an Islamic society founded. Millions, whose unbearable life gave them little to lose, were inspired to fight and be ready to die for that vision of heaven on earth.

The Islam that appealed to the urban poor was a 'modernised' version that spoke directly to their material grievances. Some of its leading exponents, such as the religious ideologue Dr Shariati, operated from modern mosque buildings using closed-circuit television and other up-to-date devices. Shariati's message to the faithful was that Islam — and especially the Shi'ite wing that predominates in Iran — was no fatalistic conservative creed, nor a purely personal faith, but rather a revolutionary ideology permeating all spheres of life and especially politics.

Modern Islam, he preached, inspired true believers to fight against all forms of oppression, exploitation and social injustice. To be a Muslim was 'to create a dynamic community in constant motion towards progress and not just a monotheistic religion'. The new social order 'would be completely united by virtue, striving towards justice, human brotherhood, public ownership of wealth and finally a classless society'. Shariati also stressed that 'Shi'ism raised the banner of revolt because their contemporary rulers, the corrupt caliphs and the court elites, had betrayed the people and given up the goals of a classless society.'[14] Ideologues like Shariati came to express the feelings and aspirations of the urban poor more effectively than the more traditional clergy like Khomeini.[15]

Ayatollah Khomeini himself had remained aloof from political struggles until the early 1960s. His active intervention into politics in 1962-63 focussed on opposition to the Shah's land reform, but also took in the regime's corruption and dependence on the USA and Israel and its neglect of the bazaar. For centuries the clergy had relied on donations from large pre-capitalist landowners as well as donations from the bazaar and money given by pilgrims at the major shrines. Land reform ended one of their sources of revenue, leaving them dependent on the bazaar — which was itself being weakened by the industrialisation drive. Khomeini and the traditional clergy increasingly faced a future in which their role as a serious political force would require state funding.

Khomeini was exiled by the Shah in 1963, essentially for his opposition to the development of capitalist modernisation and land reform. In 1968, sections of the traditional clergy protested against Shariati's 'secularist' lectures. Khomeini himself, aware of Shariati's popularity, remained silent on this question. Instead, he stole the clothes of the left and the liberal clergy, concentrating his fire on the regime's corruption, its neglect of the economic needs of the workers and peasants, its lack of freedom and its barbaric jails. Unlike the overtly traditionalist clergy, he did not publicly voice opposition either to the Shah's grant of the vote to women, or to the increasing tendency for women to work outside their homes. Instead, he issued calls for the overthrow of the Shah and the establishment of an Islamic society based on equality and brotherhood.

The Rising Revolution

As the economic crisis deepened, popular opposition revived. Beginning in the early summer of 1977, wave after wave of demonstrations and strikes propelled the Iranian masses forward, at each stage deepening the revolutionary movement and strengthening its methods of struggle. The Shah's regime had become unendurable. They began to break down the barriers separating them from political life, and to lay the initial groundwork for a new social order.

The demonstrations began in June 1977 with a peaceful march of Tehran's shanty-town population. The army, implementing the city government's planning decisions, had moved in to bulldoze their homes. The Shah's troops and police fired on and killed many of the demonstrators.

The previous month, fifty lawyers had issued a public declaration of protest at the executive's interference in judicial matters. In June, forty writers called for freedom of speech and the abolition of censorship. In July, a group of intellectuals addressed an open letter to the Shah, asking him to put an end to despotism. A growing flood of articles, leaflets and pamphlets began to circulate openly.

These activities marked a turning point in the political life of the country. Until then, protest had occurred only in the form of isolated strikes and sabotage in the factories, or attacks by urban guerrilla groups and protests by students and intellectuals abroad. After a long period in which SAVAK had ruthlessly hunted down and silenced critics both in Iran and abroad, the opposition was coming back to life. Resistance to the Shah was now voiced loudly and clearly everywhere.

Under these pressures, the regime launched a 'liberalisation programme' in the hope of relaxing tensions. SAVAK continued to maintain a close watch on the various movements, but it reduced its active harassment. There was also a slight easing of censorship. But with every concession the opposition gathered strength. Khomeini, still in exile, sent the opposition messages of support from Najaf, the Islamic holy city in Iraq. These were distributed among the population in the form of smuggled tape cassettes.

In early November 1977, the Writers' Association organised a series of public poetry readings. Each evening between 10,000 and 20,000 people attended these. On the tenth night, the police attempted to disband the session, and the poetry reading immediately turned into a mass demonstration shouting slogans against the regime. Many of the crowd were killed in the subsequent clash with the police.

On 6 December there was a further mass demonstration to celebrate *16th Azar* (the unofficial student day) when many more were killed. SAVAK seemed no longer able to intimidate the protestors, while the 'liberalisation programme' was stimulating political activity against the regime.

The same month, US President Carter visited the Shah in Tehran. For two days before his arrival, the motorway leading from the Mehrabad Airport to the Shah's palace was closed to the public, and all houses and apartments along the route were occupied by the police. At the end of his stay, Carter told journalists that he 'admired Iran's rapid progress and the enlightened monarch who enjoys his people's total confidence'.

In mid-January 1978, on the eve of *Muharram* (month of religious mourning) Khomeini called from exile on the clergy and the faithful to protest against repression. When a demonstration in the holy city of Qom was staged, the police and army attacked it, killing several people. This initiated a new series of protests every forty days. By Iranian Islamic tradition, the dead are commemorated forty days after their departure from life. Since each new demonstration created new victims, the demonstrations were repeated at this regular interval.

In the meantime the revolutionary movement was spreading fast among its various but divergent forces: the industrial workers, the urban poor, the students and intellectuals of the modern middle class, and the clergy and their supporters from the traditional middle class of the bazaar.

In Tabriz, one of Iran's main industrial cities and the capital of Azerbaijan, in February 1978, demonstrators for the first time fought back when the police attacked them and killed young students. Shouting 'Death to the Shah!', the demonstrators launched assaults on police stations, the headquarters of the Shah's official Resurgence Party, banks, luxury hotels, cinemas specialising in sex films. Many of the premises they attacked were owned by the Shah and his family.

Faced with the growing opposition, the regime attempted to build itself a new social base by coming out openly with policies favouring the petty-bourgeoisie of the bazaar and their clergy representatives. The 'anti-inflation war' against small businesses was called off; the government abandoned a plan for establishing huge state-owned markets which would have undermined the small shopkeepers, apologised publicly to the clergy for the attacks on some religious demonstrations and on clergymen's homes, and announced a ban on pornographic films. The Shah and the Empress began a public series of visits to religious shrines, while their media ran pictures of them praying, with the Empress wearing the *chador* (the long Islamic veil). In 1971, to celebrate 2,500 years of the monarchy, the Shah had ordered the rescinding of the Islamic calendar for a monarchical calendar; now, in 1978, this decision was reversed to conciliate the clergy. High-ranking clergymen who had been under arrest since the early 1960s were released.

The Shah ordered a cut in the subsidies to his Resurgence Party. He closed down 57 gambling casinos owned by the Pahlavi (royal family) foundation, and sent the most openly corrupt members of his family on extended foreign vacations. To placate the Islamic fundamentalists, he abolished the post of Minister for Women's Affairs in the government, replacing it with a Ministry of Religious Affairs. As a specific concession to Khomeini, he launched a campaign against the Baha'i religion, and ordered police attacks on the liberal nationalists of the National Front, the parties of the left and the intellectuals. SAVAK raided their homes, beat them up and attacked their meetings.

The Shah's aim was to split the forces of opposition to his rule. In an interview on 26 June 1978, he declared:

> No one can overthrow me. I have the support of 700,000 troops, most of the people and all of the workers . . . In ten years we hope to be what Europe is today . . . In twenty years we hope to be a fully advanced nation.[16]

As the movement against the Shah's regime grew stronger still, Khomeini sought to secure the maximum advantage from it. The National Front and the Tudeh Party had been crushed after the 1953 coup. The guerrilla organisations had conducted armed operations between 1971 and 1975, but were also defeated by the regime. Shariati, whose ideas had incorporated elements of Islam, liberalism, Fanonism and Marxism, had played an important role as a focus for the opposition, especially as the regime was always more tolerant to its religious than to its left opponents. After Shariati's death, Khomeini was able to win over his followers, who saw him as accepting Shariati's liberal version of Islam. Khomeini denied that he or any other clergy had any desire to rule Iran, agreed that there should be a freely elected Constituent Assembly to draft a new constitution after the Shah was gone, and declared that — as women and men were equal in the eyes of Islam — women should have the right to vote and should have equal rights with men.

In early November 1978, Karim Sanjabi and Mahdi Bazargam, leaders respectively of the National Front and the Liberation Movement of Iran, a body established in 1961 by religious supporters of Dr Mossadegh and of the National Front, left Tehran to join Khomeini in Paris. There they announced their open alliance with Khomeini and declared that 'mass movements of the previous year had shown that the people followed Ayatollah Khomeini and that they wanted the monarchy to be replaced with an Islamic system of government.'[17]

The guerrilla organisations, which had suffered heavy losses with their members tortured and murdered in the Shah's prisons, changed their tactics. In Iran their sympathisers accepted many of Shariati's ideas, and abroad they stepped up their activities within the student movement. When, in late 1978, the mass movement forced the release of many political prisoners, the guerrilla organisations moved into action, recruited new members, published leaflets and newspapers and fought the Shah's army and police. At the same time, having built no base among the workers and the urban poor in the early years of their guerrilla activity, they too accepted Khomeini's leadership.

Khomeini now began to issue calls for the overthrow of the Shah and the whole monarchical system.

The struggle escalates

Up until June 1978, the demonstrations against the Shah were predominantly made up of students and intellectuals, the urban poor, and the modern and traditional middle classes. Industrial workers were less prominent. A survey of workers' struggles during this period[18] suggests that from March to June 1978 most of the strikes, sit-ins and other industrial protests were confined to economic demands.

From June onwards, however, industrial workers' movements took on an increasingly political as well as economic character. Demands for pay increases, for improved conditions and paid holidays, and against non-payment of wages, sackings and plant closures were now combined explosively with wider issues. Calls for independent trade unions, in opposition to the SAVAK-run 'Syndicates', were now openly voiced, along with a whole series of other demands: for housing benefits and health services, for credit and insurance facilities for workers, for a five-day week, for workers' participation in 'profit-sharing schemes'.[19] Demands for changes in management and for the removal of SAVAK offices from industrial plants were more and more loudly voiced. Other popular demands that emerged in strikes included the re-instatement of sacked workers, for workplace nurseries and equal treatment for Iranian and foreign workers.[20]

As the movement advanced so the demands became more overtly political. New strike demands — the ending of martial law, the freeing of political prisoners, the return of political exiles — surfaced for the first time. In September, workers in the vital oil industry struck at the refineries in Tehran, Isfahan, Shiraz, Tabriz and Abadan, adding their weight to strikes already begun in other industries. Economic questions were combined with political demands concerning such matters as Japanese managements and political prisoners. The oil workers' list of demands was now directed against the army's presence within and outside the plants, against media censorship, against the very existence of SAVAK; they demanded a national judicial system to prosecute those identified as betraying Iran, and a revoking of all the current international oil agreements.

In September 1978, the strikes overflowed the bounds of the workplaces. Industrial workers marched from their factories to the city centres, joining into the millions-strong mass demonstrations. The oil workers now began to use their industrial muscle to weaken the regime directly. They decided to cut oil production from six million to only one million barrels a day, to halt exports and produce solely for domestic consumption. The customs workers followed suit, allowing the entry only of medicines, baby food and paper.

In October, the oil workers halted production to protest against the regime's links with South Africa and Israel. Tobacco workers struck against American tobacco imports. Oil workers cut back production further, to just 220,000 barrels a day. Coal miners struck in support of the students' and teachers' demonstrations and strikes.

Every few days a new section of the workforce came out on strike or joined the street demonstrations and protests. Every night for an hour communications workers blacked out the regime's radio and TV propaganda. Railway workers refused to allow police and army officers to travel by train. Atomic Energy workers struck, declaring their industry had been imposed on Iran by the great powers in the interests of nuclear war rather than creative industry. The Russian-built steel complex was completely shut down. Just about every industrial establishment was closed, with the exception of gas, telephones and electricity: here the workers explained they were continuing to work to serve the public, but that they supported the strikes and demonstrations to overthrow the regime. Dockers and seamen only offloaded foodstuffs, medical supplies and paper required for political activity.

The whole working class was now involved in the insurrectionary movement, united by the call for the overthrow of the Shah and his entire regime. And workers began to formulate their own political concerns for the future: the oil workers sent an open letter to Khomeini, expressing their support but also demanding workers' participation in the future government. They were followed rapidly by the communication workers. Workers in the electrical and electronic industries demanded a new labour law involving workers' control of industry. Oil workers' committees sent messages of support to airforce technicians and cadets who were now fighting the Shah's army.

Under the pressure of the developing revolutionary situation in the winter of 1978-79, Iranian workers' consciousness evolved by leaps and bounds. Their experience and combativity expanded rapidly. Many of the most important factory owners and managers panicked and fled the country. This sudden departure of their bosses promoted a strong feeling among workers of responsibility for their factories and a determination to take control of them. Elected strike committees took over management functions, deciding production limits, hours of work and hours of strike, and so forth.

The strike committees were essentially political bodies. The state-organised 'Syndicates', under SAVAK control, had been deeply hated. Time and again during disputes, workers attempting to choose their own militant representatives had had to confront SAVAK. At the Zamyad car plant in Tehran, for instance,

. . . when a militant worker had stood for the leadership of the factory syndicate, SAVAK was sure he would win the election. He was banned from entering the factory on the election day in two successive years. For this reason, in the third year, a day before the election he hid himself at the top of the factory water-reservoir for the night. The next day he was inside the factory, took part in the election and won. Immediately after his victory, he was fired.[21]

Now openly elected strike committees replaced the SAVAK Syndicates. Their position was strengthened by the power vacuum in the factories after the bosses' flight and by the generalisation of the popular revolutionary tide.

Sections of the workforce in the oil, printing and textile industries had been involved in the political and trade-union movements of the 1940s and 1950s,[22] but the majority of Iran's workers were relatively recent migrants from the rural areas, with no such traditions. Among both sections of the workforce, however, the strike committees mushroomed with equal force.

Where previously workers had felt defenceless, now they felt a deep sense of their collective power. The newly organised intervention of the working class in the revolutionary movement — which combined all the other oppressed and exploited layers of Iranian society — tipped the political balance. Together this vast popular movement overthrew one of the most repressive regimes of modern times.

The Shah departs

On 16 January 1979, after eighteen months of bitter struggle, the Shah was forced to leave Iran. His departure triggered an absolute carnival of public rejoicing. As the radio broadcast the news, the population thronged into the streets to cries of 'Shah Raft' (The Shah has gone). Strangers embraced each other. Cars sounded their horns. Confectioners' shops were offering sweets to the crowds for celebration, an old Iranian tradition.

The crowds fraternised with the soldiers, throwing flowers to them and appealing to them 'Do not kill your brothers and sisters'. The conscript soldiers, mostly from peasant backgrounds, wept and embraced people. Demonstrators pulled down the statues of the Shah and his father.

In a final effort to save the monarchy, Shapour Bakhtiar, a member of the old National Front, became prime minister. The whole country, however, refused to recognise him; immediate mass demonstrations demanded his resignation. Meanwhile army officers were secretly discussing the possibility of a *coup d'état* with their American advisers.

On 1 February, Ayatollah Khomeini returned from his last place of exile in Paris. Five days later he declared himself head of state, and published a decree appointing Mehdi Bazargan as prime minister. Bazargan was a leading member of the Liberation Movement and of the National Front. At the same time Khomeini set up a secret Revolutionary Council, consisting of a number of the clergy together with members of the National Front and the Liberation Movement, to negotiate with the army's chief of staff.

The army officers, shaken by the Shah's departure, now found they were losing the support of the rank-and-file soldiers. They were distressed, too, by the departure of the American general, Robert Huyser, deputy commander of the NATO forces, who quit Iran on 8 February after a month of negotiations with the army command in which he had dissuaded them from attempts at a coup. Meanwhile Washington advised the Shah to take a long vacation abroad. In the face of the revolutionary movement, it had become clear to the US that, if they were to protect their interests in Iran, they could no longer support the Shah. In hopes of re-securing their position, they officially confirmed their intention to cooperate with the provisional government.

The army officers were divided and uncertain. Finally they determined to remain neutral and to begin negotiations with the provisional government.

While these developments were taking place behind the scenes, the guerrilla organisations, together with the airforce technicians and cadets who had come over to the revolution, engaged in open battle with the Shah's last loyal troops, the imperial guards, defeating them and distributing arms among the whole population. On 11 February the fighting reached a climax, when the armed people took control of police armouries and barracks, together with the main army garrison in Tehran and the military academy.

As the fighting intensified, representatives of the clergy tried to disperse the armed population under 'Islamic guidance'. 'This is not yet the time for armed confrontation,' they argued, 'Khomeini has not yet issued the *Fetwa*' (religious decree). But the clergy was not yet in a position to control the movement: after two days of intense fighting, the guerrilla organisations, joined by large numbers of eager and armed volunteers, brought the insurrection to its completion and the 2,500 year-old monarchy to utter destruction. Prison doors were opened; the radio and TV, taken over by revolutionaries, announced 'This is the voice and the face of revolution' and declared to the world the end of the monarchy and the victory of the revolution.

As the Shah's state disintegrated, power passed into the hands of the people. Strike committees in all the factories, installations, offices, schools, universities and other workplaces re-formed and began to function as *Shoras* (councils): workers' *Shoras*, students' *Shoras*, office workers' *Shoras*. Peasants in the villages established their own peasants' *Shoras*. In the cities power passed to local *ad hoc* bodies called *Komitehs* (committees). The membership of the *Komitehs* was made up mainly of supporters of the guerrilla organisations but also included local clergy and other fanatical supporters of the idea of an Islamic republic. Among the national minorities, power fell into the hands of their local *Shoras*.

Factories were occupied by workers who took control of production. Peasants, with the help of their *Shoras*, began seizing land from the landlords. The Iranian left, together with the Mojahedin and with the help of students' *Shoras*, took over the offices and other premises of SAVAK, turning them into their own headquarters. From their new bases they organised meetings and rallies.

Within the oil and other older-established industries, workers with direct traditions of organisation (or with parents or close relatives who had passed on their experience), played a leading role in founding the workers' *Shoras*. But in the newer industries, whose workforces were mainly recent rural migrants, the emergence of the *Shoras* owed little either to previous working-class traditions or to the influence of the organisations of the left. In these industries, the workers' recent experience of developing and running insurrectionary strike committees, together with their hatred of the Shah's SAVAK-imposed Syndicates, provided the main impulse behind their formation of *Shoras*.

Ayatollah Khomeini became Iran's new Head of State, largely because of the organisational and ideological weakness of all the other existing opposition groups. However, for eight months after the victory of the February insurrection his power was anything but assured. In reality there was a complete power vacuum in Iranian politics. During this period, the newly created workers' councils, the *Shoras*, were to play a fundamentally important political and economic role. As long as they maintained their momentum, Khomeini could not consolidate his power.

The rise of the workers' *Shoras*

A few days after the insurrection, Khomeini ordered workers to begin work again 'in the name of the revolution'. The workers went back to the factories — to find that nothing had changed. Wages and working conditions were as before. They reacted quickly. In many factories, the absence of the manager or owner provided an opportunity to establish *Shoras* immediately. Elsewhere, the continued presence of the same manager, the same supervisor and even the same old SAVAK representative was the motive for the *Shoras*' formation.

Within most workplaces, the pre-revolutionary strike committees provided the core of the leadership of the new workers' organisations. Within the *Shoras*, workers established committees to identify and investigate the authoritarian and oppressive elements within the factory, and to weed out those having close links with the old regime. As one worker argued:

> Those who were managers under the Shah have been re-appointed. These men have oppressed us so much, how could the state have appointed them as our managers? We will never put up with this, never accept such a burden as long as we have blood in our veins. [23]

The *Shoras* began to exercise their power at every level of factory life, in purchasing, sales, pricing and orders for raw materials. Different committees were organised to carry out various tasks: guild committees to secure trade-union demands with respect to wages, conditions, insurance, health and safety; financial committees to control the incomes and expenditures of the individual factories and to watch over managerial financial affairs; communications committees to maintain contact with *Shoras* in other factories; supervising committees to oversee production and sales; political committees to organise small factory libraries, to produce wall newspapers and distribute leaflets and newsletters so as to keep workers informed of the latest news of their own and other factories; guard committees, consisting of armed workers, to protect the factories from former owners and managers and/or from counter-revolutionary elements; cooperative committees to organise strike funds; women's committees, made up solely of women, to press women workers' specific demands, especially in the chemicals and textiles industries where women constituted the majority of the labour force.

The workers were effectively in control of industry. They were discussing, planning and managing the individual factories. They had control of hiring and firing. The *Shoras* were their key instrument for exercising power over production and distribution. Typical was the Chite Jahan textiles factory near Tehran — famous under the Shah for the number of political activists among its workers and for its tradition of strike activity — where the workers' council achieved a high level of control over the factory's affairs. During the first few months of the revolution, the workers increased production, doubled minimum wages by cutting the top salaries of engineers and managerial staff, and provided free milk for the workers. [24]

The workers' task, as they saw it, was to keep the factories open and running under their control, and to win legal recognition from the government for their *Shoras*. All too soon, however, several major problems were to affect the *Shoras'* independent role.

Firstly, the provisional government of Mehdi Bazargan declared that workers' intervention in management affairs was 'un-Islamic'. Refusing to recognise the *Shoras*, the regime sought to combat their power by dividing the workers on the basis of religious belief. Through small groups of workers organised in Islamic societies, the government started to intervene in the affairs of the *Shoras* and to support the state-appointed managers. The Islamic societies began religious agitation, organising meetings on the general importance of Islam, and more specifically on the Islamic meaning of work and property and control. Their aim was ideological control of the workplace. As a worker from Roghan Pars, a subsidiary of Shell, described it:

> The revolution was victorious because of the workers' strike. We got rid of the Shah and smashed his system, but everything is the same as before. The state-appointed managers have the same mentality as the old managers. We must strengthen our *Shoras*, because the management are afraid of them. They know that if the *Shoras* remain powerful they've had it. They can't impose their anti-working-class policies directly; but they're now opposing the *Shoras* on the basis of religious belief. If we say anything, their answer is, 'This is a communist conspiracy to weaken your religious belief.' What I would like to know is, what have *Shoras* got to do with religion? Workers are exploited all the same: Muslim, Christian or any other religion. That bloody manager who's been sucking our blood has suddenly become a good Muslim and tries to divide us by our religion; so we should know the only way for us to win is to keep our unity through the *Shora*.[25]

Secondly, the *Shoras* had real difficulties with obtaining raw materials and undertaking economic reconstruction. Typical was the Azmayesh electrical and gas appliance factory, formed by private capital and employing a workforce of 900. After the revolution the factory was nationalised with a state-appointed manager. An Azmayesh worker explained:

> After the revolution, there were 60 million *tomans'* (£6 million) worth of goods in the factory. But, before we returned to work, the management had already distributed these among middlemen in the bazaar. We had no means either of getting back the goods or the money for them. Not only that: a year ago — at the time of strikes and the escalation of the fight against the Shah — the previous management stopped all orders for raw materials. In a factory like Azmayesh, 90-95 per cent of the materials have to be imported from abroad, and orders for them have to be placed a

year before delivery. So we could not start production. We didn't give up, and decided to sell anything of value from our personal belongings — our carpets, etc — to save our factory. Then we realised we wouldn't get anywhere that way, by ourselves, and we'd have to cooperate with the new management. We needed government credit and financial support to keep the factory open.[26]

Raw materials were not the only problem. Many of the modern factories were primarily final assembly plants, such as those putting together automobiles from components shipped in by such companies as General Motors or Talbot. This pattern of economic development, a crucial element in Iran's effective integration into the world market, had involved the creation of a layer of highly skilled industrial engineers. While numbers of these were foreign experts connected to multinationals, many others were Iranians educated in Europe and America. These Iranian skilled engineers lived in a world apart from that of ordinary workers. They had been through the experience of higher education. They enjoyed huge salary differentials. They worked closely with management and the foreign experts, and participated in the extraction of surplus value. They possessed a social and technical superiority which gave them authority over the workers.

The workers, through their *Shoras*, were trying to implement full control over production and distribution, and not to allow the anti-working class managements to regain control, but the whole situation was obviously putting serious obstacles in their path. The mass of the workers were unskilled or semi-skilled. As the most effective force in the revolutionary movement against the Shah, they had been strong enough to halt production, and felt strong enough now to mount an effective challenge to bourgeois relations of production. But they were caught on the horns of a dilemma. Now, in the aftermath of the revolution, if they were to restart and sustain production under their own control they needed not just the financial assistance of the state but also the skill and expertise of the engineers and other technically equipped managerial personnel.

Many owners, managers and foreign experts had fled the country; the skilled Iranian engineers who remained constituted a vital force if production was to continue. They were hostile to the idea of the Iranian working class exercising power through its *Shoras*. When the workers' *Shoras* appealed to the government for financial help, the regime had a perfect justification for sending this layer of skilled personnel to take control of the factories.

The struggle for workers' power in the factories had reached a critical point. For the workers to consolidate the power they had won at the point of production, they needed a state machinery that was directly under their control and responsive to their needs as a class. With their own power and resources at the factory level alone, they could not overcome the problems of economic backwardness. As the Iranian workers sought to develop their struggle into one for emancipation from exploitation, these problems faced them starkly and imperatively demanded further solutions.

The Iranian workers faced the danger of losing all their revolutionary gains and being thrown back to where they had started. On the one hand, the contradictory unevenness of development of Iranian capitalism had produced the immense popular upsurge of the February 1979 revolution. Now the same contradictions were leading to the breakdown of the economy, whose maintenance was crucial for the survival of the working class. The smashing of the Shah's state was relatively simple compared with the difficulties the Iranian workers now faced.

Yet the working class, having gone so far, did not want to stop. They wanted to continue the revolution, and to make it genuinely theirs. No doubt the fact that they were still a minority within the country was an objective difficulty, but not necessarily an insuperable one. The numbers of the industrial proletariat, their concentration, their culture and their political weight are all affected by the degree of capitalist development, but these matters are not the only determinants. The power of the working class is dependent not only on the level of development of the productive forces, but also on workers' traditions, initiatives and readiness to fight. Among the Iranian workers these were certainly not in short supply.

The Founding Council of the Iranian National Workers' Union (*Shoraye Moassesse Ettehadieh Sarasariehe Karegarane Iran*) was established to strengthen the individual councils and develop unity between them. On 1 March 1979 this body published a set of 24 demands:

> We the workers of Iran, through our strikes, sit-ins and demonstrations, overthrew the Shah. During these months of strike, we tolerated unemployment, poverty and even hunger. Many of us were killed in the struggle. We did all this in order to create an Iran free from repression, free of exploitation. We made the revolution in order to end unemployment and homelessness, to replace the SAVAK-oriented Syndicates with independent workers' *Shoras*, formed by the workers of each factory for their own economic and political needs. Therefore we demand:
>
> 1) government recognition of the *Shoras*; 2) abolition of the Shah's labour law and enactment of a new labour law written by the workers themselves; 3) wage increases in line with the cost of living; 4) tax-free bonuses; 5) a free health service instead of the present semi-private insurance system; 6) housing benefits in the shortest possible time;

7) sick pay; 8) a forty-hour five-day week; 9) the sacking of all elements closely linked with the old regime; 10) the expulsion of all foreign experts and foreign and Iranian capitalists and expropriation of their capitals in the interests of all workers; 11) an end to discrimination against blue-collar workers and an increased annual holiday of one month; 12) improved health conditions in the factories; 13) sick pay; 14) an end to disciplinary punishments and fines; 15) an end to the intervention of the police, army and government in labour disputes; 16) inclusion of workers' *Shoras* in industrial decisions such as investment and the general condition of the plant, as well as buying, selling, pricing and the distribution of profit; 17) determination of hiring and firing by the *Shoras*; 18) freedom of demonstrations and protests, and legalisation of strikes; 19) return of the capital of co-operatives to the workers; 20) free meals, washing facilities and improved safety at work; 21) provision of ambulance, nurse, bath and nursery services at work; 22) official employment and job security for all temporary workers; 23) creation of a medical consulting body to review the condition of unhealthy and sick workers and to grant them exemption from work and retirement; 24) reduction of the retirement age in the mining and moulding industries from 30 to 20 years' service.[27]

The provisional government of Bazargan had a definite project in view: the establishment and consolidation of an 'Islamic Republic'. What this term meant was becoming increasingly clear: there was to be no place in an 'Islamic Republic' for anything but orthodox capitalist relations of production. The workers' *Shoras* stood in the way.

The provisional government declared that, because of their interference with management and production, the *Shoras* were 'anarchistic'. Darioush Frouhar, minister of labour and social affairs, announced at a press conference, 'The Ministry of Labour is in favour of Syndicates and believes that workers can defend their interests only through a healthy Syndicate; therefore the Ministry will support such organisations and intends to dissolve any other forms of organisation which are wasteful.'[28]

While ordinary trade unionism — which is restricted to collective bargaining and involves recognition of management rights — is perfectly compatible with capitalist production relations, workers' councils are a very different matter, and infinitely more dangerous to capitalism. Yet despite the government, the struggle for workers' control within the factories continued.

The oilfield workers' *Shora* expelled the entire membership of the state oil company's board of directors for being 'corrupt and anti-working class', locked them out and occupied their offices. Hassan Nazih, the company's director general, complained that 'to threaten the management in such a way is seriously to damage our economy, especially in the absence of foreign experts who have left Iran and are not prepared to return because we cannot ensure their safety and security in the existing atmosphere'.[29]

Khomeini himself publicly avoided expressing any views about the *Shoras*, although he made comments in various speeches about industrial disputes, wages, conditions and unemployment. But he revealed his real position in the speech for the May Day celebration:

> Workers, especially the oil workers, played the most important role in the victory of the revolution. And it is still you who can continue the revolution with your production. But you have to be aware that the hands of the devils are waiting to divide you and weaken your power; you must be aware and awake, and serve your country, Islam and the Koran. The whole of Iran and all Islamic countries are one Islamic society; each of the Islamic Societies are small branches of that Islamic society which is under the leadership of God and the absent Imam [the Messiah]. We have to be together in these Islamic societies.[30]

The Struggle of the Unemployed

The workers also had to contend with a serious problem of unemployment. According to government statistics, only 50 per cent of industrial units were operating, and they were functioning at only 80 per cent of capacity. In the conditions of revolutionary excitement, private capital was neither secure nor prepared to invest, and the government itself lacked the means to pay for the reconstruction of the economy.

The drop in oil revenues, combined with international and domestic inflation, made the economic crisis especially intractable. Iran's oil revenues had paid in part for imports of food, raw materials, goods and services, together with foreign experts and foreign workers. The fall of the Shah had resulted in some necessary economies, by cutting corruption and by saving of funds previously spent on expensive weapons and extravagant showcase projects. But these savings were insufficient to bring better economic conditions for the mass of the people: Iran remained far too dependent on oil revenues for these reforms to have the required impact.

The government's response to the economic crisis was to close newly nationalised factories, sacking part of the workforce, lowering wages and cutting such services in the workplace as nurseries, washing facilities and canteens; at the same time the government loudly promised to build new houses for the poor, to start unemployment benefit and even to raise wages in the near future.

Unemployed workers especially bore the brunt of the financial crisis. After the revolution these unemployed workers — according to official figures, some four million out of a total workforce of ten and a half million — remained in the big cities. The worst affected were construction workers, who provided the largest number of the unemployed. They had already been hurt in the Shah's last year by the fall-off in large-scale construction — itself a factor in creating the revolutionary situation.

Often the unemployed were former rural migrants, unskilled and on low incomes. Generally they had been hired on a daily basis, and thus had proved exceptionally difficult to organise in the period of the Shah's regime. But the months of anti-Shah mobilisations had had a tremendous effect on the consciousness of the unemployed. After the revolution they joined and supported political meetings organised by students and different left political organisations, and participated in factory meetings organised by employed workers. They themselves organised various demonstrations in large cities against unemployment, demanding jobs or state benefits.

In Isfahan, one of the big industrial cities in the south, their demonstration was attacked by pro-Khomeini 'Revolutionary Guards' and one worker was killed. This outrage led to more demonstrations and sit-ins in other cities. In Tehran, unemployed workers occupied the Ministry of Justice and the Ministry of Labour. They demanded that news of their protests be given on radio and television, and a lifting of the censorship newly imposed by Sadeg Ghotbzadeh, Khomeini's appointed head of broadcasting. They sent an open message to Khomeini: 'We have been shot at by the *Komitehs* and have been accused of being subversives. We are unemployed workers, we made the revolution and we now want to rebuild our country. We will continue our protests until we get what we want.'[31] One of the workers occupying the Ministry of Labour said:

> I suggest that we remain in this place until this ministry of bosses becomes a ministry of workers. The Minister of Labour should know that he is a minister of a provisional government, and is himself only provisional, not permanent. It is his duty to tell the owners and managers that for 25 years they robbed millions and millions, so how are they now suddenly bankrupt? We don't want your promises, we want action. Don't accuse us of being non-believers. You meet our demands, and we will pray 37 times a day instead of 17.[32]

The unemployed converted the former headquarters of the old SAVAK-controlled Syndicates in Tehran into a centre for their meetings. They named the building '*Khaneh Kargar*' (Workers' Home). Every day unemployed workers from different cities sent delegates to *Khaneh*

Kargar to discuss local unemployment problems, to determine further actions and to participate in sit-ins, demonstrations and occupations. Delegates from *Shoras* in different plants also sent delegates to *Khaneh Kargar* to announce their solidarity with the unemployed and to invite them to join in the fight to defend the *Shoras*.

The unemployed workers also played a major role in the First of May demonstrations. These demonstrations represented a trial of strength between the working-class movement and the provisional government. The Founding Council of the Iranian National Workers' Union called on all employed and unemployed workers to celebrate May Day, by joining a workers' march from *Khaneh Kargar*. On the day, unemployed men and women and their children led the march, carrying their banners and congratulating each other on the celebration of Workers' Day. They were followed by employed workers, each plant or industry represented with its own banners. School and college students and political organisations also supported the march.

The workers' demonstration was massive: it took six hours for the one and a half million marchers to pass in the streets of Tehran. Slogans in Farsi, Arabic, Kurdish and Azari expressed the marchers' demands: 'Education for children, not child labour'; 'Nationalisation of all industries'; 'There is no kind capitalist in the world'; 'Long live real unions and real *Shoras*'; 'Death to imperialism' and 'Death to America'; 'Pay the Workers' Wages' and 'Equal Pay for Men and Women'; 'Today is Workers' New Year: In our first new year, we remember all those who gave their lives for the revolution'; 'Unity everything; disunity nothing'; 'Free speech, free press'; 'Down with the old labour law; compile a new law with workers' participation;' 'Workers, peasants, unite and fight'; 'Work for the Unemployed' . . .

At times the march was harassed by small groups of Islamic thugs shouting anti-communist and pro-Islamic slogans. The demonstrators replied: 'The workers will be victorious, the reactionaries will be defeated.' When the thugs threatened violence, the march organisers and political groups decided not to confront them as 'they were only a small group'; indeed, they even agreed to change the route of the demonstration to prevent confrontations with these agents of the regime. The Islamic group, however, took this to be a victory for themselves; they tore down placards and banners, shouting 'Long Live Khomeini, Long Live Islam, Death to Communists'. Thus, despite the massive size of the workers' demonstration, the organisers permitted the political initiative to pass, in part, to their numerically much weaker opponents.

Meanwhile, the newly formed Islamic Republic Party organised a separate rally from 'Iman Hussein Square' in East Tehran. They only managed to gather a few thousand demonstrators, whose slogans expressed the anti-working-class character of this rival rally: 'Workers and peasants, Islam is your real supporter'; 'Muslim workers we must work hard today'; 'Splits and agitation are the tasks of betrayers'; 'We are followers of the Koran, we don't want communism'; 'Islam is victorious, conspirators will be defeated'.

The Mojahedin refused to join in with the independent workers' rally, for fear of seeming to oppose the Islamic Republic. They too held their own separate demonstration in Karaj, near Tehran, but this was joined by only a few thousand, chiefly their own members and supporters. Their contradictory position was revealed in their slogans, which sought to reconcile utter opposites: 'Support Khomeini' and 'Support *Shoras*'; 'Support the provisional government' but also 'Support nationalisation of all industries'.

The Islamic reaction

The events of May Day revealed the potential strength of the workers' movement, but also two other factors: first, the regime's open opposition to independent activity by the working class; and, second, the confusion of the Iranian left. The activity of the groups of Islamic thugs was nothing new. Within days of the Shah's overthrow, the new regime had been encouraging fanatical Islamic groups to launch attacks on the democratic rights and demands of every section of society, and using its own forces to the same end. Women's rights, the national minorities, the peasants, the unemployed and the left had all suffered from the onslaught. But the resistance was divided in its response. Why were the thugs not dealt with on May Day, and prevented from gaining a symbolic victory? Indeed, why were they allowed so many other victories?

Essentially, the problem was that the left thought it should simply *tail after* working-class and other oppositional activity, rather than intervene and propose alternative strategies. They believed that they should avoid having ideological arguments with various currents within the working class. In practice, this meant that the left ended up taking its lead not from the most advanced but from the most backward sections — those who were most influenced by Khomeini's supporters. Numbers of the members of left organisations tried to conceal their middle-class origins by dressing and trying to sound like workers, believing that this faking was necessary as a way of winning workers' confidence. *Later*, they hoped, they would be able to put forward their ideas. In the meantime, they avoided supporting potentially unpopular causes, leaving the field open to the Islamic reaction.

This attitude — and its dangerous consequences — first revealed itself over the issue of women's rights. On 26 February 1979, Khomeini's regime opened an assault on women by suspending the Shah's minimal reform, the Family Protection Act. By this means Khomeini restored to the husband the exclusive right to divorce, permitting him at the same time to take four permanent wives and an unlimited number of temporary wives (*Sighe*) without the first wife's permission. A few days later, on 3 March, another decree forbade women judges to work since, according to Islam, women are not fit to judge. On 6 March, the Ministry of Defence barred women from military service (which some women had used as a way to get weapons training). And on 7 March Khomeini proclaimed that women, while not prohibited from taking jobs, must wear the Islamic veil (the *hejab*).

The next day, when millions of women celebrated International Women's Day and protested against the anti-women Islamic laws, thugs from the Hezbollahis — the 'Party of God' — attacked women with stones, while Islamic fundamentalist members of the *Komitehs* and the Pasdaran (Khomeini's guards) shot at women demonstrators. Every day for a whole week several million women came out to protest against Khomeini's Islamic rules, as these affected every aspect of their lives. The Iranian left did not try to rally support among workers for the women's cause, but largely evaded the issue. Some indeed argued that the women's demands were merely 'bourgeois demands' which it was not important to support.

The position of Khomeini and his forces was thereby strengthened, not least within the *Komitehs*. These, it will be remembered, were formed after the revolution, and took over much of the local administration. Initially they were made up of revolutionaries and young men from the working class and the urban poor who had been exposed to revolutionary ideas during the months of mass struggle against the Shah. In Tehran and the other big cities, the Fedayeen and Mohajedin had considerable influence within the *Komitehs*.

Among the national minorities, the local *Komitehs* were generally under the control of the leaders of their movements. Thus the Kurdistan *Komitehs* were led by the Kurdish Democratic Party and a radical Sunni clergyman, Shaykh Ezaldin Husseini, who was sympathetic to Marxist ideas. The *Komiteh* members in Azarbaijan were followers of the liberal Ayatollah Shariatmadari; in Khuzistan (the land of the Arab minority) they were followers of the guerrilla organisations and the radical Ayatollah Al Shabir Khaqani; in Torkamansahra and in Baluchistan, again, the guerrilla organisations provided the leadership, and under their influence the *Komitehs* expropriated lands belonging to the royal family and large landowners who had escaped the country. All of these groups were opposed to Khomeini's plans for an Islamic Shi'ite Republic. Of course, in other areas where the left political groups had no influence the *Komitehs* were under the control of the bazaar and of the mosques run by the Shi'ite clergy and Khomeini's followers.

The top police officers and army officers had fled the country, and those who remained were disillusioned and not in favour of the new regime. The regime therefore lacked a reliable army and police force, and needed to develop new forces to defend its own existence and further its interests. It began to transform the reliable *Komitehs* into state organisations, while setting out simultaneously to smash the oppositional ones. It began to recruit those elements who had strong ideological links with the regime, giving them a social and ideological role in areas under the control of Khomeini's supporters. These men became part of the new state apparatus, and in turn went on to recruit their relatives (a significant factor in Iran, where the extended family plays an important role). The left did not conduct any kind of systematic political struggle within the *Komitehs*.

As a result, in a very short time the *Komitehs* became the regime's police force, and began to purge revolutionary elements within their ranks. In March — only a few weeks after the victory of the revolution — they strengthened their position by establishing the Revolutionary Guards (Pasdaran) as a fanatical elite group within the *Komitehs*, taking on the job of savage suppression of any activity against the Islamic Republic. To all intents and purposes, they became Khomeini's SAVAK, viciously active in the streets, in the factories and among the national minorities.

After the women came the turn of the national minorities. On 18 March Kurdish villages were bombed for demanding national self-determination, and for seizing land from the landlords. On 29 March, troops shot down Torkaman peasants in Gonbadkavoos, again for seizing land. The Iranian left organisations stood apart from this struggle, in that they did not support the major Kurdish organisations' demand for self-determination, including the right to secession from Iran — thus they subordinated their politics to Iranian nationalism.

Bazargan's government sought to strengthen its position by pushing ahead with its proposals for an Islamic constitution. It announced that 30 March would be 'Referendum Day for the Islamic Republic'. The Tudeh Party and the Mojahedin both backed the regime's proposals, but the rest of the left, the women's organisations, the national minorities and the *Shoras* of many of the factories argued for a boycott of the referendum. They demanded, not a narrow Islamic form of government, but a constituent assembly of elected representatives from the different sections of society, which was itself to determine the form of the new republic.

The government began its preparations for the referendum by lowering the voting age to sixteen, announcing that 24 million voters should now participate. They began, at the same time, to rebuild the atmosphere of intimidation and fear that people had so recently experienced under the Shah. To 'combat counter-revolutionary activity', they announced, the armed forces would remain on alert until after the end of the referendum.

For the referendum itself, they produced two different voting slips, a red one with 'No' and a green one for 'Yes'. Members of the local *Komitehs* handed individual voters their preferred voting slip, at the same time stamping the identity cards of those who participated. The identity card had for years been used as an effective means of policing individuals' activities in Iran; people had had to use it for a whole variety of activities, including school and university attendance, buying and selling, marriage, travel abroad, military service, and so on. For years people had lived with the mentality of fear produced by the secret police and the suppression of any genuine elections. Now, once again, they were afraid: if they boycotted the referendum, their identity card would not be stamped; if they chose the 'No' card, their names would be recorded by the local *Komiteh*.

Despite this intimidatory atmosphere, there were reports from all over the country of severe clashes between sections of the people and the local *Komitehs* and Pasdaran. In Kurdistan and Torkaman-sahra, people burned the ballot boxes.

Though they did not reveal the overall figures, the regime declared a clear majority in favour of the Islamic Republic. Armed with this result, the provisional government spurned the demands for a constituent assembly that came from workers, women, national minorities, students, intellectuals and *Shoras*; instead they began to prepare an assembly of Islamic experts to approve the Islamic constitution. The Revolutionary Guards (Pasdaran) were now formalised under the leadership of Hashemi Rafsanjani, later to be head of the Islamic parliament, in order to 'save the Islamic Revolution'. These organised and armed groups of fanatical Islamic fundamentalists now formed the core of the police force of the new Islamic state machine. A new party, the Islamic Republic Party, was set up to counter the influence of the left groups, and to organise counter-demonstrations when revolutionary demands were raised.

On 10 April, as we have seen, the Pasdaran opened fire on an unemployed workers' demonstration at Isfahan. They also launched attacks on bookshops, burning books while shouting 'Allaho Akbar' (God is the greatest). The regime took control of the radio and television stations, sacking 'un-Islamic' women and representatives of the left. Gangs of thugs armed with knives and clubs attacked the headquarters, bookshops, meetings and demonstrations of both the left and the Mojahedin. Anyone not fanatically Muslim was labelled a 'counter-revolutionary'.

The regime intensified the level of repression, banning progressive newspapers and monopolising the official media. The Shah's army officers were reinstated, and used to lead extensive military offensives against Kurdistan and Khusistan. The local Komitehs, now called Islamic Komitehs, were purged thoroughly of revolutionary elements, whose places were taken by Islamic fundamentalists.

There followed a gradual series of attacks on the labour movement, including purges of the Shoras and the sacking of individual workers. The regime used Islamic ideology to divide the working class. The Shoras, they declared, must be Islamic. Their purpose was to reduce the influence of revolutionaries among the mass of the workers. New terms for capitalists and workers were introduced: workers were now to be known as Mostazafin (the downtrodden) and capitalists Mostakberin (oppressors). Khomeini announced himself the protector of Mostazafin, while all those who opposed his regime were labelled Mostakberin.

It was amongst the most backward sections of the working class that these ideas appeared attractive. They identified with Khomeini's Islamic terminology, and with the idea of the Islamicisation of the Shoras. At the same time, their support for Khomeini was deeply contradictory, as many of them partly grasped. For they opposed the state-appointed managers and believed that the Shoras should make all decisions. One worker put the matter as follows:

> If they don't recognise the rights of our Shoras, there will be sit-downs and sabotage. If they outlaw the Shora, the workers will never let them inside the factory. If they dissolve the Shora, they themselves must go.[33]

The reality was that, despite the regime's anti-capitalist and anti-imperialist slogans, and despite Khomeini's claimed 'support for Mostazafin', the development of the Islamic state rested upon the revival and strengthening of capitalist relations of production.

The situation was further complicated by the fact that the Mojahedin were in favour of Islamic Shoras, though the way they interpreted this was much more liberal than Khomeini's. The Fedayeen and others, rather than oppose Islamicisation on principle, believed they should concede to the ideas of the most backward sections of the working class, so as to 'gain their confidence'. The process of Islamicisation, as a result, was by no means evenly accomplished across the whole of industry. The outcome in different workplaces was shaped by the level of workers' consciousness and the variable influence of the left.

On 9 August, Khomeini declared the formation of a new Islamic organisation, the 'Reconstruction Crusade', with which workers would be required to cooperate fully. From now on, he explained, strikes would be crimes, for the time for 'reconstruction' had come.[34] Hot on the heels of this announcement, the Islamic Societies and Islamic *Shoras* argued for going back to the Shah's 48-hour week. They began sending workers out of the factories to work on the land or on cleaning the streets, washing the windows of ministry buildings and so on.

Workers from large assembly plants such as General Motors, Caterpillar, and Iran National — all highly dependent on imported parts — now found themselves being sent out on 'reconstruction crusades', on the grounds that with a cut in production workers should not be left idle. Many workers refused and took part in strikes and sit-ins. One worker from Iran National, a subsidiary of Talbot, argued: 'With millions unemployed, still they move us from the factory floor where we can be productive, and send us on the reconstruction crusade.' Another, from General Motors, asked, 'Why doesn't the government force the capitalists, who've salted away their capital in European banks, to bring it back so we can carry on production and modernise industry and agriculture? That's real reconstruction.'[35]

Of course the regime had a specific political purpose in seeking the removal of the skilled and semi-skilled workers from the factories: if the most militant and conscious sections of the workers could be got away from the factory floor, it would be that much easier to strengthen the Islamic Societies and *Shoras*.

In the wake of Khomeini's decree, strikes and sit-ins were labelled 'communist conspiracies' and came under attack from armed *Komitehs*. In early October, the unemployed workers' centre, *Khaneh Kargar*, was occupied by the local *Komiteh*. It was then taken back twice by the unemployed workers.

The autumn of 1979 was a critical period for the regime. For despite the intensive repression, all manner of popular struggles continued. Large numbers of women were in opposition to the revived Islamic laws; factories were still being occupied; all over the country demonstrations and meetings of the unemployed were still occurring. Peasants were still involved in land seizures and in battles with the regime's guards, while the war between the national minorities and the central government was reaching its highpoint.

The Iranian ruling class was also divided, with the fight for power among the different factions of the regime intensifying. The Bazargan government represented a bourgeois nationalist tendency, looking for a pro-Western kind of capitalist reconstruction programme; while a state capitalist tendency within the Islamic Republican Party wanted extensive nationalisation and economic centralisation; and the Islamic fundamentalist Hojatieh Group favoured a policy of Islamic private capitalism based on a strengthened bazaar and petty bourgeoisie. No single wing of the bourgeoisie yet had dominance over the others; no-one within the regime seemed to have a clear view of the way forward.

It was in this situation, with the Iranian revolution facing a relative *impasse*, that a wave of 'anti-imperialist' activities began which led to the occupation of the US Embassy on 4 November. The 'anti-imperialist struggle' was to provide the means both to settle the argument within the ruling class and to bring to an end the movement for workers' control.

The American Embassy Occupation

On 4 November 1979, the 'Islamic Students Movement Following the Imam Khomeini's Line' occupied the American Embassy in Tehran. The regime organised demonstrations 'against imperialism', throwing its domestic opponents within Iran into utter confusion. All political attention and activity was diverted towards the 'anti-imperialist' campaign. The political groups of the left, deeply confused about what was going on, deserted independent activity against the Islamic regime as they began heated debates about the 'anti-imperialist' nature of Khomeini's government.

The Iranian left forgot that, despite the victory of the revolution and the destruction of the Shah's imperial regime, much of the old state machine remained in place. According to a US government estimate,[36] while 30 per cent of the Shah's officer corps had been removed, 70 per cent remained. There had been some nationalisation of banks, insurance companies and some private industrial concerns, but under the control of Islamic laws and Islamic organisations rather than under workers' control. Past promises concerning the demands of the national minorities had been forgotten and broken: Persian chauvinism, together with the Islamicisation of society under Shi'ite rule, left no space for minority rights.

Khomeini's exploitation of the religious issue had already seriously divided the opposition; now, with the US Embassy occupation, Khomeini played his militant nationalist card to complete their disorientation. He was able to split the left opposition completely. Khomeini now declared that all problems arising in factories, among women and among national minorities were due to US imperialism. It was US imperialism that was fighting the governent in Kurdistan, in Tabriz, in Torkamansahra and in Khusistan. Women opposing Islamic laws were US and Zionist agents. Workers resisting Islamic *Shoras* were imperialist agents.

The Tudeh Party fell in with Khomeini's argument, and backed his line. The biggest left organisations — the Fedayeen, the Mojahedin and the Paykar[37] — also broke away from the struggle, abandoning the militant workers, the women and the national minorities, among whom they had some significant presence.

In an attempt to justify their position, all the left parties now spoke of the 'low level of consciousness' of the workers. After all, they claimed (very inaccurately), the *Shoras'* demands were no more than economic demands. The Fedayeen and Paykar declared that the *Shoras* needed to be led, under the left parties' guidance, towards political demands. This might sound like socialist sense, except that the proposed political demands were no more than nationalist. The Mojahedin's attitude to the *Shoras* was that a bridge must be built between workers' control and Islamic ideology, so that the socialism of *soviets* could be combined with Islam. Under the circumstances of the US Embassy occupation, the left agreed, all forces must be united with the 'progressive anti-imperialist bourgeoisie'.

The national mobilisation around the occupation of the American embassy provided Khomeini with a favourable political climate in which to silence the opposition. He seized the opportunity with both hands. A new referendum for the proposed Islamic constitution was announced. Anyone opposing the referendum was branded as a Zionist and agent of imperialism.

All the left political groups supported the referendum 'so as not to jeopardise the anti-imperialist struggle'. However in Tabriz, home of the Azari Turks, supporters of Ayatollah Shariatmadari, a leading representative of the liberal clergy, organised a general strike and mass demonstration against Khomeini's Islamic constitution. This was brutally suppressed. By such means, even a section of the clergy and the liberal bourgeoisie who opposed the new constitution were driven into silence.

Under the new constitution, personal liberty, freedom of the press, of association, of assembly, of speech and of religion (with the exception of the Baha'i faith) and similar rights were constitutionally guaranteed — but only according to the 'Islamic standard'. Women appearing in public had to wear Islamic dress. Music and alcohol were forbidden. Anything critical of either the Islamic Republic or Islam was banned from the press and other media. Other religions beside Shi'ite Islam — again, except the Baha'i faith[38] — were permitted, but their followers must behave according to the Islamic rules, for example as regards women, alcohol and music. Other nationalities might exist, but their languages and cultures were not recognised.

In the factories, the Islamicisation programme was pushed ahead, using the Islamic *Shoras* and Societies. A wave of wildcat strikes mounted again, demanding the expropriation of private capital, and especially capital involved in joint ventures with foreign capital. Many of the *Shoras'* leaders were arrested, and their strike funds were expropriated by the Islamic *Shoras*.

Once the Islamic constitution had been ratified, the next step was the establishment of the presidency and parliament. This was the occasion for the eruption of a factional struggle within the regime. Two especially influential forces were contending with each other. On one side was the liberal nationalist tendency, led by Khomeini's former adviser and foreign minister, Bani Sadr, with a programme for relatively orthodox bourgeois reconstruction. On the other side was a tendency within the Islamic Republic Party, led by Ayatollah Beheshti, who was seeking a state capitalist solution to the problems of economic reconstruction; it had been the Islamic Republic Party which had actively intervened in the struggle in the factories, and brought the Islamic *Shoras* under its control.

The first round in the power struggle went to Bani Sadr, who was elected president in January 1980, chiefly because the Islamic Republic Party was internally divided and unable to agree on a single presidential candidate. The Mojahedin put forward their leader, Massoud Rajavi, for president, on a programme of support for the rights of women and national minorities, and for the workers' *Shoras*. Rajavi, however, was forced by the government to withdraw his candidacy on the grounds that 'according to the constitution he was not a real Muslim and he was really a counter-revolutionary'. Bani Sadr then adopted the Mojahedin's programme, including support for workers' *Shoras*, and on that basis gained the victory.

After his election, the conflict between Bani Sadr and the Islamic Republic Party (IRP) sharpened. The party mobilised its supporters in parliament and the cabinet to weaken his position. In the factories, the Islamic *Shoras* under IRP control also became vehicles for the consolidation of the clergy's power. They opposed both the workers' *Shoras* and the liberal managements, introducing '*Maktabi* management' (Islamic management), which together with the Islamic *Shoras* campaigned against the workers' *Shoras*.

Bani Sadr's minister of labour, Mohammed mir Sadeghi, who favoured recognising trade union rights within bourgeois democracy, was replaced by Tavakoli, an Islamic fanatic and a member of the Hojatieh faction within the IRP. Tavakoli disapproved even of Islamic *Shoras* on the grounds that 'property, factory, government and everything belonged to God, his prophet and the 12th Imam; in the absence of this Imam (the Messiah) they belong to the deputy of the Imam' — in other words, to Khomeini.

During this period many factory *Shoras* were closed down, among them the *Shoras* for the Tool-making, Lift Track, Pomp Iran and Kompidor factories in Tabriz, the Union of Workers' *Shoras* of Gilan (with 30,000 workers), the Union of Workers' *Shoras* of Western Tehran, the Ahwas oil industry *Shoras* and the railway workers' *Shoras*. *Khaneh Kargar*, previously the free headquarters for workers' assemblies, became the centre of pro-IRP *Shoras* and Islamic Societies.

In August 1980 the regime abolished the former profit-sharing law. This had been one of the Shah's industrial reforms, through which enterprises paid part of their profits to their workers. As one worker in Tehran stated: 'This was part of our wages, which the previous regime paid us each year in the name of profit-sharing. Now the Islamic regime is taking even this from us.'

Industrial disputes still rumbled on. The main issues were the closing down of the *Shoras* and the sackings of workers for opposing *Maktabi* managements. Though the regime's aim was a complete end to every vestige of the *Shoras*, workers' continuing resistance made the task difficult. In August 1980 the Iranian parliament ratified a law on Islamic *Shoras*, granting them only a consultative role. The majority of workers refused to recognise this law, protesting strongly. In a survey carried out by **Keyhan**, one of the national newspapers, workers expressed their strong objection to the new law. 'We do not recognise this law,' said one, 'we want a law giving us control over production, distribution and management.' Another said:

> This law aims to weaken the power of the workers; this is in effect the recognition of semi-Syndicate rights, which only preserves the rights of the capitalists. *Shoras* are the basis of our power in the factories. It is now clear that as long as capitalists are running the factories, they will continue to weaken our power.[39]

In September 1980 Iraq invaded Iran. The effect was to give a huge boost to the counter-revolutionary Islamic Republic in Iran. The Islamic *Shoras* passed resolutions declaring, 'We are at war, we must sacrifice and be united' and 'We must work even at the weekend to win the war'. Khomeini launched his 'cultural revolution' to Islamicise all educational and cultural institutions. Revolutionary Guards and

Komitehs attacked the left in their last sanctuaries, the universities, which were closed down indefinitely. The wearing of the veil became compulsory; women without the veil were beaten up, had their bones broken and their faces burned with acid.

The left shattered and split. The Mojahedin allied themselves with Bani Sadr, a representative, at best, of the liberal bourgeoisie. The Fedayeen split into two wings: the majority joined with the Tudeh Party, arguing that Khomeini's regime was anti-imperialist and hence progressive; while the minority held it was a reactionary capitalist regime. As the left, the *Shoras* and even the liberal nationalists were weakened, so the Islamic Republic grew stronger.

In June 1981 Bani Sadr was dismissed as president. A country-wide campaign of urban guerrilla warfare against Khomeini's regime began, launched chiefly by the Mojahedin but also the Fedayeen minority. A bomb killed 72 of the IRP's top leadership, including Ayatollah Beheshti. Bani Sadr and the Mojahedin leader, Rajavi, fled to France. Another bomb killed the new president, Rajai, along with his prime minister, Bahonar. The guerrilla campaign, and the war, provided the final excuse for the regime to begin militarising all the factories and liquidating every opposition element still remaining there.

Nothing remained of the gains of the popular revolution of February 1979. The Iranian workers' movement had been crushed. The left had collapsed back into its old mistakes: either uncritical support for a murderous anti-working-class regime, or the terrible isolation of guerrilla politics.

Conclusions

The Iranian working class provided the key force in the struggle to bring down the Shah's appalling regime. But power did not pass into the workers' hands. Instead, the provisional government under Khomeini's leadership determined the policy content and the form of the new state power that emerged on the ruins of the old. As the Khomeini government worked to develop a new system of bourgeois state rule, the working class became its prisoner. In the final outcome, the workers found themselves subjected to a new, Islamic regime in which their rights and powers were no greater — and in some important respects even less — than those they had possessed under the Shah.

The counter-revolution was pushed forward under the guise of Khomeini's phoney 'anti-imperialism' and consolidated with the development of the Gulf war. Some of the popular enthusiasm for the war, especially in the backward areas of the countryside, can be explained by the way it was presented as an 'extension of the revolution'. The appallingly high number of deaths was defended with the grotesque claim that dying for Islam meant 'liberation for paradise'.

The war also provided a perfect cover for the regime's wiping out of any remnants of left-wing opposition. Independent trade-union organisation and the right to strike were abolished as 'un-Islamic', returning workers to the situation under the Shah; here Islam found a perfect unity with the needs of capitalism. Women were subjected, in the name of God, to a patriarchal humiliation that destroyed all their basic rights to choose their own fate as far as such matters as marriage, divorce, custody of children, right to work and the like are concerned. National and religious minorities were fiercely repressed.

The 'Irangate' scandal of 1986 exposed the real nature of the Islamic regime. Rafsanjani, Khomeini's second-in-command, suggested in his arms dealings with the Reagan government of the US that Iran should resume its role as policeman in the Gulf. Fundamentalist Islam is now poised, in a sinister fashion, to throttle other progressive developments throughout the Middle East, Near East and North Africa, while the ruling classes of the West are adjusting and beginning to make overtures to this strange new ally.

This tragic outcome need not have occurred. The history of the Iranian workers' struggle, over the months after February 1979, points to the possibility of a very different result. Iran's workers wanted a very different kind of society from that imposed on them in the name of the Islamic Republic. They wanted a society directly under their own control. The demands they advanced through their *Shoras* indicated this clearly.

The workers' struggle for power through their *Shoras* linked together demands of an 'economic' and a 'political' character. The *Shoras* were revolutionary instruments, initially forged in the fire of the battle to remove the Shah, through which the workers' aspirations to their own power were given expression. The demands they posed did not simply concern pay, hours, conditions of employment, but involved centrally issues of control over production and indeed over the whole of social and political life.

For a number of months after the Shah's overthrow, there was to all intents and purposes workers' control in industry. But for this to be consolidated as the basis of a new social order, the question of state power had to be confronted. From the beginning, the Islamic Republic had sought to undermine the *Shoras*, the instruments through which the workers sought to develop their control over production, distribution and the like. It was the Khomeini regime which backed the 'Islamic' managers and the middle-class technical experts against the workers' committees, and whose laws and regulations inhibited the full extension of working-class power.

A political struggle over the form of the new Iranian state was a vital precondition for victory in the workplaces. Socialist relations of production at work can only be guaranteed if the working class can extend its collective power beyond the factory to the state itself. The demands of the *Shoras*, and especially of their National Founding Council, revealed a strong awareness of this among the leading militant workers.

Had the workers succeeded in developing their power in this way, they would have had to broaden out the basis of their demands and thus of the Iranian revolution as a whole. Not only would they have had to push ahead with their own specific demands, but they would also have needed to take up and unify the demands of other oppressed sections of Iranian society: the unemployed, women, the peasants, the various national and religious minorities. For the interests of these various overlapping groups, like those of the workers, were bound up with the further development of the revolution. All these groups were the workers' potential allies in the struggle against Khomeini's provisional government.

However, almost from the start, Khomeini and his allies were able to divide the forces opposed to his project for an Islamic Republic. Why was Khomeini's offensive against the democratic and working-class potential of the Iranian revolution so successful? At least two of the explanations that have been offered seem very inadequate.

Some commentators have suggested that Iran was peculiar, in the hold that Shi'ite Islam held over the minds of the Iranian masses. This is firstly to exaggerate the degree of religiosity of the Iranian workers and peasants; secondly, the mere existence of widespread religious belief does not explain why a section of the Islamic clergy should have come to political power in the way they did. The reality is that the Islamic Republic was the *form* taken by bourgeois counter-revolution in Iran. The same essential result — the defeat of the revolutionary forces of the working class — has been produced in a whole variety of different guises in a host of different countries during the course of the present century.

Nor can the defeat of the workers' movement be explained in terms of Iran's economic backwardness. After all, in proportional terms the modern Iranian working class is very much larger than was the working class in Russia at the time of the 1917 revolution. In both cases, certainly, the contradictions of uneven capitalist development within an imperialist world economy pushed the working class to the forefront of the political struggle against the old regime. In Iran, as in

Russia, the Marxist thesis of 'permanent revolution' proved crucially correct: the working class occupied the centre of the revolutionary arena, and sought to press the revolution onward from an unstable 'bourgeois democratic' stage towards socialist, working-class democracy.

Alas, in Iran the left badly misread the situation. The parties of the left consistently saw their historic tasks as no more than the overthrow of the Shah and the inauguration of a democratic structure. For them, the principal content of the revolution was to be a 'democratic revolution' only, with the socialist revolution pushed away into some indefinite future. Insofar as they perceived the proletariat's struggle for power, it was only through the lens of the 'bourgeois-democratic' revolution.

The exploited and oppressed peoples of Iran, having tasted their potential power in the struggle against the Shah, sensed the possibility of carrying the revolution onward towards a socialist society under their own direct control. Not so the bourgeoisie: they had no impulse to continue the revolution, indeed they wanted it rapidly halted and the popular forces demobilised. Thus the revolution against the Shah was immediately transformed into a bitter class struggle over the future form of Iranian society. The workers and the other oppressed sections did not want the revolution to stop: they wanted to continue it until all their urgent needs and aspirations were met.

This was the significance of the *Shoras*, the women's groups, the peasant bodies that seized the land, the organisations of Iran's various national minorities. Together, these various movements had immense potential power. But in practice they were cut off from each other: the workers' struggle for the *Shoras* was conducted in isolation from the women's battle for emancipation, from the movements for national self-determination, and from the peasants' struggle for the land; and in turn these movements were equally isolated from the workers' struggle. The Iranian left proved incapable of unifying these different movements, for they lacked the overall perspective within which this unification would have been seen to be necessary. While they discussed the issues of rights for women and national minorities in their papers and meetings, they never campaigned actively for them within the *Shoras* and the unemployed workers' committees.

A revolution in a backward country poses with particular sharpness some fundamental issues of socialist politics. The working class cannot gain power by itself, in isolation from and in opposition to a struggle for the emancipation of society from all forms of oppression, whether national, sexual, cultural or religious. The fullest extension of democratic rights is an essential precondition of workers' power.

When the Mojahedin and Tudeh Party fell in with Khomeini's proposals for an Islamic Republic, they condemned Iranian women and the religious minorities to a continuation of their repression. When the left as a whole failed to argue for the rights of women and the national and religious minorities among the workers, they merely strengthened their opponents. And when they fell in with the utterly reactionary call for 'national unity' in Khomeini's phoney 'anti-imperialism', they cut their own throats.

A complete victory for the popular revolution was only possible on condition that it broke with the bourgeois provisional government and began a decisive struggle for a new form of society *centred* on workers' power, on the realisation of the demands of all the different revolutionary forces, and the complete shattering of the Islamic state. That meant a fight to extend the power of all the different kinds of secular *Shoras*, to coordinate their activities and to make them the basis of a new kind of society.

As it was, the establishment of the Islamic Republic represented the complete end to any revolutionary enthusiasm on the part of the Iranian bourgeoisie and petty bourgeoisie. In reality, not even the original project of the left, the creation of the institutions of a normal 'bourgeois democratic' regime, had been achieved. In the specific conditions of Iran, that project was always utopian: the real choice lay between on one side a democratic workers' and peasants' republic, able to lay the foundations of a socialist regime, and on the other the re-establishment of a highly authoritarian capitalist regime.

For some months after the fall of the Shah, there existed in Iran a potentially revolutionary situation. But for the outcome to have been different, a revolutionary socialist party able to break decisively with the failed politics of the Iranian left — the Tudeh Party, the Mojahedin and the Fedayeen alike — was an absolute pre-requisite. Unfortunately, such a party did not exist.

The Iranian left's theoretical armoury completely lacked the central Marxist conception of socialist revolution. Whatever the differences among those various parties, they all shared two inter-related ideas, both of them rooted in the theory and practice of both Stalinism and social democracy. The first was that the perspective for social transformation must be limited to the democratisation rather than the overthrow of bourgeois social relations. The second was that the role of a revolutionary party is to act *on behalf of* the exploited and the oppressed, rather than to encourage and lead them in their own revolutionary self-activity. In the history of Iran, as of so many other countries, the application of this false perspective by the left has regularly led to the defeat of revolutionary movements, whenever the workers' struggle has created a revolutionary situation with the potential for socialist development.

The Tudeh Party and the Mojahedin supported Khomeini's proposals for 'Islamicisation', despite the fact that this meant the weakening and destruction of autonomous working-class organisation in the shape of the workers' *Shoras*. The Mojahedin and the Fedayeen, alike, never broke with the elitist politics of the guerrilla struggle, which involved them in substituting their own activity and courage for the self-development of the struggle of Iran's workers and peasants. None ever centred their politics on the development of the popular struggle, and especially the workers' movement, towards the creation of a democratic workers' and peasants' state. Other organisations which might have shown a revolutionary socialist alternative were too small and too weakly rooted in the working-class movement to make any significant difference to the outcome, however formally correct their politics.[40]

Socialist revolution is centred on the self-emancipation of the working class. In such a process, it is the job of a revolutionary socialist party to point the way forward, but not act for the real subjects of history, who are the exploited themselves. Such a party cannot substitute itself for the action, consciousness and organisation of the workers themselves. Nor can it make the revolution *for* the workers, or for the rest of the oppressed and exploited population. It has to argue with them, consistently and patiently, for the necessity of their taking power into their own hands. What it cannot do is abstain, as the Iranian left did, from political argument within the workers' movement.

The absence of a revolutionary socialist party in Iran during the first eight months after the Shah's fall meant that no one was able to propose a means for filling the power vacuum, or to prevent the various left organisations from vacillating in a way that helped the Islamic regime to consolidate its position. As a result, immense possibilities were missed. The workers' *Shoras* revealed an amazing resilience in their courageous effort to build an independent national organisation. A large part of the population, as a result of the battle to remove the Shah, possessed arms. Yet no party argued that the *Shoras* should advance from being a kind of militant pressure group, acting on the newly emerged Islamic state, towards arming themselves and developing their power as the embryo of a new state.

Of course, the national organisation of the *Shoras* did not amount to a full network of workers' councils (*soviets*) of the kind that characterised Russia in 1917. But it was not impossible for them to have developed in just this way. To do this, they would have had to assume political responsibility for the administration of the towns and cities, thus competing with the new *Komitehs* and absorbing their best elements. This was by no means impossible: the *Komitehs* were, at first, extremely unstable formations. Their membership often comprised many of the best of the guerrilla fighters from the period of the struggle against the Shah. Many of them could have been drawn towards a revolutionary socialist perspective had such a clear political lead been given within the *Shoras*. Instead, in the absence of such a vital pole of attraction, those militants were drawn towards the Islamic Republic as Khomeini's regime began to consolidate itself.

A revolutionary socialist party would have had to be uncompromisingly atheist, opposing the clergy's influence on political life and the constitution, and uncompromising in its support for the struggles for women's liberation, for peasant land seizures, and for the rights of the national and religious minorities. It could not hope, immediately, to overcome the deeply contradictory brew of Islamic ideas that coexisted with advanced socialist ideas in the minds of many of the most militant workers. But it could have organised a clear minority faction in the factories which would have been prepared to break completely with the notion of the Islamic revolution.

The condition for all of this, of course, was precisely the existence of a revolutionary organisation that consistently presented a clear case for carrying the revolution forward to a socialist conclusion. Such an organisation would have had to understand, and patiently explain, the anti-working-class nature of the Khomeini regime. On such a basis, the project of a struggle for socialism could have won majority support within the *Shoras*, even among workers who retained illusions in Islam.

The question for the future of Iran, and thus of the whole Middle East, is whether such a socialist organisation will be created within and through the struggles that now inevitably arise between Iran's Islamic Republican government and the mass of the population whom that regime now oppresses so severely. Unless and until such an organisation is developed, the tragedy of the Iranian revolution of 1979 is liable to be endlessly repeated.

FIVE

POLAND 1980-81
The self-limiting revolution
Colin Barker

'PEOPLE'S POLAND' was born at the end of the Second World War. By the end of the 1970s what had been a backward, predominantly agricultural country had become the world's tenth industrial power (with the world's eighth largest military budget). Rapid, state-directed development had created great factories and industrial cities. The working class was now the biggest class, and the majority of workers were no longer former peasants but an educated and culturally more sophisticated 'second generation'. That working class had several major experiences of battle with its rulers, in 1956, 1970 and 1976, and was to produce, between July 1980 and December 1981, the most advanced workers' movement of the post-war world.

For at the end of the 1970s 'People's Poland' was racked by crisis. Beginning in 1979, it was to experience the largest collapse of production yet seen in any post-war industrial country: GNP fell in 1979 by 2 per cent, in 1980 by 8 per cent and in 1981 by 15-20 per cent. Poland's debts were phenomenal: as well as millions of rubles owed to the USSR, the regime owed between $20 billion and $25 billion to Western banks. The 'economic miracle' of the early 1970s had come to a shuddering stop.[1]

The crisis was more than merely 'economic'. Rapid growth in the first half of the 1970s had been accompanied by a widening of inequalities. Public corruption had become endemic. Popular belief in the regime was at an all-time low. And the prospects of improvement seemed thin. The housing shortage remained acute; food supplies were a permanent source of difficulty; Poland was the most polluted country in Europe; the women of the textile city of Lodz suffered the continent's highest still-birth rate.

Among the Western left there are still those who fondly suppose that Poland and its sister regimes are somehow more 'advanced' than their Western capitalist rivals. 'State planning' and 'nationalised property', they imagine, give Eastern Europe a superior form of society. The reality is very different: like the Western capitalist powers, the state-capitalist regimes of the East manifest increasing tendencies to stagnation, cyclical 'stop-go' movements in their economic mechanisms; the class antagonisms between the workers and peasants on one hand, and the ruling classes of these countries on the other, are quite as acute as anywhere in the West. And they have erupted in some of the sharpest class battles of the post-war world.[2]

For socialists with more than cloth between their ears, the experience of 'Solidarity' in Poland powerfully demonstrated the continuing vitality of the heart of Marxist politics. Firstly, it laid bare the sharp class antagonisms within Eastern Europe's apparently monolithic regimes. Secondly, Solidarity revealed the continuing and developing power of the modern working class to organise itself for its own emancipation, and to become thereby the beacon for all the other oppressed and exploited layers of class-divided society. For the workers' movement in Poland became the real leadership of the whole mass of the people. And thirdly, and tragically, Solidarity in its defeat also showed how even the most highly organised trade union movement in the advanced world could be crushed and atomised for lack of a political analysis and strategy adequate to its achievements and its problems.

Lighting the fuse

The supply and price of everyday necessities, including foodstuffs, has been a persistent thorn in the side of every Polish government since the war. In the later 1970s, as the economic crisis deepened, the regime led by Edward Gierek attempted to solve the problem of shortages by doubling up the rationing system: beside the price-controlled shops, where queuing dominated the rationing system, there developed a second set of stores, where rationing was by price alone. On 1 July 1980, a government spokesman announced that better cuts of meat would in future be available only in the 'free price' shops.

The announcement was the signal for a wave of strikes that rolled across most of Polish industry for the next six weeks, to reach its climax in the coastal cities of Gdansk-Gdynia and Szczecin in mid-August. That strike wave had a number of notable features.

It was fully expected. Over the previous four years, the Polish regime had become more than accustomed to strikes. There had been at least a thousand, predominantly in the larger (and stronger, and more politically significant) 'flagship' enterprises that are the pride of industrialised Poland. The regime's reaction to those strikes had been, mostly, compromising rather than militant. The Polish ruling class was running scared of its working class. Time and again, refrigerated trucks loaded with good sausage and other supplies had driven through the gates of major enterprises to assuage Polish workers' militancy. In July 1980, industrial managers were instructed to buy peace by granting substantial pay rises.

The regime was nervous for good reason. In 1970, the party leader, Gomulka, had been toppled from government by the workers' reaction to price rises. Riots and street battles, the burning of party buildings and then factory occupations had forced prices down. Many workers had died in these struggles, especially in the coastal cities, leaving a heritage of bitterness and mistrust. In June 1976, the regime had again attempted to raise prices: strikes, street demonstrations and the ripping up of major railway lines by industrial workers had forced a retreat — this time within 24 hours.

Thus in 1980 the regime faced a working class already possessed of a certain confidence in its own power to win concessions. Indeed, the balance of forces was such that some workers were granted pay rises without even asking for them — an event which actually precipitated strikes! In other cases, as if determined to prove that militancy pays, managements granted pay increases only to workers who actually went on strike, leaving the less active to reflect — in the mirror of smaller pay-packets — on the practical advantages of militancy. 'Those who do not strike will not eat meat' ran the tantalising rumour.

Although the strike movement had no coordinating centre, the workers had developed an information network by which they spread news of their struggles, their demands, their victories and their defeats. Lorry and train drivers carried messages, telephone messages were passed, kinship and friendship links were mobilised to spread news rapidly. (The official media provided almost no news at all of the 'work stoppages'.)

In addition, a key group of 'dissidents' played a major role in publicising the workers' movement. The Committee for the Defence of Workers (KOR) was set up originally in 1976 to organise aid for the victimised workers of Radom who had struck and demonstrated against the price rises; but it had moved beyond fund-raising towards working-class organisation. From 1977, some of KOR's best activists drew around them small circles of working-class militants in major industrial centres, with whom it produced and distributed cyclostyled bulletins, entitled 'Worker', 'Coastal Worker' and the like. These news-sheets reported on working-class conditions and struggles and publicised a 'Workers' Charter' whose demands included 'free trade unions'.

The workers' circles provided a focus for developing a rank-and-file workers' leadership that was to play a fundamental role in Polish life from August 1980. The groups around the bulletins gathered in news of the strikes, and spread it back to the workers; they gave tactical advice on how best to organise, crystallising and generalising the hard-won working-class experience of the previous decade.

The early successes of the strike movement emboldened the workers during July and their demands, and forms of organisation, underwent a process of development. In Lublin there was a three-day general strike, coordinated loosely by a strike committee based in a number of workplaces. Demands broadened out from wages to encompass other issues: family allowances equal to those received by the police; closure of the special 'free price' shops; a five-day week; new union elections; freedom of the press. In the setting of growing working-class confidence and combativity, there was nothing forced or artificial about this transition from purely 'economic' to more and more 'political' demands.

The government strategy was to pay additional wages when it must, in hope that the strike movement would gradually fade away. With any luck, pay rises would be limited to the larger factories while smaller and weaker enterprises would pay the costs of inflation. In the second week of August, indeed, a plump government spokesman affably assured Western journalists that 'work stoppages' had almost ceased. But within days the movement rose to a whole new level.

Explosion in Gdansk

One of the KOR-inspired workers' circles had been set up in Gdansk around the paper 'Coastal Worker'. From 1979 the group had already tried to organise in a few local factories to prevent sackings and to contest factory elections. They had circulated KOR's 'Workers' Charter', and held demonstrations in memory of the workers killed in 1970. In August 1980, one of the group, a 50-year-old woman crane-driver, Anna Walentynowicz, was victimised by the management at the giant Lenin shipyards. Meeting on the night of Wednesday 13 August, the group decided it was time for them to act. They prepared hand-written leaflets and posters, and the following morning smuggled these into the shipyard and a few other workplaces.

Once inside their sections, they pinned up their posters and called meetings, demanding strike action. Previous propaganda and agitation bore fruit: their sections stopped work, and marched around the shipyard calling out the rest of the workforce. By the end of the morning, a mass meeting was arguing with the shipyard manager, who tried to address the strikers from an abandoned bulldozer. A member of the Coastal Worker group, Lech Walesa — himself sacked from the shipyard — climbed over the wall and joined the crowd. He now jumped up beside the manager, announced himself to the crowd, and declared the start of an occupation strike.

The Gdansk strike spread rapidly to other local workplaces, largely through the initiative of other members of the 'Coastal Worker' group.[3] Delegates from these workplaces, including the Paris Commune shipyards in neighbouring Gdynia and from the city's tramdrivers, gathered in the Lenin yard.

By Saturday, the shipyard workers' immediate demands had been met. They had been granted their largest ever pay rise, the reinstatement of Walentynowicz and Walesa, improved family allowances, plus permission to erect a memorial to the workers killed by the police in the riots of 1970. Walesa announced the end of the occupation over the shipyard's tannoy system. The workers began streaming out of the gates. There the matter might have ended, with one more sectional victory to be added to the list of local concessions already made by the regime over the previous seven weeks.

Except for one thing: other workers had struck in solidarity with the Lenin yards, and they had gained nothing. Henryka Krzywonos, a Gdansk tram-driver, angrily accosted Walesa and demanded that the shipyard workers stay out until all other local workplaces had also won satisfaction. Walesa immediately agreed. But the shipyard management now refused further access to the tannoy system. The leading activists — among them Walentynowicz, Walesa and a shipyard nurse, Alina Pienkowska — ran to the gates to try to turn back the flood of workers going home. Only about a tenth of the workforce were persuaded to stay, but the gates were closed again and the occupation resumed.

This was the start of a qualitatively new development. Over the weekend, a new body was formed: the Inter-Enterprise Strike Committee (MKS), comprising delegates from all striking workplaces in the region. This new organisation formulated a new and much more advanced set of demands, which were to crystallise into '21 Points'. No longer concerned simply with immediate local issues, the list began with the demand for new, independent trade unions. It went on to call for relaxation of censorship, new rights for the church, the freeing of political prisoners, improvements in the health service.

Overnight the MKS negotiated with local church authorities, and on Sunday morning a parish priest came into the shipyard to bless a makeshift cross and conduct an open-air mass. This had the desired effect: large numbers of workers who had quit the yards the previous day now returned to strengthen the occupation.

The MKS now expanded rapidly. By Tuesday there were more than 250 enterprises represented on the Gdansk committee. A newssheet, '*Solidarnosc*', began appearing: produced on the shipyard's printing press with the assistance of KOR members, it reached a print-run of 30,000 copies daily. The authorities cut off Gdansk from all telephone contact with the rest of Poland. (One government representative claimed a week later that the Warsaw telephone exchange had been demolished in a hurricane.[4] Even his colleagues on the government negotiating team looked pained at this blatant lie.) But news of Gdansk's new organisation and new demands spread rapidly through Poland's industrial centres. A further MKS was established in Elblag, and then another along the coast in Szczecin, scene of the mass shipyard occupation of 1971. The Szczecin MKS entered into liaison with Gdansk. A fourth MKS appeared in Wroclaw, to the south, and yet another in Walbrzych. In other centres, workers threatened to strike if the Gdansk demands were not met.

At first the regime refused to recognise the new workers' committees, attempting to divide and rule by entering into separate negotiations on a plant-by-plant basis. But the MKSs held together, and the regime was forced to agree to open talks directly with the Gdansk and Szczecin MKSs, inside the shipyards.

Until almost the end of August, hardliners in the party leadership still hoped that repression rather than concessions might be used to handle the crisis. The government still hoped that at least the mining areas of Silesia — traditional stronghold of party boss Gierek — would hold out against the tide of working-class revolt. But on 29 August, yet another MKS emerged against a background of major strikes in the Silesian mines, at Jastrzebie, where miners' and other representatives were even joined by a delegate from a striking beauty salon. It was clear that, short of a massive blood-letting, the regime would have to make major class-wide concessions.

On 30 August in Szczecin, and on 31 August in Gdansk, government ministers signed documents accepting the '21 Points'. The Szczecin MKS had been rather self-enclosed, suspicious of outsiders. In Gdansk, however, the MKS had sought maximum publicity: there the agreements were signed in a huge ceremony before the world's TV. Three days later, at Jastrzebie, with strikes mushrooming in the pits, a further agreement was signed, granting a major reduction in the working week.

Soviets in Poland?

The formation of the Inter-Enterprise Strike Committee (MKS) had been a specific response to the problems generated in Gdansk in the aftermath of the shipyard's isolated victory. The MKS form, once adopted, proved to be brilliantly adapted to the Polish workers' problems.

The whole movement was based on a huge wave of workplace occupations. Each striking enterprise sent a delegate to its local MKS. The delegates elected an inner executive committee, under their immediate control. The major negotiations with the state were conducted in front of microphones, which were linked into the shipyard tannoy system so that thousands of workers could follow the proceedings and assess the progress being made. Delegates returned to their workplaces with tape-recordings of the day's proceedings, to report and renew their mandates.

No longer, as in 1956 and 1970, or even in 1976, did workers' anger boil over into street riots. That form of resistance had been conducted on terrain that the state could easily — and bloodily — control. Polish workers are credited with the invention of the tactic of factory occupation. They carried the memory of it to the United States where it was used in the great organising battles in the later 1930s. Now, in 1980, it had returned to its birthplace on a scale never previously witnessed. An estimated 4,000 enterprises had joined the strike and occupation movement by the end of August.

Within days of its establishment, the Gdansk MKS had begun taking control of essential services in the area. The striking tram-drivers and railway workers returned to work, covering their transport with posters: 'We are on strike too, but we are working to make your life easier'. A fleet of 300 taxis was placed under the MKS's direction. The MKS instructed bakeries and canneries to continue producing food supplies for the working class. Lorries operated with MKS licences.

On the MKS's initiative, the production and sale of alcohol in the Gdansk region was halted. At the gates of the occupations, workers' guards confiscated and destroyed vodka and cider bottles. At the port of Gdynia, where cases of thieving occurred, offenders were subjected to a form of proletarian justice: men and women were made to stand on a stack of pallets to be hooted at by the workers they had betrayed. The early stages in the growth of workers' control, even of a democratic workers' state form, could be discerned.

As we have seen, the actual demands for which the workers were now fighting were no longer restricted to immediate 'economic' issues but stretched towards the very heart of political powr. This was symbolised by the final argument between the Gdansk MKS and the regime. Early in the occupation movement, leading KOR members in Warsaw and elsewhere were placed under preventive arrest. The Gdansk workers' assembly refused to allow its leaders to sign the agreement on the '21 Points' until these intellectuals were guaranteed immediate release. As Anna Walentynowicz put it, 'If we don't defend the political prisoners today, then tomorrow our agreements are worthless; for we are all political, and they will call us that, and simply lock us up.'[5]

The MKS was a strike committee of delegates from occupied workplaces, without regard to trade or industry, putting forward and fighting for political as well as economic demands, beginning to take control of aspects of production and distribution. This form, improvised to handle the concrete problems of the struggle, was also the organisational summary of bitterly-won lessons from previous battles, and an immense advance over previous modes of self-organisation. Though they did not know it, the Polish workers had re-invented, out of the logic of their own experience, the organisational form first adopted by Russian workers in 1905 — the workers' council. In 1905 and 1917 it bore the title of 'Soviet of Workers' Deputies'. But the *form* has re-appeared regularly in workers' struggles when they have reached a revolutionary peak.[6]

Such class organisations have the *potential* to develop into organs of revolutionary popular power and become the foundations of a new social order. However, that potential is not automatically realised; for the MKS to develop in this direction, its members would need to be able to *see* the potential. In Poland in 1980 no significant body existed within the MKS (or indeed outside it) to propose any such notion. Rather, from the beginning, the MKS consciously limited its aspirations.

When the '21 Points' were being drawn up, the demand for the *abolition* of censorship was raised by workers. On the advice of a local KOR member, this demand was 'toned down' so as not to frighten the authorities. Similarly, a proposed call for free elections to the Polish parliament, the Sejm, was dropped.[7] In the second week of the Gdansk occupation, numbers of intellectual 'advisers' were incorporated into the circle around the MKS leadership. Their role, as various participants and commentators have noted, was predominantly to act as the advocates of compromise.

The church hierarchy, too, preached moderation. At the height of the strikes, Cardinal Wyszynski delivered a widely broadcast sermon effectively calling for an end to the occupations. His call was not much heeded by the Polish workers; in an effort to recover their position, the bishops issued a further statement more supportive of the workers' action.

But not all tendencies to moderation can be ascribed to the influence of the Warsaw intelligentsia or to the church. In Szczecin, where intellectuals played no significant role, the same phenomenon of moderation within militancy was apparent. If the form of organisation adopted by the workers was *potentially revolutionary*, the content of their demands was not. What they sought — and what they won most impressively — was above all the right to form their own independent trade union organisations. That right was embodied in the first of the '21 Points' agreed by the regime; but the written agreement also suggested that the workers, in accepting the 'leading role of the party', recognised the continued existence and rights of their rulers.

Nonetheless, the outcome of the workers' victory was pregnant with explosive contradictions.

A Rising Tide

The Polish workers had won a massive victory. They knew it, and the regime knew it. Within days of the Gdansk agreements, there was a burst of recriminations in ruling circles. Szczepanski, the corrupt head of Polish television and a Gierek protégé, was sacked in a blaze of publicity. Gierek himself was retired from the leadership of the party, to be replaced by Stanislaw Kania. In 1956 and in 1970, changes at the top had been the immediate prelude to a decline in the popular movement. But in 1980 the workers were unimpressed. Their own organisations had now entered directly into the making of history.

Three weeks after the Gdansk agreements, delegates from the various MKSs held their first national meeting. Even at that early stage, they represented three million workers. Some, including Walesa, urged the establishment of separate regional unions, but the majority favoured a single unified organisation based on regional branches. They called their new union NSZZ *'Solidarnosc'* (Independent, Self-Governing Union 'Solidarity'). A Provisional Coordinating Committee (the TKK) was elected to run the union in between meetings of the larger delegate body. In effect, the *form* now adopted was a centralised federation of *soviets*.

Over the next months, new members flooded in. By late autumn something like ten million members were registered. This was some 80 per cent of the total Polish workforce: a higher level of organisation, won in a few weeks, than had been achieved over decades by the trade union movements of Western capitalism. The heart of the new union was constituted by the great industrial enterprises, among whom commonly the skilled manual workers took the leading roles. But the attractive pull of Solidarity was felt far more widely: in small workshops, in food shops, in offices, in cafes, among lower-rank state employees the tide was irresistible. Only among school-teachers did Solidarity not gain a majority (only 48 per cent joined).

Solidarity also changed its members. The very act of participating in a founding meeting, often in defiance of local bosses, involved a breach with old habits of deference and submission. New bonds of solidarity and a new sense of strength were forged.

All over the country, this process involved strikes and other conflicts. Far from the Gdansk agreements having ended battles between workers and the regime, they merely opened the door to a swelling flood of popular demands and sharp regional and national conflicts. For seven months after August, the Solidarity tide continued to rise.

In October, delays in winning recognition produced a national one-hour warning strike. When Solidarity's leaders went to court to register the new union's statutes, the judge unilaterally amended them to include the 'leading role of the party' formula. There was a national eruption of protest, and the threat of a further national strike. The appeal judges, on instruction from the government, reversed the lower court's decision. In Czestochowa, the provincial governor had expected the court to rule against the union, and jumped the gun by outlawing the union. A strike called for his removal — successfully.

In Szczecin, the local party newspaper attacked Solidarity. The union's response was to print 400,000 leaflets, commandeer the trams, festoon them with posters and man them with student volunteers who toured the city with loudhailers and inserted a copy of Solidarity's reply in every single copy of the next day's edition.

In November, security police raided the Warsaw union offices, where a volunteer printer, Jan Narozniak, was running off copies of a secret government report on repression of dissidents. This had been leaked to Solidarity by Piotr Sapielo, a junior civil servant in the Prosecutor General's department. The arrest of the two men was answered with a city-wide strike. Even their release did not stop the strike wave, for the workers now expanded their demands to include a cut in the secret police budget. Eventually it took pleas by Walesa, and finally by Jacek Kuron of KOR, to get the militant Warsaw steelworkers to end their defiant strike.

As Solidarity grew, so its members' horizons and demands expanded. Much of the '21 Points' had been conceded on paper, without anything much being done. Now the demands became insistent, backed with occupations and strikes, and began to touch new areas of social and political life. One target was the security police. Another was the misuse of public resources: corrupt officials were tumbled from office, and buildings devoted to private state functions were turned over to socially useful purposes such as clinics, nurseries and schools. A Gdansk medical workers' and students' occupation won promises of improvements in the health service. In Katowice, workers' commissions entered food warehouses to check if there was any cheating in the rationing system (there was).

Time and again these initiatives came from local and regional organisations of the union, without official sanction from the national leaders, who tried unsuccessfully to limit them.

Even among the workers, Solidarity had been from the beginning more than a trade union movement concerned with wages and working conditions. Solidarity touched the ever-present nerve of Polish national independence aspirations; it won the church the right to weekly broadcasts of mass; it posed questions about political and civil liberties, the democratisation of society, the place of the Polish state in international military alliances. As such, it drew behind its banner all manner of other oppressed and exploited groups in Polish society.

The students were among the first to move. The autumn of 1980 witnessed a rash of student occupations and the formation — and official recognition — of new independent, self-governing student unions: Student Solidarity. Among the peasants, previously spasmodic agitation now bore fruit in a spate of demands for a Peasants' Solidarity; over the winter and spring that issue grumbled on with peasant occupations, and worker agitation in support. Prisoners in most of Poland's jails set up their own committees and agitated and demonstrated for improved conditions, often with Solidarity members demonstrating outside the walls. And a variety of other movements and organisations were inwardly transformed by the impetus of Solidarity: tenants' organisations, allotment holders, ecologists, philatelists, journalists, artists, actors, writers. 'Self-governing, independent unions' sprang up everywhere. Queues outside shops established their own self-government, organised systems of place-saving for the old and those with young children, and negotiated with shop managers for fair treatment.

Polish society enjoyed an orgy of self-governing participation. In a society where every form of union, club and association had been under party supervision, all this was immensely liberating. *Except* for the authorities. On every side their power was being weakened. Large numbers of officials at every level lost their positions. Every attempt by the party and state to recover lost ground seemed to set in motion an avalanche of protest, in which the popular demands and movements expanded and the rulers became more disorganised.

Dual Power

There was in reality an incipient 'dual power' situation in Poland. On one side stood the regime, still holding the major levers of official economic and political power and still firmly in control of the forces of repression (the security police and the army in particular), though demands rumbled within the civil police for the right to form their own Solidarity union. But the normal mechanisms of control over the mass of the population were rapidly breaking down. The regime was isolated, regarded now with an openly articulated scorn and contempt. Against them stood Solidarity, a flooding torrent of popular power and aspirations, growing in confidence, and centred on the huge regionally-based delegate bodies that comprised the workers' union, the heart of the opposition.

As far as the ruling class was concerned, any long-term accommodation with Solidarity was out of the question. The economic crisis was deepening all the time, and its resolution along acceptable lines must involve the re-disciplining and re-subordination of the workforce. By one means or another, Solidarity must be broken and normal political life restored. Some party leaders dreamed of achieving this by a dual strategy: breaking the essential class solidarity that characterised the new organisation, and returning to 'industry' or 'trade' forms of unionism; and corrupting the leaders.[8] But Solidarity was too damn democratic, too urgent in its demands for this to succeed. Others set out to provoke Solidarity, in hopes of finding the weaknesses within the union that could enable them to go onto the offensive. Others again merely hung on and hoped for fairer weather.

On Solidarity's side, if its full potential and its members' dreams were to be realised, if the principle of self-organisation which fired that expansive movement were to become the real basis of everyday life in Poland, the existing state would have to be pushed aside. For two fundamentally different modes of social organisation were in conflict, each embodied in an opposed force. The state and the ruling party represented class rule, exploitation, the subordination of the people to the drive to accumulation. Solidarity represented, in essence, the idea of popular power, the subordination of the state to the expansion of people's needs, a democratic re-ordering of the entire priorities of society. Such an opposition was fundamental. The logic of the situation was that one side must *destroy* the other, by whatever means suited their aim.

But what also characterised the situation was that neither side was yet in a position to win outright. The rulers' machinery was gravely weakened, and thus *could* not achieve their aims in the immediate future. On the workers' side, the predominant idea was that they *should* not attempt their opponents' destruction.

Solidarity's leaders and their advisers gave the impression that they had set in motion tidal forces they could not fully control. Officially, Solidarity was a 'trade union', but that formula hardly encapsulated the members' aspirations and demands. On paper, Solidarity recognised the 'leading role of the party', an ambiguous phrase, but one the union leaders understood to mean they must not challenge the bases of party and state rule. The phrase implied the party must 'lead' Polish society out of the crisis, yet the party seemed incapable of initiative. No one trusted it; everyone looked to Solidarity for a lead.

This was a dilemma for a movement that did not aspire to power. The union leaders' response, by and large, was to seek to stem the onward rush of their own side. Bogdan Borusewicz, a KOR supporter from Gdansk, expressed the problem well in a discussion in late 1980:

> At this moment, people expect more of us than we can possibly do. Normally, society focusses on the party. In Poland nowadays, however, society gathers around the free trade unions. That's a bad thing . . . In the eyes of the people the new trade unions should do everything: they should fill the role of trade unions, participate in the administration of the country, be a political party and act as a militia, that is confine drunkards and thieves, they should teach morals — and that's a great problem for us.[9]

Why should it be a 'bad thing' or a 'great problem' that the workers' movement was drawing around itself all the newly aroused hopes and expectations of the great mass of society? Fundamentally, because the leaders and their advisers were committed to a political perspective whose central proposition was: Don't go too far.

The trade union formula was proving far too constricting for the real character of the movement, but no viable alternative was developed. There were sizeable groups of Solidarity members who argued, in relation to specific events, that the union was in danger of becoming 'soft', but these criticisms were not generalised by any organised left-wing opposition inside the union.

It took a while for these issues to come to a head. The first three months of 1981 saw Solidarity's combativeness continuing to rise. At the beginning of January, peasants occupied a public building in Rzeszow, demanding recognition for Rural Solidarity. And the union entered into a major confrontation with the government over the question of free Saturdays. The regime, arguing the classic employers' case that 'the country couldn't afford it', attempted to claw back the reduced working week they had finally agreed at Jastrzebie in early September.

Solidarity's members were in no mood to compromise. The national leadership called on their members to stay away from work on the first designated 'free Saturday', 10 January. Millions did so. In essential services, workers wore red and white armbands to show their support. The following week, workers in numbers of centres struck again, demanding pay for the day off. The second 'stay-home' strike, on 22 January, was even larger, with a million party members ignoring a specific instruction to scab. At the end of the month, faced with the threat of yet another national strike call, the government conceded.

Hardly was the ink dry on the new agreement on Saturday working when the whole Bielsko-Biala region launched an indefinite general strike, calling for the removal of corrupt local officials. After a week, and intervention by the church, the officials were removed. Then, at Jelenia Gora, a strike burst out demanding not just the ousting of corrupt officials but also the turning over of a special luxury hospital from the police to the civil health service, and the opening to the people of a huge area of prime hunting land.

In mid-February, in response to the sharpening social crisis, there was a further game of 'musical chairs' in the government. Prime minister Pinkowski, who had gained office only the previous September, was replaced by the defence minister, General Jaruzelski, who now occupied both posts. Jaruzelski's call for a period of 'peace' was echoed by the Solidarity leadership. But the strikes went on.

Some sense of the character of the movement is provided by Mieczyslaw Rakowski, speaking for the regime a little over a month later:

> In Kalisz there has been a strike alert and a threatened strike. In Suwalki, a threatened strike on account of some personnel in leading positions in the regime.
>
> In Katowice the interfactory committee has put forward political demands. It demanded the speeding up of the legislative work of the Sejm and abundant food supplies for the country. The ultimatum says that, should the government not agree to it, there will of course be a strike.
>
> In Radom there have been demands for the dismissal of members of the provincial and central authorities, and many other demands connected with the events of 1976. We have come to a provisional agreement with Radom Solidarity. In Bielsko-Biala, despite the fact that we had already concluded an agreement, local Solidarity demanded the elimination of more people from leading posts . . .
>
> In Nowy Sacz there is conflict against the background of various local issues with demands to change the use some public buildings are put to.
>
> In Szczecin, Solidarity of municipal workers threatened to strike if their

pay and other demands were not met. In Krakow, Solidarity of employees in institutes of higher education have demanded personnel changes at government level, and trade unionists from colleges of education have submitted a number of demands of a political nature. In Lublin there was a strike alert at the post office, connected with paper deliveries.

A particularly large-scale propaganda attack was conducted by Solidarity in 33 provinces against the militia and security services . . . This is what Solidarity's reply to General Jaruzelski's appeal for 90 peaceful days really looked like . . . During the few weeks since I took office I have not worked as a deputy prime minister, but only as a fireman, putting out large or small fires . . .

I cannot help feeling that an ever-growing number of Solidarity groups are being transformed into political parties. The country is flooded with leaflets, placards, gazettes of an anti-Communist nature. I have seen such a leaflet showing a gallows with an explanation of who is going to hang from it. One factory paper wrote: 'ninety days of Jaruzelski's government — 90 gallows for 90 leaders of the party'. It is difficult to call this 'partnership'.[10]

Rakowski's bitter listing was accurate but ignored a critical factor in the situation. All this time, Solidarity's militant temper was being raised by a whole series of testing provocations initiated by sections of the ruling order. Members of the apparatus still tried to rule in the old way. At Lodz, the director of the local hospital appropriated for his own use ham supplied for patients by the church. The theft of the 'Pope's ham' provoked a million-strong strike on 10 March to remove him. Whole sections of the apparatus, who had never accepted compromise with the workers, sought to provoke confrontations which would force the state to smash the union or give the Russian army excuse and reason to intervene. The ruling class's position and privileges were under threat: small wonder that militants of that class should attempt various offensives.

Solidarity complained that

recent weeks have brought a resurgence of official arrogance and malicious propaganda, and attempts to confront society and our union with *faits accomplis*. Work on preparing the new laws on trade unions, on censorship and on workers' participation has been blocked, a number of activists of independent organisations have been arrested with the intention of staging political trials in violation of clause 4 of the Gdansk agreement.[11]

In early March, Jacek Kuron was arrested and held for six hours. When a similar action was attempted against Adam Michnik, another KOR member, Wroclaw workers formed a 'workers' guard' to defend him. Antoni Pajdak, an 86-year-old KOR founder, and other Solidarity members were given savage beatings by 'unknown assailants'. Sections of the apparatus began to promote and sponsor anti-semitic propaganda and demonstrations.

Crisis at Bydgoszcz

In March, a massive crisis erupted out of just such developments. All over Poland, agitation for the legalisation of the peasant union, Rural Solidarity, was continuing. In the city of Bydgoszcz, Solidarity members had been occupying an office in support of the campaign. On 19 March, they went to the local prefecture to negotiate with party representatives. The talks broke down, and the workers refused to leave. After further negotiations, in which it appeared a peaceful resolution was agreed, a couple of hundred police invaded the room and systematically beat up the Solidarity men. Twenty-seven were injured, among them a national leader of the union, Jan Rulewski.

This was the first time open force had been used against union members. Half a million workers across the whole Bydgoszcz area erupted into strike, and thousands of Solidarity members crowded outside their local union office to defend it against the danger of attack. By the time a national delegate meeting, 300-strong, was held on 23 March, the pressure coming from the grass roots for national action was overwhelming.

Initially the angry mood was expressed at the meeting in a call for an immediate all-out general strike. Walesa marched out when his calls for restraint were ignored, but returned. Eventually a compromise was agreed. There would be a four-hour national strike on 27 March, after which the authorities would be given four more days to meet the workers' demands. These included the punishment of those responsible for the Bydgoszcz beatings, recognition of Rural Solidarity, release of political prisoners, a halt to proceedings against oppositionists, and full pay for all strikers. If these demands were not met, then an unlimited general strike would begin on 31 March.

The atmosphere in Poland was electric, as both sides prepared for a decisive confrontation. The four-hour strike was completely solid. Even the official TV programmes were blanked out by a notice on the screens: 'On Strike'. If it was a dress rehearsal for a full-scale general strike, it seemed the performance would be a success.

In preparation for 31 March, strike headquarters were designated in the largest factories in each region. These were fortified with barricade materials, and supplies of food and sleeping bags were stored. A young woman from Warsaw's Solidarity office recalled:

> We dossed down on sleeping bags on the office floor since there was no possibility of getting home. Scouts came in with flowers for us, old men

with ration cards for sausages, old ladies with cold drinks, jam and blankets. The whole country was like a coiled spring, we were ready for 'them' to do their worst. The spirit was incredible, and the people were 120 per cent behind us.[12]

The regime reacted by mobilising large numbers of police into Bydgoszcz, and issuing dark warnings that 'our friends' (meaning the Russians) would intervene. Warsaw Pact military exercises were extended owing to 'the seriousness of the situation'. But the regime was unsure of its footing. When a Politburo majority favoured declaring an immediate state of emergency and using the police and army to smash the strike, Jaruzelski threatened to resign as premier and head of the armed forces.[13] He seems to have estimated that victory by that method could not be assured.

Instead, Jaruzelski played a sharper card. He turned to the church for support. Cardinal Wyszynski and the Pope called for restraint. The church's appeals — as in the previous August — had little effect on the mass of union activists. But they were effective at the top of the union. Direct pressure was applied to Lech Walesa, both through an hour's private meeting with the cardinal, and more importantly through the church's 'advisers' in the union leadership.

While the rest of the union leaders, who were actively preparing the organisation of the general strike, were kept completely in the da‿ ‿, Walesa at the last moment negotiated secretly with the regime along with a handful of members of the TKK, the union's co-ordinating committee, and several 'advisers'. He then persuaded Andrzej Gwiazda from Gdansk to appear with him on TV to announce the strike was called off.

Reaction in Solidarity was confused.

Many of the activists accepted the deal, for it seemed to let the union off the hook of a major battle whose outcome was uncertain. A considerable minority were bitterly angry, some referring to the deal as Walesa's 'Munich'. Many workers thought the cancelled general strike should have been replaced by other more restricted forms of action, though it was notable that not a single factory continued the strike unofficially. One young woman from Warsaw spoke for many:

It was the beginning of the end, a breaking of the spirit. For three days after that betrayal, I felt physically ill, so depressed I wanted to die. It was such a terrible mistake. I don't think it would actually have come to a strike, the authorities would have backed down. The Russians? They wouldn't have come. It would have meant too bloody a struggle. They knew we'd fight to the end.[14]

Jan Rulewski and the other Bydgoszcz activists denounced the deal from their hospital beds. Karol Modzelewski resigned as union press spokesman in protest. In Gdansk, Anna Walentynowicz's bitter criticism of Walesa led to her removal from the local branch praesidium. Gwiazda, who felt he'd been duped, offered his resignation, but it was rejected. He later published an Open Letter to Walesa, accusing him of undemocratic practices.

Whatever else, Solidarity was never as united after Bydgoszcz as it had been before. Inernal tensions mounted: the moderates were angrily defensive, and the critics began to develop the beginnings of 'radical' tendencies within Solidarity.

Crisis in Solidarity

The general strike's sudden cancellation was a serious setback. The union had gained very little from its negotiations. The government agreed to suspend certain officials involved in the Bydgoszcz attack, and to seek those responsible. Nothing more was ever to be heard about that matter, for the organised character of the attack suggests it was authorised from very high up. The regime agreed to 'study' the problem of Rural Solidarity: in May, the peasant union was legally recognised. Solidarity won the right to begin publishing its own weekly newspaper, but this was still subject to state censorship and only published in a limited edition. The majority of the union's members rarely saw it. In return, the union accepted that 'there was some justification for police interference in Bydgoszcz because of a climate of tension in the city,' a concession of amazing potential scope . . .

At the end of March, the balance of forces could hardly have been more favourable to the union: the entire membership, in total solidarity, had just demonstrated its active unity in the four-hour national strike. The ruling party's million working-class members had joined that strike with at least as much determination as the rest. After nine months of a rising movement, workers' confidence was high, while the state's forces were shaky, divided and uncertain. As for the Russian threat, that was omni-present. It had not stopped the birth of Solidarity, a much more significant enterprise. Objectively, the risks had been even greater in August 1980 than in March 1981.

After nine months of continuous upward development, the workers' movement had met with its first major check. The general strike's cancellation produced a serious de-mobilisation of Solidarity's rank and file. For the next three months, there was not a single significant strike in Poland. The membership were confused, disoriented, their confidence knocked back. Not till July was there a revival of organised activity by wide sections of Solidarity members.

But why had the debacle taken place? Whatever the merits of the decision for the general strike, or its abandonment, what a way to call it off! And what a breach with the principles on which the union had been founded! In place of the open democracy of the MKS had been substituted the dictatorship of a tiny handful of national leaders and a few advisers. In place of open negotiations, the talks had been completely secret. Regional leaders of Solidarity staying in the same Warsaw hotel with Walesa and the advisers had been deliberately shut out of all news of what was going on. The Bydgoszcz crisis agonisingly illuminated the degree to which Solidarity had become bureaucratised.

But the movement's own development posed a more general question: what exactly was Solidarity, and what should its largest aspirations be? Officially, what had been born in August 1980 and had developed over the succeeding months was a 'trade union'. The term was never very adequate to capture Solidarity's dynamic, the hopes placed in it, or the demands it pressed forward. It became even less adequate. Zbigniew Bujak, the activist from the Ursus tractor factory who chaired the Warsaw regional branch, told his factory: 'If we consider ourselves merely as a trade union, as the government expects us to, then we must think of ourselves as a trade union of seamen on a sinking ship.' Increasingly the union was forced by the logic of its situation to re-define itself.

The Bydgoszcz debacle crisis was not Solidarity's terminal crisis, a sign of its complete exhaustion and limit. But it was the end of its first phase of development. Thereafter, it had to move in new directions.

After Bydgoszcz, therefore, there was to be a growing argument within Solidarity, both theoretical and practical, about the course that should now be steered. How should the union develop? What issues should it take up? How high should it aim? By what methods should it struggle? Who should lead, and with what policies? The argument would be about the movement's very life and death.

Paralysis in the Party

A condition of existence of a 'dual power' situation is the *flabbiness* of both contesting forces. Solidarity's problems, revealed over Bydgoszcz, might have provided an opportunity for the regime to strike hard and consolidate a victory. But only if it could itself gather the strength for such a blow. The regime was itself still stricken with sickness, partially disarmed, incapable of major offensive action. Hence the damage Walesa and the advisers inflicted on the workers' movement did not have an immediately decisive and destructive effect.

A central instrument of rule in People's Poland since the war had been the Polish United Workers Party. That instrument had no organic connection with the pre-war Communist Party of Poland. The leadership of the old Communist Party were men and women with a real heritage of working-class struggle, who could trace their lineage back to Rosa Luxemburg's party. But they had been massacred by Stalin in the later 1930s, and the party had been dissolved. What was constructed during the later days of the war and after was an entirely new body, built from above. An agency for pursuing industrial development and capital accumulation, it was never a party of workers' struggle, but always a party whose *raison d'être* was the optimisation of exploitation, a party of struggle *against* workers. Its closest kinship was with the 'movement parties' of post-colonial countries; it shared their central concern with national economic development, competition with other states within world capitalism, and control over the working population.

The party operated to select and coordinate ruling personnel, and to transmit the rulers' plans into the communities and workplaces. Its members were given various rewards, including better career prospects and access to valued commodities: both scarce material goods and equally scarce political 'inside dope'. Over the years, the strictly *ideological* aspect of party doctrine declined.[15] Less was required of party members. Attendance at occasional party meetings and participation in annual May Day parades were the chief requirements. Adherence to a particular set of beliefs was no longer demanded. In tone and social composition, the PUWP came increasingly to resemble a Western conservative party.

With the decline of ideological commitment went a growing everyday corruption of political and economic life. At the same time that industrialisation was producing a more sophisticated and educated working population, the ruling stratum was becoming more overtly cynical, more self-seeking, more inwardly corrupted by its monopoly of office. Among wider and wider layers of the people, the rulers' venality produced a growing sense of everyday disbelief and outrage, a feeling amplified by the fact that their rule was also seen as grossly ineffective.

The party, in reality, was undergoing a gradual crisis of moral decomposition. But, given its political monopoly, neither electoral competition nor democratic renewal movements within its structure could enforce reform. There were possibly numbers of individual members — including some who had inherited the old Communist and Socialist Party traditions — who were still subjectively socialists of some kind or were privately critical of aspects of their party. Many were uneasy in the 1960s when the Moczar wing of the party promoted open anti-semitism; many more were disturbed by the party's unpopularity among their colleagues at work, by the ever-more prevalent smell of corruption and the lack of opportunity to criticise systematically. On the whole, however, they tended to bite their tongues rather than risk open criticism.[16]

The advent of Solidarity, which unlocked so many tongues and aspirations in Poland, had a deeply disturbing effect on the PUWP. First, it revealed the depth of the gulf between the party regime and the population, and especially the core working class of the great industrial enterprises. Second, Solidarity rained blow after blow on the personnel of the apparatus, among whom dismissals, resignations, exposures and turnover became an epidemic. (An example: in 'normal' times, nine out of the 49 provincial first secretaries would change each year: in the last four months of 1980 there were 22 such changes, and in the first six months of 1981 31 more.)[17] And third, Solidarity provided an altogether new and more appealing framework for political engagement for wide sections of the party's lower ranks. Something like a million party members joined Solidarity, many becoming keen activists.

Solidarity's emergence inspired sections of the rank and file to attempt party reform. What became known as the 'horizontalist' movement first emerged in the industrial city of Torun. Here a factory branch secretary, Zbigniew Iwanow, initiated an inter-enterprise party committee — modelled on Solidarity's organisational form — and began issuing calls for an emergency party congress. The aim was to win the principle of free election of delegates (rather than the normal selection from above) and to push the whole party towards closer development of joint agreement with Solidarity, economic reform and the like. However, the 'horizontalists' did not challenge the principle of the one-party political monopoly. Like Solidarity's leaders, they did not transgress the limits of the 'leading role of the party'.

Iwanow himself was expelled in February for breaching party rules, but his branch re-elected him as their secretary. In mid-April 1981, the 'horizontalist' movement reached its highpoint, when a national conference in Torun drew in party branch delegates from a third of Poland's provinces. In the meantime, the leadership had agreed to the demand for a special congress, and to the principle of free election of delegates.

The 'horizontalists' were by no means the only faction to develop within the party. Against them stood the slightly shadowy 'Katowice Forum', made up of apparatus hard-liners, which held no public conferences but whose calls for tough action against Solidarity were regularly publicised in the Polish and Russian party media. And in the spring, an anti-semitic grouping — the Grunwald Patriotic Union — was rapidly registered as a legal organisation and began issuing leaflets whose tone, as one writer remarked, was reminiscent of the Nazi paper **Der Stürmer**.[18]

The party congress was scheduled for July 1981. The early summer witnessed a bitter election campaign inside the party branches. Many high party leaders failed to win nomination. Only 40 of the 143 members of the existing central committee were elected as conference delegates. The Kremlin responded to this affront with a long denunciatory letter. Yet few of the 'horizontalists' managed to get elected either. Predominantly, those elected were chosen on the grounds that they were not identified with any clear position either *for* or *against* the existing leadership.

The great majority of the delegates to the congress — 80 per cent — were people who had not been delegates before. And the party's real class character was revealed in the delegates' social composition. Previously 'from-the-top' selection procedures had ensured a reasonable proportion of workers. Now, with free elections, only 20 per cent of delegates were 'workers', and a quarter of these were foremen. The congress was a meeting of 'middle-aged, middle-class intellectuals'. Only 5 per cent were women.

In the event, the party's 'reform' congress decided nothing of importance. A largely new central committee and Politburo were elected. But no significant programme for economic or political reform was determined. What the congress revealed was the party's practical incapacity to offer any real solutions to the crisis. Even the demands for internal reform amounted to nothing: within a month the new central committee complained that it was not being kept informed; provincial party secretaries who had failed to win election were co-opted on to the central committee anyway; and Kania, the first ever first secretary to be elected by secret ballot, was to be removed within three months in favour of Jaruzelski, who would combine in his person — against party rules — the offices of party first secretary, defence minister and prime minister.

Within days of the congress, marchers in Lodz protesting at food shortages bore signs with the bitter slogan: 'The only outcome of the Ninth Congress: Hunger'. Critics who remained vocal inside the party — such as Journalists Association president Stefan Bratkowski or the Gdansk Solidarity activist Bogdan Lis — were summarily expelled. What had previously been a slow leakage of working-class members out of the party (about 13 per cent up to the congress) now grew to a flood (42 per cent by 13 December, and many more after the military coup).

The party, as an effective mechanism of rule, was finished. After the congress, the centre of the government system shifted away from the party to the army.

Solidarity's Impasse

With both the regime and Solidarity suffering a degree of internal paralysis, what would matter, from now on, was the relative speed with which each side would re-organise itself. The tragedy of Poland, in one sense, can be reduced to this — that the forces of reaction achieved theoretical and practical clarity before the workers' movement did. After the party congress, Poland's rulers would increasingly militarise the regime and develop an open offensive against the workers' movement, gathering and testing their own forces and working to weaken their adversaries, until the time was ripe to strike their deadly blow. The price they would exact was immense.

Within Solidarity, the Bydgoszcz crisis produced a shock, throwing the union back on itself. It had to change. Marx once wrote that every revolutionary movement, at a certain point in its development, requires the 'whip of reaction' to drive it forward. At Bydgoszcz, the whip had certainly cracked. The question now was whether some section of the union could achieve a new clarity of vision, and offer a lead adequate to the new situation.

Yet what actually characterised the situation in Solidarity over the next months was not so much clarification as deepening confusion. In this sense, the last eight and a half months of Solidarity's legal existence are difficult to summarise, for there is no clear pattern of development. A whole overlapping series of different tendencies and movements interacted. All testified to the critical situation and the need for a radical sharpening of Solidarity's political edge, but none managed any adequate resolution. Only in the very last days were there signs that a significant re-orientation might be occurring within the leadership — but by then it was too late.

Provisionally, we can identify some of those tendencies.

Moderation and Bureaucratisation

The predominant orientation of Solidarity's leadership was 'moderate'. They wanted to treat the August 1980 agreements as the basis of a permanent relationship with the regime: Solidarity would grant partial legitimacy to the government and treat it as a 'partner' in a joint enterprise to reform Polish society. There would be elements of antagonism, but these would no more threaten the overall system than does a Western trade union movement. On some points Solidarity would compromise with the regime, while hoping to make advances on others.

Where did this idea come from?

One apparently obvious answer is the church hierarchy, whose role in Polish society is fundamentally conservative. Far from being complete antagonists, the leaderships of party and church in Poland have over the years achieved a complex balance of mutual antagonism and accommodation. Regularly since 1956, in times of crisis, the church's leaders have given the regime their support; in return they've gained increasing space for a large apparatus of priests and nuns, buildings, ceremonials, publications, religious education in state schools and the like.[19]

It was nothing new therefore when, with the workplace occupations spreading in August 1980, Cardinal Wyszynski — at the direct behest of party leader Gierek[20] — delivered a directly strike-breaking sermon. Nor when, during the Bielsko-Biala regional strike in February, Bishop Dabrowski intervened to assure the workers they could trust the authorities. In the Bydgoszcz crisis, the Pope's message — 'voices were reaching him from Poland saying workers did not want to strike' — was widely publicised by the government. Cardinal Wyszynski pressed Walesa to call off the general strike.

Right up to the coup, and afterwards, the church hierarchy continued to preach moderation. They were suspicious of, and often openly hostile to, forces to their left, even moderate ones. Thus the secretary to the episcopate issued an attack on KOR in December 1980 (he was forced to withdraw it).

Many Polish workers listen to the church, not least because the church tells them their general complaints are justified. Polish Catholicism plays a political role rather like that of the Labour Party in Britain: it gives mild legitimation to popular grievances, but discourages workers from actually fighting for their demands. Where the Labour Party suggests the ballot box as a solution to all ills, the bishops offer prayers. But the principle is the same. The church speaks for suffering workers — not for a fighting working class.

However the church hierarchy is not necessarily obeyed. The most religious workers are by no means the most conservative. The dangers of their job, for example, promote a high degree of religiosity among Silesian miners, but their militancy contributed enormously to the eventual victory of Solidarity in August 1980; they were also to fight the regime hardest at the time of Jaruzelski's military coup. Some of the sharpest critics of the Cardinal and the Pope were in fact the strongest believers.[21] Belief in God by no means involves an automatic belief that the bishops should run the union! In any case, the church is not politically homogeneous: numbers of priests, closer to the everyday lives of the workers and peasants, also come close to espousing a 'radical liberation theology'. Their interventions in the strikes — the holding of masses in occupied factories and the like — often contributed to a *strengthening* of workers' solidarity.

Besides, Solidarity was a predominantly *secular*, working-class movement. It is symptomatic that the Solidarity Congress in September 1981 voted not to have a daily mass during its proceedings. If conservative ideas *like* those of the bishops ruled in practice in Solidarity's top leadership, something else is needed by way of explanation. Those ideas had an independent transmission belt. And this was provided, predominantly, by the 'advisers'.

No other workers' movement has ever had anything like Solidarity's advisers. A stratum of the Warsaw intelligentsia — ex-members of the party, members of the Catholic intellectual circles, members of KOR — was directly represented in the union's ruling councils. At a Warsaw regional conference, indeed, two separate 'top tables' were provided: one for the union praesidium (elected workers) and one for the advisers (co-opted intellectuals). All major proposals for action had to pass through the advisers' sieve.

The advisers' entry into Solidarity had been achieved from the beginning, at Gdansk.[22] The Warsaw intelligentsia's delegation to the shipyard brought more than 'solidarity greetings': they came offering 'advice' on the conduct of negotiations. Jadwiga Staniszkis and Tadeusz Kowalik, members of this delegation, have both described how its members were shocked by the workers' militancy, and how it intervened throughout to moderate the workers' movement. Staniszkis suggests the intellectuals imported a different 'language' into the talks: not the language of class consciousness, but a muffling 'liberal semantics' in whose terms the government's and the union's 'experts' could converse with ease.

On the advice of their new 'experts', the MKS leaders accepted a formula recognising the 'leading role of the party' — and allowed this to be slipped into the final agreement without a vote among the delegates. The advisers' developing role in the Gdansk talks was associated with a decline in the MKS's democratic functioning: detailed negotiations were now carried on behind closed doors, meetings between the executive and the main body of the MKS became less frequent, and issues of principle were no longer put to a delegate vote.[23]

Once Solidarity was established these advisers formed a kind of 'court officialdom' around Walesa, playing on his uncertainties, writing many of his speeches, exerting a continually moderating influence. This was not only true of the former Catholic deputy in the Sejm, Mazowiecki (from April 1981 he was editor of Solidarity's weekly paper), the historian Geremek, or the former Christian Democrat lawyer Sila-Nowicki; it also applied in full measure to the former revolutionary Marxist and later founding member of KOR, Kuron. Indeed at critical moments the more radical dissidents, who had been the objects of state repression, could be more effective in a moderating role than the more apparently right-wing advisers, who had no previous connection with working-class struggle.

Part of Solidarity's strength, clearly, lay in its support outside the working class, but there was also a risk in its cross-class appeal. Solidarity might become a 'popular front' whose politics were determined by the intelligentsia's predominance in its leadership. And that was a *class* problem.

The Polish intelligentsia tends to be elitist, the limits of its imagination set by Poland's national frontiers, its history and social role intimately tied to the growth of the state. Its members share with workers an interest in freedom of speech and non-interference by the state in private life, yet the division of mental and manual labour is also central to its special existence. If it tends to 'represent' a class, it is the 'new petty bourgeoisie' of lower-level functionaries.[24] Its natural sphere of operations is that of intra-bureaucratic manoeuvring; its instincts are not revolutionary.

The intelligentsia, via the 'advisers', exerted a profound influence on the inner politics of Solidarity. Whether from within or outside the party, they represented a variety of admixtures of Catholicism, nationalism and liberalism. What they never represented — indeed, what many regarded with overt hostility — was any tradition of *socialist* politics, of working-class internationalism and struggle for real proletarian hegemony over society. The formulae in which the intelligentsia tried to encapsulate Solidarity played down its working-class character in favour of an emanation of a national movement. It sowed illusions of 'national unity' and 'rational solutions', smothering issues of class antagonism and the necessity of a struggle for workers' power.

The pursuit of a moderate strategy required that the leaders hold back the movement, inhibiting and stopping movements from below which might threaten the development of long-term consensus. In the aftermath of the Warsaw strikes over the arrests of Narozniak and Sapielo, Walesa argued that the legalisation of the union should mean the end of 'wildcat' strikes:

> It may indeed appear that unrest is rampant in the country, with stoppages here, sit-ins there, and hunger strikes somewhere else . . .

Even when there is just cause, there are other ways to settle our grievances without striking.

The summer and autumn of 1981 saw Walesa touring the country,
calling for a halt to strikes, pressing workers not to raise new demands,
urging patience.

The task of enforcing moderation is eased considerably if the
movement is bureaucratised, if there develop separate layers of leaders
who decide and members who merely follow. The same tendencies
kept re-appearing. On his return from a visit to the Pope in January
1981, Walesa immediately went to private talks with the then prime
minister, Pinkowski. The key negotiations over the Bydgoszcz crisis
were conducted secretly. As late as November 1981 Walesa went to
talks with Jaruzelski and the Church without previously consulting
the union's national commission.

Membership apathy and bureaucratisation are two sides of the
same coin. The aftermath of Bydgoszcz saw a partial demobilisation of
the membership. For more than three months after March there were
no strikes. Attendance at union gatherings declined. In early summer,
election meetings to select delegates to Solidarity's first national congress were held: numbers of these meetings were inquorate,[25] and
working-class candidates withdrew their nominations. In the same
period, the intelligentsia's grip over the machinery of Solidarity was
strengthened. They tended to predominate at the election meetings:
they were more articulate, and they won many of the nominations.

It was the intelligentsia, rather than working-class delegates,
who were to predominate at the Solidarity Congress in the autumn of
1981. That congress approved a resolution increasing the formal
centralisation of power within Solidarity and giving Walesa a free
hand in his dealings with the government, against opposition from
regional activists.[26] Walesa, once elected as president, was freed to
select an 18-person praesidium which was mostly made up of intellectuals, and which excluded all those who had stood against him in the
election for presidency.

The moderates' influence contributed to what Staniszkis[27] refers
to as 'areas of silence' within the union. A variety of needs and
aspirations among the members were not properly articulated. Especially after Bydgoszcz, union leaders tried to censor local Solidarity
bulletins and posters, and several regional offices held short protest
strikes over this. There was a degree of freezing of criticism and open
debate within the union. One effect was the turning away, in disappointment, of many workers from active involvement in Solidarity's
affairs. Controversial issues were not aired openly: the advisers' influence, for example, or the fact that the leaders voted themselves

salaries well above average wages. Regularly the advisers would attack critics, accusing them of attempting to 'split the unity' of Solidarity: the regime, it was claimed, would exploit open differences within the union. Often that argument sufficed to stifle debate.

Reformism — for what else did the moderates represent? — is a strategy involving specific theories and tactics. At the most general level, the moderates tried to distinguish between those parts of the existing system that could be changed and those that must be preserved. The 'state' must not be threatened, but 'civil society' could be liberated: the distinction was very cloudy, especially in Polish conditions, but its implications were clear. Efforts to undermine the unity of the state's own forces, especially the army and police, should be inhibited. 'We should not threaten our partner.' The party's 'leading role' defined, however loosely, the 'limits beyond which we must not go'.

The moderate strategy in a sense *demanded* a government capable of giving a lead and acting decisively. Kuron reported in the summer that there were many people in Poland who longed for a 'Government of National Salvation'.[28] In October 1981, Walesa expressed cautious pleasure at Jaruzelski's accession to the party leadership: Poland, he declared, needs strong government.

There is of course nothing unusual in the rise to leadership of a reformist layer in the early stages of a great workers' movement. It has been a regularly occurring phenomenon. In the Polish case, the reformist wing of Solidarity was never a very stable formation. For the actual situation in Poland was one of dual power: two rival and incompatible forces contested the country's future. The moderates were seeking to convert this fact into a constitutional principle, to make the duality of 'society' and 'state' the basis of a new order. But the scale of the crisis and the nature of the regime, added to the insurgent character of Solidarity as a mass movement, combined to make the 'moderate' schemas into utopian fantasies. The regime, especially from the summer of 1981, kept attacking the union, breaking up negotiations, demanding instant and total submission. And broad sections of Solidarity's membership, under the sharp pressures of the crisis, kept demanding more militant responses.

If all the intelligentsia were agreed, in broad terms, about the need for 'self-limitation', this does not mean they were a homogeneous formation. The KOR members, for example, were often more radical than the church advisers, and more open to radical impulses from the rank and file. Apart from anything else, they were the ones who went out to speak to the membership, and they often had to duck and weave to defend their main orientation. Adam Michnik, addressing a factory branch, heard complaints from workers at the local managers' incompetence and corruption. Yes, he explained, but the problem is not just individual personalities, it's the *system* that produces these distortions, and new managers would be the same. 'Right!' shouted one of the workers, 'So let's get rid of the whole system!' Michnik backtracked rapidly: account must be taken of 'certain geo-political realities . . . you couldn't just . . .' etc.[29]

Plain speaking, under these limitations, was difficult. The leaders tended to stifle their own sense of the precariousness of the situation by retreating into unfinished arguments, intellectual language games, amusing tricks. Touraine noted: 'Michnik's vocabulary, and indeed that of the militants in general, was peppered with ambiguous phrases and jokes playing on these contradictions.'[30] The moderates never gained any sense of sure footing, any certainty of direction. They might hamper the articulation of alternative perspectives, but they lacked any stability of purpose themselves.

Radicals

The moderates' leadership was by no means unchallenged. Especially after Bydgoszcz, various more 'radical' tendencies emerged within the union. However none of these ever took definite shape as an organised faction or succeeded in clarifying any alternative strategy. Rather the radicals' responses were confused, often moralistic rather than political. Some developed as local cliques, built on the basis of personal likes and dislikes rather than worked-out political differences.

In Szczecin from the autumn of 1980, a grouping around the local Solidarity paper, **Jednosc**, published articles defining Polish society as shaped by an irreconcilable antagonism between the regime and the working class, and concluding that a decisive confrontation between these two forces must (sooner or later) come to a head.[31] Similar ideas were expressed by a 'fundamentalist' grouping that issued its own manifesto at the union congress in autumn 1981:

> The party apparatus has become a new ruling class, which has seized three essential elements of power: ownership, force and propaganda. Instead of the promised classless society, the most class-ridden society in history has been built, a society whose one extreme is political, economic and doctrinal power, and the other, masses of people deprived of everything who, as Karl Marx would have said, have nothing to lose but their chains.[32]

But neither group appears to have drawn any specific organisational conclusions from its views, and in this sense they disarmed themselves. Indeed, the fundamentalists' manifesto ended with the statement, 'Solidarity does not struggle for power for itself, nor to become a political party.'

In Gdansk, Anna Walentynowicz, appalled at the way the decision to call off the general strike had been made, delivered highly personal-ised attacks on Walesa. She was voted off the shipyard committee, and became increasingly isolated. Andrzej Gwiazda, feeling he had been tricked into appearing on TV with Walesa to call off the general strike on 31 March, issued an 'Open Letter' to Walesa expressing concern at undemocratic practices within the union.[33] Rank-and-file activity, he stressed, is essential to maintaining Solidarity's strength, and 'A dictatorship in the union is an essential (and sufficient) condition for the absorption of Solidarity by the system, returning us back to square one'.[34] An informal grouping, known locally as the 'constellation' (after the Polish for 'star' — Gwiazda), developed around him, but it lacked any clear perspective.

In part, Walesa had defined the radicals' problem at the meeting to decide the union's response to Bydgoszcz. Demanding that the TKK follow his advice, Walesa had declared: 'I have the support of the factory workers, I could even go against the whole national coordinat-ing committee'. This was not simply an idle boast, and the radicals knew it. When Karol Modzelewski resigned in protest as Solidarity's press spokesman after Bydgoszcz, he complained:

> The union has created a king which rules over it. Around the king is a court, and power lies in his court, and then in a parliament. And since the king is no dummy, power resides in his court rather than with the parliament. It is a suicidal arrangement for the union.[35]

If this was part of the problem, what were the radicals to do about it? To fight the issue simply on personalities would condemn them to defeat in advance. And to pose the issue of 'democracy' in the abstract, similarly, led nowhere. For millions of Solidarity members, Walesa symbolised the union's strength and unity; the fact that he was needed as such a symbol was also a measure of the membership's uncertainty about their own power. The only way to weaken Walesa was to strengthen the rank and file's own self-reliance and self-confidence. What they needed was to develop a whole alternative programme for the union, in which the question of internal democracy would be a living issue.

At the autumn congress, three regional leaders — Marian Jurczyk from Szczecin, Jan Rulewski from Bydgoszcz and Andrzej Gwiazda — stood against Walesa in the elections for union president. Between them they collected 45 per cent of the votes. Yet their election speeches were notably lacking in clarity: indeed, Gwiazda, asked why he was standing, could only reply 'Because the union statutes permit me to'. One reason for their diffidence was that they knew they must not win: a referendum amongst the membership at large would have won Walesa 90 per cent of the vote. More fundamentally, none offered a clear alternative. The size of the vote against Walesa was an indicative protest vote, a 'warning' to the leadership to take account of rank-and-file dissatisfaction, rather than a real challenge.

The more radical activists were often the most opposed to the role of the experts and advisers, but they translated this into a suspicion of any kind of ideology or theory. Governed by feelings of distrust and hostility, they were often highly moralistic, and found no articulation of their feelings in programmatic terms. The French sociologist, Alain Touraine, who conducted an extremely valuable study of Solidarity members, uncovered a powerful sense of anger and mistrust at the whole Polish social system and the ruling regime. However, as he also noted, the members' widely-held aspirations to radical change remained 'an inner language', which was never transformed into a political strategy.[36]

The Self-Management Movement

The absence of a clear opposition tendency itself affected various other potentially promising developments within Solidarity.

One of these was the 'self-management' movement. Back in August 1980, the revival of workers' councils did not figure prominently among the demands. True, the final agreement did propose 'a radical increase in the independence of enterprises' linked to 'genuine participation by workers' self-governing institutions in management'. But those clauses were there, thanks not to pressure from workers but to 'influence exercised by the advisers of both sides'.[37] Discussion in reformist intellectual circles before August 1980 had focussed on the need for economic reform, and in those schemes workers' participation in the factory had played a significant role.

For some months after August, self-management attracted little interest. Solidarity's attention was focussed on the struggles to gain recognition and on the mass of immediate issues thrown up by its battles with the regime.

But the workers' control question could not be evaded. It was increasingly obvious that the self-limitation of Solidarity within a 'trade union' formula was impossible. The membership, in one battle after another, kept pushing the frontiers of the movement's aspirations outwards. And the scale of the economic crisis was such that the classic union demands — more pay, shorter hours, better working conditions — ran hard into regime propaganda that the union was preventing economic reform. Solidarity activists felt a growing need for arguments to counter the regime, and for a programme of demands which could advance their position within the workplaces.

The primary impetus came from the large factories in the spring of 1981. A new grouping, the 'Network', linking together activists from a number of the union's regions, began a series of discussion meetings which formulated a programme of demands. This activity expanded in the aftermath of the Bydgoszcz crisis, just when the rank-and-file membership was partly demobilised. Thus the Network emerged, predominantly, as a movement of the *militants* in association with a number of interested intellectuals. This circumstance affected the way its ideas developed. The Network — rather like the 'Institute for Workers' Control' in Britain in the 1960s — had a tendency to be a 'talking shop': it formulated some interesting ideas without, however, any immediate connection with the living practice of the workers' movement itself. Under these conditions, the intelligentsia's formulations tended to play an especially significant role.

The leadership grouping around Walesa fairly soon adopted the Network's arguments as their own. They became a major feature of the union's programme, adopted at the autumn congress.

A central target of the Network[38] was the state's bureaucratic stranglehold over the economy. Two key aims were identified: the de-centralisation of economic decision-making, and the democratisation of enterprises. Each enterprise should be self-financing and decide its own production targets, relying not on central directives but on criteria of economic rationality. Within the enterprise, a democratic workers' council should choose its director and control everyday running. To this should be added major steps towards local democracy through 'territorial self-management'.

The basic idea was that the whole of economic life should be treated as a clear space, free of political influence, where power would lie not with political decisions but instead with 'rational' market forces. The state's influence over 'civil society' would be limited to 'indicative' means, such as taxation, incentives and the like.

These ideas had several serious weaknesses. Some of the 'Network' thinkers tended to idealise the free market, and to treat it as the sole alternative to bureaucratic planning. They played down the consequences of 'profit-oriented' enterprise: unemployment, widening pay differentials and the rest. Nor did they explain how workers' control would in fact be compatible with a market-orientation. (Some of their advisers[39] openly advocated reliance on decision-making by 'efficient' managers — a position that implied no real workers' control at all!) A socialist alternative to bureaucratic control — namely, a democratically formulated planning mechanism, flowing out of workers' councils in the factories — was nowhere considered.

The Network's proposals were not essentially different from those of economic reformers within the ruling party. They only really went beyond the regime's own proposals in two respects: they wanted to stop party interference in the enterprise, and to abolish the party's 'Nomenklatura' control over the appointment of managers.

A further weakness was that they formulated their proposals as 'good ideas', to be adopted by the existing regime, rather than as a fighting programme to be won by workers' action in the workplaces. This was immensely contradictory, for the Network's ideas implied a fundamental challenge to the regime: workers' self-management requires that workers must control the overall direction of the economy. The Network programme stated thus: 'The central plan must mirror the aims of society'. Yet serious pursuit of this aim would inevitably involve a head-on challenge to the state.

The programme fudged on the vital question of power. Here, again, the influence of the intellectual 'experts' can be seen: in classic reformist manner, the programme suggested combining workers' councils with a 'second chamber' in the Sejm, this second parliamentary chamber to be composed of 'economic experts'.

On paper, the self-management proposals implied a more radical stance by Solidarity, but they were formulated in separation from the day-to-day experience of the mass of the membership. 'The fight for authentic self-management', wrote the Marxist sociologist Staniszkis, 'seems more important for the union's activists than for its masses'.[40] Zbigniew Bujak of Ursus referred to this problem during the summer:

> People were wary of me in an Ursus meeting. Only when I explained that this self-management leads to a taking of power did people understand and agree with me.[41]

But it was not clear at all, in practice, that the self-management idea *did* lead to a taking of power . . .

When, from July 1981 onwards, a new wave of workers' militancy erupted in the form of local strikes and hunger marches, many of the Network activists were as anxious as the Walesa group to bring these to an end. Rather than seeing the revival of working-class mobilisation as a chance to start putting their ideas into practice, they opposed the strikes as an interference with the serious work of preparing a plan for legislation. The result was that, although 'self-management' became a part of Solidarity's official programme, it developed little in the way of a basis in the factories themselves. The point was admitted in November, when the union reported that few steps had been taken to establish the beginnings of 'self-management committees' in the actual workplaces.

Resurgent conflicts

The economic crisis deepened in the spring and summer of 1981. All the main production indices turned more sharply downwards. Between January and July the official statistics recorded the following falls: 13.6 per cent in the value of goods sold through official outlets; 21.3 per cent in coal production; 21.1 per cent in investment; 29.2 per cent in housing construction; 18.3 per cent in exports; 9.4 per cent in imports.[42]

Shortages of components and raw materials increasingly disorganised production. The supply of everyday goods was steadily worsening. Meat rations were cut; soaps, detergents, toilet paper were all in short supply. Officially, basic necessities were rationed; in practice, even the possession of a ration card was no guarantee of supply. 'What is a Polish sandwich?' ran a bitter joke: 'A meat coupon between two bread coupons.' Huge food and fuel prices were announced. The black market expanded. The strain of endless queuing, of the struggle to ensure three meals a day, was telling more and more strongly. From every side the Polish workers were told they would have to tighten their belts. The union's experts said it too.

After Bydgoszcz, Solidarity's rank and file may have been partly demoralised, but they retained their membership, and still looked to the union as their chief source of hope. By the summer, the crisis provoked a new eruption of working-class protest. Only this time the majority of the actions were 'wildcat': the response of the leadership was cool, and sometimes hostile.

On 8 July postal workers went on strike. The next day the Polish airline, LOT, was shut down; the LOT workers protested at the appointment of an army general as director and demanded the right to select their own.

These strikes were quickly followed by a wave of hunger marches and demonstrations in various cities, beginning in Kutno. In the textile centre of Lodz, tens of thousands paraded through the streets for three days with angry placards: 'A spectre is haunting Poland: the spectre of hunger'; 'The hungry will eat their rulers'. Lodz was followed by Szczecin. In August, half a million struck in Warsaw; when a protest demonstration of cars and lorries was stopped from driving past the party offices, the whole city centre was blocked for two days. In the Silesian mining districts a million workers struck. Gdynia port workers refused to load food for export. In Bydgoszcz transport workers struck against a corrupt manager. In Radom, strikes erupted again demanding an inquiry into the repression of workers in 1976. On 19 and 20 August, much of the national press was halted by a strike of printers objecting to media slanders against Solidarity. This strike continued unofficially for a further 17 days at Olsztyn. There was a strike at Czestochowa over food rations.

The union leadership's response to the strikes was mostly negative. When the regime alleged that Solidarity was sabotaging the economy, the leadership called for a two-month moratorium on strikes. It went further, asking the miners to work the remaining 'free' Saturdays in 1981 on a voluntary basis:

> The national commission asks all the members of the union, all the workers of the country to sacrifice our own free time to save ourselves; let us work the eight free Saturdays until the end of the year. We know that this is unprecedented in free union countries. We appeal to all the organisations and union authorities not to undertake isolated protesting activities.[43]

Meetings in the mining areas produced numerous angry exchanges between Solidarity leaders and miners. One miner told the national commission: 'You dare to call on people to work their free Saturdays because the government has to be propped up. But who says we have to prop it up?'[44] Nearly half the miners refused to work the free Saturdays, despite massive additional bonuses offered by the government. The miners were split and discouraged.

The tide of strikes continued to rise in September and October. At one point in late September two-thirds of Poland's provinces were affected by strikes. Katowice, the steel centre in the south, erupted into strike action over the food crisis. At Zyrardow, a textile centre near Warsaw, the women workers had been accustomed to doing their shopping in the capital; now their ration cards restricted them to the local shops, which were empty. They struck for three weeks. Visits from national leaders, including Walesa, failed to persuade them to restart work. They sent an angry delegation to interrupt a national union meeting: 'Enough of your discussions and your projects for resolutions! . . . *Do* something! Are you men or not?'[45] This predominantly women's strike was organised on a 'shift' basis: each shift coming on would take over the occupation from those who were leaving. One Warsaw activist who visited them asked if they'd consider a full-scale occupation strike. If it would win, they assured him, they'd do it: they'd draw on neighbourhood resources, use grannies and aunties, work out creche arrangements for babies, and so on. He concluded (privately) that the union was failing to draw on its members' commitment, that it was misusing and denying its available strengths.

One thing which marked the strikes of the summer and autumn was that they brought new layers of Solidarity's members into autonomous activity for the first time: airline workers, printers, women workers, housewives, and others. Forced into action by the desperate economic circumstances, and by growing frustration at the regime, previously 'backward' sections of Solidarity were seeking to push the movement forwards. All manner of issues boiled up in these strikes: food supplies, challenges to the party's role in the factories, local managerial power, export policy, censorship, victimisation. Implicitly and explicitly, the strikes represented a call to Solidarity to act.

But the union tried to head off the strikes and protests. Jan Litynski, editor of **Robotnik** (The Worker), symbolised this. For three years before 1980, he had reported and encouraged often tiny economic strikes; now he described the hunger movement as a negative phenomenon, 'a danger the union has not known how to avoid' which 'risks degenerating into unofficial strikes'.[46] Union leaders rushed round Poland urging workers to halt their actions. In September, Solidarity's weekly paper featured an article, 'Extremists and Stupid Children' by Krzystof Wyszkowski, secretary to the editors, which argued that the union's role must be to defend the interests of the nation as a whole.

In October, the union's praesidium backed an appeal from the Sejm for an end to strikes by 350,000 workers in mining and other key industries, but without effect. Shortly after this, the leadership called a one-day national stoppage in hopes that this might permit a simple 'letting off of steam'. But the strikes continued for several weeks more. The bitter desperation and anger of whole sections of the union's members were simply not reflected in the leadership.

All these upsurges from below remained fragmented and incoherent, isolated from each other. No section of the leadership attempted to link them together, showing how they might be combined in a new assault on the regime. The radicals had nothing practical to say or offer. Eventually, from mid-November, the strike wave died down: the membership was increasingly exhausted, turning away in disappointment from the union.

Paralysis and reformulation of aims

Among widening layers of Solidarity's leadership the situation provoked a profound sense of unease, which was well expressed in a frank round-table discussion of activists organised by KOR in the summer of 1981, and published in **Robotnik**.[47]

Jan Litynski, editor of **Robotnik**, declared:

> We are now in what seems to be a dead-end. The economy and the state are disintegrating . . . it seems that waiting to see what the authorities do and negotiating compromises has proved ineffective. Solidarity is slowly losing points. It is disappointing members.

Bronislaw Geremek, a leading intellectual adviser, said:

> I may be wrong, but it seems to me that nobody among us, sitting at this table, knows the way out of the crisis. The catastrophe is evident. It overwhelms us . . . The biggest danger the union faces is its loss of impetus: a situation in which the union might become a conservative force . . . restraining an increasingly radical society.

Zbigniew Bujak from the Ursus plant, chairman of Warsaw Solidarity:

> Our movement grows weaker. At the outset it was based upon great hate towards the authorities, towards the party. But this is not enough any more. Motives must change. The members of our union do not understand the policy of their leaders . . . Protests, strikes, local struggles do not form a coherent whole . . . At the moment, people are waiting for a clear programme. Whether they understand it or not, they want to hear that it is the way out of the crisis.

The discussion brought out Solidarity's need for a new conception of its own role and aims. In September Grzegorz Palka, a member of the Solidarity Praesidium, described the bind the union was in: 'When we do not have our own conception of how to solve economic and social problems we protest against bad government programs, but after a while we must collaborate in their realisation.'[48]

These pressures led Solidarity's leaders, in the late summer and early autumn and especially at Solidarity's National Congress, to elaborate a new programme.[49] Now Solidarity defined itself, not as a 'trade union', but as a 'social movement' aiming at the complete reform of Polish society. Now its stated aspiration was a 'Self-Governing Republic'.

In one sense, the public development of the Solidarity Programme was an immense step forward. It codified and made public what had previously been the 'inner language' of masses of Polish workers: the demand for wholesale social transformation. At the programme's heart lay a demand for 'people's power', a principle whose realisation required 'a true socialisation of our government and state administration'. The vision the programme expressed was of a fully democratic society, in which working people controlled their own political, social, economic and cultural life, without fear or hindrance, and without any muzzling of freedom of opinion.

However the programme was also immensely contradictory. It proposed a whole series of immediate measures to deal with the economic crisis, and longer-term reforms in the functioning of economic and social life. Many were excellent. But the programme evaded the critical question: how were these reforms to be implemented? In field after field of discussion, it proposed *revolutionary* goals, but denied the need for revolutionary means. Its aims could not be realised within the existing political framework — except on the utopian supposition that the regime would agree to dissolve itself — yet the need to break that political framework decisively was nowhere faced.

When it had called itself a 'trade union', Solidarity also declared itself bound by 'self-limitation'. Now, despite its formal leap from the limits of trade unionism into acknowledging itself as a political actor, Solidarity was still torn between wanting to rupture the regime completely and anxiety to remain within existing legal bounds. In reality, the tensions of 'self-limitation' had not been overcome, only lifted to a higher plane.

Any adequate political programme must not merely specify ultimate goals, it must propose how the movement is to get there. Here Solidarity's programme failed completely, evading the real problem: how were the members to be *won* to fight for the programme? Like the 'maximum programme' of the pre-1914 German Social Democratic Party, there was a real danger that Solidarity's in many ways brilliant programme would be a mere decorative garment, not a real plan for advance.

Solidarity's move towards a more 'political' self-definition was taken by a congress where the intelligentsia rather than workers tended to predominate. Touraine comments: 'The trade union element of the movement was in itself hardly represented at the congress: Solidarity appeared much more as a movement for the liberation of society.'[50] If there was an *advance* in this respect, there was also a *retreat*. For Solidarity risked cutting itself off from the immediate economic concerns of its working-class base, as these expressed themselves all autumn in the form of strikes and other local movements. The actions and concerns of the membership and of the leaders were as dissociated as ever.

The regime prepares for war

Within weeks of the Bydgoszcz crisis, in April 1981, the regime held army exercises, checking its ability to use military means against the Polish workers.[51] But it had probably not yet decided to pursue this method.

By the summer, however, it was clear that the use of purely *political* means would not defeat Solidarity. The party — the regime's chief political instrument — had by now demonstrated its incapacity. Poland's rulers therefore turned to the army for salvation. Jaruzelski told the party congress in July, 'In the present period our armed forces have not been shaken. They have maintained their cohesion and discipline. They are always ready to defend the fatherland and its socialist achievements.'

The regime moved cautiously, testing out the ground at each step, preparing its forces and weighing up its opponents' strengths and weaknesses. Its first move was to increase the role of the military in civil administration. In the summer, several generals were brought in to direct major enterprises and ministries. (This was the occasion for the July strike at the state airline, LOT.)

In numbers of state enterprises — among civilian employees in military establishments, in military printing enterprises and elsewhere — Solidarity membership had not been recognised. Solidarity established a 'commission' to examine this question. But the commission, on the leadership's advice, negotiated secretly with the government without reference to the workers involved. Finally the talks were blown when angry printing workers from Szczecin picketed the ministry building in Warsaw where the negotiations were being held. The union remained unrecognised in these sectors.[52]

A movement among civil police, demanding the right to form an independent union, was repressed by sacking the leaders. Solidarity took no action to defend union rights for the police, though a substantial proportion favoured unionisation.

On the political front, the regime began a propaganda offensive against Solidarity, initiated in early August by the deputy prime minister, Rakowski, who broke off talks with the Solidarity leaders accusing them of seeking power. In September, a new law on 'self-management' was presented to the Sejm, denying workers in 'essential industries' the right to choose their directors. Despite the fact that the union congress had voted, only days before, to refuse any such limitation, Walesa and a handful of leaders agreed to accept the restriction. This provoked a row at the resumed congress, where Walesa's action was defended by Kuron and others.

By this time the regime had hardened up its plans. Albin Siwak, a notable hard-line Stalinist worker, revealed the main outlines in a speech as early as September: a six-man committee, headed by generals, would use army and police to smash popular resistance; they would wait several months, until Solidarity's support had weakened. But the Solidarity leadership ignored the warning.

At October's central committee meeting, Stanislaw Kania was removed as party first secretary. He was replaced by General Jaruzelski, who now combined in his hands the office of party secretary, defence minister and prime minister. Further militarisation of ministries followed. Walesa made a speech almost welcoming Jaruzelski's assumption of power: 'At least it means power is concentrated in one man's hands. What we need is a strong reasonable government we can negotiate with.'[53] By now the regime was drawing up lists of people to arrest: this was indicated by the fact that, after the coup, the arrest lists included people who had left Poland in October.

Still the regime camouflaged its preparations. Jaruzelski announced that conscript soldiers, due to be demobbed in October, would have to remain in the army for a further two months, 'to assist with the economic crisis'. There were protest letters to Solidarity from soldiers, but the union did not respond.

In late October and November, the regime began taking open offensives against Solidarity activists, testing the union's readiness to fight back. Police in Katowice and Wroclaw arrested Solidarity members engaging in street propaganda activities, and violently dispersed protesters. At Sosnowiec in Silesia, 'unknown persons' attacked a Solidarity meeting with gas grenades. At Chorzow, Solidarity members were beaten up. Attacks of this kind, in the spring, had been signals for mass strikes; now nothing more than scattered local protest strikes occurred.

From late October, small army squads were sent out into the countryside and the smaller towns: the declared purpose was to assist in overcoming the economic crisis. In reality the regime was testing out its machinery, checking its troops' loyalty, and seeking to win popular support for the army. No alarm was raised by the union.

In November, similar units were sent out to the factories 'to check on civil defence preparations . . .' Still the union leaders responded complacently.

Also, from 28 October, the Sejm was informed it would soon be voting in a law giving the government martial law powers in an emergency. No immediate vote was taken: the impression was given that, if the regime was going to deploy force, it would give due warning via a parliamentary debate. Solidarity fell for this trick.

In November, partly to divert attention from the military preparations, Jaruzelski invited Walesa and church leaders to participate in tri-partite talks on government reform. Despite opposition from sections of the national commission, Walesa and some of his advisers went along to participate in Jaruzelski's talks, only to find the general was offering them nothing but a token representation in a 'Front for National Reconciliation' in which they would be out-voted on every issue. In return, they'd have to take responsibility for huge price rises without any guarantees of reform. They had no choice but to turn this down flat and walk out, leaving the official media to attack Solidarity for the lack of progress.

Turn to politics

Solidarity's leadership was divided and uncertain in its response to the growing threat. As the strike wave continued, so the union praesidium repeated its calls to stop 'elemental and unorganised' protests. In the first week of November there were still 65 separate strikes going on, the largest at Jelenia Gora, where 160,000 workers were out over the sacking of a Solidarity activist, with the leadership urging them back to work.

Not till the middle of November did the strikes largely stop, and that through sheer exhaustion and disappointment. Many workers sank back into angry apathy. Some showed signs[54] of accepting the regime's propaganda and blaming the union for the economic mess. Certainly the readiness to act if called on by Solidarity was declining. Karol Modzelewski undoubtedly spoke the truth when he stated in Radom on 3 December: 'The trade union has not become stronger, it has become weaker, and all activists are aware of this. There are several reasons for this: weariness as a result of crisis, weariness at the end of a line. Some people blame us for the prolongation of this state of affairs.'[55]

Solidarity was born accepting a self-denying ordinance, declaring it would not involve itself in 'politics'. The position was never tenable, and by the autumn the sense of crisis and of paralysis in Solidarity pushed many activists into a search for openly political solutions.

Some moved towards purely nationalist politics, particularly the Confederation for an Independent Poland (KPN). The KPN's attraction was that it articulated the widespread hatred of Russia. The KPN — whose roots lay in the pre-war right-wing parties — was by no means a workers' party. It interpreted Polish politics in purely 'patriotic' rather than class terms. But it seemed to numbers of Solidarity militants to offer at least a more militant *rhetoric* than the Solidarity praesidium. In reality, its strategy was essentially 'moderate', and its nationalism diverted attention from the possibility that 'our Polish army' might actually be deployed against the Polish people. Jaruzelski would reap the benefits of that illusion.

Others sought different solutions. On 22 November, Kuron, who only a month previously had been attacking the idea of establishing political parties, organised a founding meeting in his apartment of the 'Clubs for a Self-Governing Republic'. The aim was to establish the nuclei of parties in a democratic state. Yet the document issued by the meeting (which the police raided) was still contained within the self-limitation formula. It spoke of the need for central government to be 'as much as possible, circumscribed by organs of workers' and territorial self-government', not of breaking and replacing the central state power.

In numbers of factories, resolutions were carried demanding the removal of the party apparatus from the workplace. Calls for free local elections in February 1982 were increasingly insistent, along with a variety of calls for a popular referendum on the future form of Polish government.

The moves towards the idea of political parties and political solutions were, at the minimum, a further break with Solidarity's previous self-limitation. But all these developments treated 'politics' as something belonging *outside* Solidarity, in a special 'political' field of action focussed on the weak Polish parliament, the Sejm. None implied the direct mobilisation of the industrial strength of the Polish workers as a part of a political programme. All remained constrained by the need not to challenge directly for state power. No one argued for developing a party whose task would be to fight *within* Solidarity for the direction of workers' industrial strength towards replacing the state power with workers' power. Thus the shifts towards 'politics' remained the special province of interested activists, and did not involve the rank and file.

In that sense, new developments within the self-management movement were much more promising. Already in the summer, groups of militants from some of the regions expressed their dissatisfaction with the moderate 'Network', and established a rival 'Lublin' grouping. They emphasised workers' control more strongly; they opposed purely indicative planning, favouring 'economic planning from below' in association with a second chamber in the Sejm.

Crucially, they were sceptical about the use of mere legislative means to obtain improvements, and treated self-management bodies in *activist* terms as 'organisations of struggle for self-management and instances of control over production.' They began to argue for the use of 'active strikes' in which workers would continue production, but under their own control.[56]

This group's influence among activists grew in the autumn. In some areas (notably Lodz) they began preparing to put the active strike into practice. The idea was simple: workers would seize the means of production and distribution, and run them directly in line with popular needs. Some grasped the potential revolutionary significance of the idea: the active strike would be part of 'a strategy of struggle for workers' power.' (Some of the praesidium's intellectual experts attacked the plans on the same grounds, as 'an idea launched by leftists and Trotskyists'.)[57]

The 'Lublin Group' was evidence of a hardening radical current within the workers' movement in the late autumn. Their proposals had the great advantage that they might be able to re-mobilise the rank and file around meaningful activity, though their ideas still suffered from several weaknesses. First, they remained still at the discussion stage: they developed late, and never had the opportunity to put them into practice. Second, if the ideas had a revolutionary potential, they were still mixed up with reformist perspectives: using the active strike to force negotiations, or to win free elections to the toothless Sejm. Third, as one participant has noted, they never directly confronted the question of 'the struggle to win over the army'.[58]

The final days

By late November it was becoming obvious that a major confrontation was looming. The regime was pressing ahead with its emergency powers legislation, and deploying its army units in the industrial centres.

Within Solidarity, as we have seen, new currents of radicalism were developing among the activists. Militant resolutions were carried in some workplaces, calling for a popular referendum on a motion of no confidence in the regime. Preparations for active strikes were being made in some regional centres. Plans for large-scale demonstrations were announced.

In early December the regime suddenly raised the temperature. Though workers' struggles had been generally demobilised, Poland's students were involved in a major wave of occupations. One of the occupied colleges was the Warsaw Fire-Fighting School, which the regime claimed as part of the military sector. The school was surrounded with a ring of ZOMOs (riot police). Large crowds gathered to support the students. On Wednesday 2 December, hundreds of ZOMOs smashed their way into the school and expelled the occupiers. For the first time the regime had deployed open force against Solidarity.

The next day, Solidarity's leaders met in Radom. The regime bugged the meeting, and published extracts from the leaders' speeches. The extracts suggest that the crisis was finally, if belatedly, pushing Solidarity's leadership towards more radical perspectives. The previous day, Walesa had told the crowds outside the fire-fighting school: 'The union is a powerful weapon hanging over the authorities — but it can't be triggered all the time.' Now he declared: 'Confrontation is inevitable and will take place. Let us abandon all illusions. They have been thumbing their noses at us.' Kuron, previously an influential prophet of self-limitation, now said:

The issue of elections and a new electoral law, total negation of the so-called provisional pre-reform system, and the state of emergency, should become the field of confrontation. The ground must be prepared now by actions designed to overpower the authorities.

Other delegates spoke of the need to launch active strikes, and to form a workers' militia. One suggested they should seize the radio and TV. Speakers urged the formation of a provisional government. Seweryn Jaworski from Warsaw told Walesa: 'If you retreat even one step, I myself will cut your head off; and if I don't, someone else will.'[59]

The delayed tendency to radicalisation was all too clear. Over the next few days, factory meetings in Lodz voted for active strikes and the formation of workers' guards. Andrzej Slowik, a Lodz leader, declared the situation was now 'revolutionary'. On 12 December, the union's national commission met in Gdansk, in the most radical mood since before Bydgoszcz. The delegates voted that they would oppose emergency powers legislation with strikes, including a general strike. They would hold their own referendum on popular confidence in the regime. The church advisers objected.

But if the last days witnessed a shift to the left among the union's leaders, it came too late. As the national commission members slept in their hotel that night, the regime struck. The hotel was surrounded and invaded by riot police, the delegates arrested and interned. Up and down the country, thousands of Solidarity activists were seized in their beds and dragged away. At six o'clock on Sunday morning, Jaruzelski announced his military coup, the suspension of Solidarity, martial law.

Cardinal Glemp broadcast an appeal for people not to fight back. The workers' response to the coup was patchy. There were a couple of hundred strikes and occupations, chiefly in the largest plants and in several of the Silesian coal-mines. After a few days, they were broken by brutal police and army interventions. Nine workers were killed at the Wujek mine. At the Ziemowit and Piast mines, there were three-week underground occupations. When the Piast miners finally came up to the surface, they were shocked to discover they were alone in their action. They could not believe the whole of Poland was not on strike with them.

The element of surprise, the sudden communications black-out, the fierce sanctions announced by the regime against anyone leading or participating in a strike, the arrest of their leaders, all contribute to explaining the relatively low level of response from the workers to the coup. But it was also the case that, even before the coup, a sense of defeat had already spread among large sections of Solidarity's members. The relative success of Jaruzelski's coup depended on the de-mobilised condition of Solidarity's rank and file.

Could it have been different?

The question, like all historical 'ifs', is of course strictly unanswerable. But it was always part of the logic of the situation that something like Jaruzelski's coup would occur. The deep structural antagonism between Poland's rulers and the workers' movement meant confrontation was inevitable. The scale of the crisis, the insurgency of Solidarity's demands and the regime's dependence on the Kremlin made longterm compromise impossible. Thus those who advocated such a solution misled the movement. And the tactics they followed made Jaruzelski's victory easier. They disorganised and demobilised their own side, while refusing all manner of opportunities to weaken their opponent's forces.

Over the course of the sixteen months from the Gdansk strikes to Jaruzelski's coup, Solidarity underwent an enormous evolution. It began as a 'free trade union', went on to demand elements of workers' control of industry, developed the demand for a 'Self-Governing Republic' and finally began to turn towards specifically political solutions to the crisis. Yet through all these developments, one element remained constant: Solidarity's leadership remained trapped within a classic reformist perspective, and restrained the movement from considering the overthrow of the state. To use their own expressions, they sought to liberate an area many termed 'civil society', while leaving the state intact.

They guaranteed, in that sense, the state's own forces and interests. Given the stakes involved, the strategy was bound to lead to disaster. When it did, they were taken completely by surprise, as many of them admitted.[60] But to be taken by surprise meant they were theoretically mis-prepared: their reading of the situation was wrong.

Jaruzelski's victory was not inevitable. It depended on the discipline and unity of the state's armed power, the army and police. Over the months before martial law, Solidarity had had many opportunities to undermine that discipline and unity, but had deliberately not taken them. It did not make propaganda among the largely conscript soldiers; nor did it respond when those soldiers protested at the extension of their conscription. It did not organise support for the civil police who were demanding union rights. It even accepted the principle of *secret* negotiations over trade-union rights for civilians in state printing works, naval establishments, and so on, rather than campaigning openly on the issue. Solidarity members who made suggestions for undermining the unity of the state machine were eased off key committees.[61]

Yet, right to the end, the possibilities kept appearing. Outside the fire-fighters' occupation at the beginning of December 1981 stood a line of armed ZOMOs, Poland's feared and hated riot police. Beyond them, a crowd of supporters threw food and packs of cigarettes over the ZOMO heads through the fire cadets' windows. The occupation committee, improvising brilliantly, took all the best quality cigarettes, and went out to offer them to the ZOMO troops, chatting to them, sympathising about the cold weather, and so on. When the order came to occupy the school, that ZOMO unit had to be withdrawn as 'unreliable'. Again, after the armed seizure of the school, 'the Founding Committee of the Trade Union in the Civil Militia' protested at the use of police in the raid on the fire cadet school. 'The militia was formed to protect the interests of society as a whole, and not those of the ruling minority', it declared; all police officers should protest at 'the use of the police in political conflicts and the suppression of justified popular actions.' No doubt this was a minority within the police, but what a significant minority!

Undermining the state machine was anathema to those who urged negotiation and compromise. For them, 'we must not antagonise our partner unnecessarily'; the state's sphere of action, its rights and powers, must be protected. In the interests of 'agreement' with its enemy, Solidarity must constrain its own forces when they tried to move forward, when they raised new demands, when they 'wildcatted'.

In that sense, Solidarity's leadership prepared its own defeat.

The element that might have made a difference was an organised socialist tendency within Solidarity, actively promoting the idea that Polish workers should prepare to take power. None of the various 'radical' tendencies that emerged within Solidarity ever sufficiently grasped the problem. None engaged directly with the strike wave of the summer and autumn of 1981; none challenged the predominance of the reformist intellectual 'advisers' in the union's leading bodies; none drew organisational conclusions from their criticisms of the Solidarity leadership, by working to build a radical faction rooted in the militant tendencies within the rank and file.

Even a small minority could have made a difference. After all, between 1976 and 1980, the tiny group around KOR prepared the way for the birth of Solidarity. KOR's contribution in that period was absolutely indispensable: without it, there would have been no *cadre* of working-class leaders ready, in Gdansk and elsewhere, to seize the time and lead the August strike movement into brilliant, expansive new forms.

But for all its courage and initiative, KOR was a reformist alliance, whose contribution was largely finished after August 1980. KOR lost its sense of direction,[62] symbolically announcing its own dissolution at the Solidarity Congress in September 1981. What is most tragic about developments after August is that no new grouping emerged, as clear in vision and as bold in determination as KOR in its prime had been, to point the mass movement forward towards power.

Of course, the development of a revolutionary socialist current inside Solidarity would not have been easy. There were some hard arguments to win: the history of the Russian invasions of Hungary and Czechoslovakia gave the case for 'not going too far' a powerful appeal. Yet the Russian empire is weakening: what was remarkable was that the Russians never did intervene militarily in Poland. They had too many reasons for keeping out.[63] In any case, fear of the Russians could have prevented the very birth of Solidarity,[64] but didn't — in August 1980 the workers simply refused to allow the threat to inhibit them. After August, the Russian threat was used as a weapon both in the regime's armoury of self-defence, and as part of reformism's case within Solidarity; it was an argument for disarming and weakening Solidarity, making its actual defeat certain.

A Polish workers' victory, of course, depended on spreading the movement outside Poland's borders. Any adequate socialism has to be uncompromisingly internationalist. Solidarity met with far fewer echoes from the rest of Eastern Europe than it had hoped; the resulting sense of isolation strengthened conservative and nationalist trends inside the workers' movement.

Nonetheless, the absence of a revolutionary alternative guaranteed defeat. And it made the defeat harder, too: up to the time of writing, five years after Jaruzelski's coup, there is still no clear sign in Poland of socialist organisation emerging within the underground movement. Among the hundreds of thousands of Polish workers, students, teachers, intellectuals and others who have kept that underground alive, there is therefore no clarity about what went wrong with their magnificent movement in 1980-81, and what is now the way forward.

At present Polish militants are cut off, practically and theoretically, from the best traditions of the left in the rest of the world. The fact that the regime has monopolised, and utterly perverted, the language of 'socialism' and 'Marxism' makes the recovery and development of a viable tradition even more difficult.

Yet part of the legacy of Solidarity is that the Jaruzelski government is the loneliest and least effective regime in Europe; it survives, not because of any positive achievements, but only because the working class has not yet found the means to remove it. The regime knows perfectly well, as the workers know, that they will rise again. But a new insurgent movement must have some inkling of a perspective of victory, some means to learn from previous mistakes, and some scent of how to act more effectively next time. Without the clarifying input of revolutionary socialist ideas, it is difficult to see how that barrier will be overcome.

The development in Poland, or elsewhere in Eastern Europe, of a genuine organised socialist current, may well be a difficult process. It is also our only hope, and a crucial task.

SIX

PERSPECTIVES
Colin Barker

THE EVENTS described in this book reveal the continuing and developing revolutionary potential of the working class, its capacity to make great creative leaps in consciousness and organisation and to offer fundamental challenges to the existing structures of power. As such, these events are a practical reply to those who declare that the working class is finished as a political force.

In the late 1980s, world capitalism's ability to meet the growing needs and demands of its population is becoming ever more problematical. Growth rates are falling, mass unemployment shows no sign of disappearing, debt mountains are growing, governments everywhere are seeking to make their working classes pay for the crisis. In these circumstances, we must expect more revolutionary explosions. The movements described here are precursors of immense social convulsions to come. They are rich in materials for socialist theory.

GREAT social crises like those described here provide crucial evidence for assessing real shifts in the balance of class forces.

A notable feature of all these events was the *scale* of working-class struggle. In France and Poland especially, mass strikes involved larger numbers of workers than ever before in history. Capitalism's development during this century has massively increased its most crucial productive force: the working class. In many parts of the so-called 'Third World', the working class has already become the largest class. [1]

Qualitative changes have occurred as well. By comparison with workers' movements before the Second World War, for example, the involvement of 'white-collar' sectors of the workforce was a marked feature. [2] Similarly, women were involved centrally, in huge numbers. [3]

In purely numerical terms, these events are witness to the immense expansion of the forces of the world working class. But numbers alone are not sufficient. Politics are vital.

What makes these movements especially significant is that all of them were, in different degrees, inspired by the heart of the revolutionary socialist vision. Not that the participants were necessarily conscious of this: in Poland, for example, the language of socialism and Marxism is so corrupted by the ruling class that the workers' movement had to struggle to find other *words* to express its aspirations. But the central dynamic of every one of these movements was a general demand for popular, democratic control over economic and social life, for collective self-emancipation. In just that sense, these were revolutionary rehearsals.

ONE ISSUE has been continuously debated throughout the history of the working-class movement: by what method can socialism be won — by 'social reform' or 'social revolution'? At issue has been an argument, not simply about what *means* should be used, but equally about the meaning of the socialist goal itself.

In 1845, in **The German Ideology**, Marx and Engels summarised the reasons why social revolution is necessary. A communist society requires the development of a 'communist consciousness', which must involve 'the alteration of men on a mass scale'; this can be achieved only through a practical movement, a revolution:

> revolution is necessary . . . not only because the *ruling* class cannot be overthrown in any other way, but also because only in a revolution can the class *overthrowing* it succeed in ridding itself of all the muck of ages and become fitted to found society anew.[4]

The first reason is more familiar. Ruling classes do not retire voluntarily from the historical scene. For them, the defence of class society is synonymous with the defence of human civilisation itself, so their own self-defence takes on the aspect of a vital crusade. They will employ any means necessary to protect the essentials of their power. The violent fury of ruling classes against assaults on their rule and privilege has regularly exceeded any violence of the oppressed and exploited: the case of Chile in particular is a terrifying reminder. Only if the ruling class are forcibly disarmed, deprived of the material means to restore the conditions of exploitation, can the development of a classless society founded on popular self-government succeed.

But Marx and Engels' second argument is even more important. The central idea of revolutionary socialism is that 'the emancipation of the working class must be conquered by the working class itself'. Labour's self-emancipation cannot be achieved within the existing social framework. Class society divides and subordinates us, denying us our capacity to rule our own society. 'In every epoch,' as Marx expressed it, 'the ruling ideology is the ideology of the ruling class.'

Capitalism continually reproduces a working class whose daily experience teaches that it *cannot* rule society. The 'muck of ages' — the learned necessity of subordination to the rule of an alien class — contains us all within the bounds of class society. It may be that 'power corrupts', but powerlessness corrupts even more, so that socialism appears an impracticable dream.

It is precisely the function of social revolution to permit the breaking — in practice — of this subordinate consciousness. Socialist propaganda cannot by itself surmount this barrier. Only practical experience of ruling-class weakness and of the real power of collective solidarity can open the way for a sense of working-class hegemony to develop. The only way that workers can acquire the capacity to rule is by beginning to exercise it, overcoming both external and internal obstacles to their developing power. As they themselves lay the vital foundations of a new form of society workers transform their own consciousness. For revolutionary socialism, the most basic process involved in social revolution is not the violent dispossession of the ruling class, but the self-development of workers' capacity to rule society. Only through social revolution can that self-transformation occur.

The case for social revolution is tied, inextricably, to a vision of socialism as a new social order where class rule is abolished and where all processes of social, economic and political life are characterised by popular and democratic decision-making and control. This was the central meaning of Marx's 'dictatorship of the proletariat' or 'the rule of the associated producers'. In Hal Draper's happy phrase, the revolutionary socialist vision is one of 'socialism from below'.[5] It cannot be realised unless the central presuppositions of capitalist society are swept away by the mass of the population themselves, in a deliberate and conscious act of collective re-making both of society and of themselves.

Against 'socialism from below' are ranged, not only the power and ideologies of the world's ruling classes, but also a variety of theories and practices all constituted around 'socialism from above'. All the politics of reformism and Stalinism, along with the essential politics of guerrilla movements, are deeply contaminated with this poison.

Central to this alternative tradition, whose roots lie at least as far back as the bourgeois Enlightenment, is a key idea: that the wise few, the trained, the educated, the heroic minority will solve society's problems *on behalf of* humanity. The disorder and anarchy of capitalism will be replaced by a well-governed, planned society administered by the socialist élite, those who know best. The essential presupposition of class society — the division into rulers and ruled — is preserved in 'socialism from above'. Reformism, in all its 57 varieties, has an essential affinity with such visions. It is, in reality, perfectly compatible with the bases of class society. Its projects for 'socialism' turn out, always, to be merely proposals for the development of capitalism in new forms.

In every one of the movements considered in our earlier chapters, it was politics of this kind which proved disastrous. Reformist ideas and practices appeared *within* these movements and led, every time, to their defeat. This issue confronts 20th-century revolutionary socialism with its most important stratetic and tactical problems.

EVERY social revolution in history has begun with a 'revolutionary situation', a specific condition of society. By no means every revolutionary situation ends with a successful revolution, but such a situation is an indispensable beginning.

Lenin's definition is excellent: a revolutionary situation is one where the ruling class is no longer *able* to rule in the old way, and the exploited are no longer *willing* to be ruled in the old way.[6] All five sets of events discussed earlier had elements of a revolutionary situation about them, more developed in some cases than others. A revolutionary situation is a moment of social crisis, a historic turning point when society faces a real fork in the path of development: *either* the mass of the population imposes a new shape on society, *or* the ruling class re-establishes its power in some new form. It is always an unstable period, of relatively brief duration.

How do situations of this kind arise? Much of the time, after all, social revolution appears a forlornly improbable and utopian hope. The dominant images of society emphasise order and continuity, mere reproduction. Socialists — and especially revolutionaries — are a small minority, whose views seem at best eccentric.

What is missing in such 'normal' periods of development in class society, we often say, is 'class consciousness'. The term is commonly misunderstood. 'Class consciousness' is more than a passive, intellectual recognition of class division and domination. That, after all, can coincide with a high degree of practical conservatism, along with cynical disbelief in the possibility of change. In 'normal' conditions, it is above all the *active* side of class consciousness that is absent, the sense of practical confidence in the collective power of the working class to transform the structures of social reality.

Yet we can also misunderstand 'normality' in an opposite and one-sided way. Marx's aphorism that 'the ruling ideology in every epoch is the ideology of the ruling class' is often taken to mean that the ruling class dominates *absolutely* over the minds of its exploited classes, that no subterranean streams of critical dissent flow, that the working class is like the 'proles' of George Orwell's science fictional **1984**. Such images are utterly exaggerated and élitist.

In reality, if there is such a thing as a 'typical' pattern of working-class consciousness under conditions of capitalist 'normality', that pattern is deeply uneven and contradictory. For the everyday workings of capitalist society *force* conflict on the working class, *force* it into struggle and therefore into forms of organisation. Class conflict is the very marrow of capitalism.

Because class conflict is experienced as uneven, discontinuous, and partial, its organisational expressions normally reflect this. The working class is sectionalised and fragmented. One section is fighting while others are not. Workers are opposing the symptoms rather than the root causes of exploitation and oppression. The overall level of conflict — measured, say, in the pattern of strikes — rises and falls in intensity and extent. Particular kinds of organisation, with definite kinds of politics, are erected to express this contradictory pattern of consciousness and struggle. What characterises them is 'reformism'.

'Reformism' is a difficult phenomenon to pin down, for it is defined by its internal contradictions. It expresses a complex mixture of opposites: it arises from the structural antagonisms and conflicts of class society, yet it also contains protest and opposition within the limits of this society. In one of its shapes, as trade unionism, it gives organisational expression to workers' everyday experience of capital-ism, in demands for an battles over wages, improved working condi-tions and job security; it demands a very discontinuous commitment from the majority of its members; it contests some of the effects of capitalist power, through 'collective bargaining', while simultaneously recognising and accommodating to capitalist power in general. In another shape, as parliamentary politics, it offers the promise of reforming legislation to improve the lot of workers, while accepting the overall structures of state power. It works at once *within*, *for* and *against* the existing system. It takes over, from the world it only partly contests, all manner of organisational forms and assumptions. Aping its adversary, it reflects back capitalism's own demarcations between 'political' and 'economic' questions.

Because, under 'normal' conditions, reformist unions and parties provide a limited capacity to resist capitalist power, they attract workers' loyalty. At the same time, these forms of organisation also act to demobilise their own supporters, to constrain them within safe limits. Naturally, given their internal contradictions, they develop bureaucratised forms of internal organisation, distinctions between officials and rank and file, leaders and led, MPs and electors. Reformism simultaneously expresses the desire for change and erects decided barriers to its possibility.

The more advanced the process of capitalist accumulation, the more developed become the institutions of reformism, as the potential capacity of the modern working class to damage capitalist production grows. Trade union bureaucracies and moderate socialist parties are essential shock-absorbers for modern capitalism and its states, effective precisely because of their capacity to smooth out and contain opposition.

Nonetheless, they arise because such opposition is constantly regenerated. At various times, different balances are struck between militancy and conservatism in workers' action and consciousness within capitalism. An immense variety of circumstances advance and constrain class consciousness, but always the seedbed of class conflict is being re-sown and re-fertilised by the everyday experience of exploitation. The 'containment' of labour is anything but a simple and automatic process, even in quiet times. It is always precarious, and takes effort and organisation to achieve. The *potential* for explosion is endlessly renewed.

EVERY one of the upsurges discussed in these pages was preceded by a growth in the level of everyday struggle. A common index was a rising level of strikes. The issues at stake in these battles were commonly localised, narrow, 'economic'. Yet they were witness to two important features. First, the gap between workers' needs and the system's practical delivery of satisfactions was manifestly widening. Second, popular confidence was notching up by a small degree. Not uncommonly, this combination was produced when ruling-class attempts to make workers pay the costs of economic difficulties were less than completely successful. These failures strengthened workers' self-assurance, simultaneously diminishing their respect for their rulers' power.

Factors other than a growth in the strike level can produce the same kinds of result. In 1934, for example, the large-scale demonstrations that drove back the French fascists were an important prelude to the general strike movement of 1936.[7] In Iran in 1978, the swelling popular offensive against the Shah, the poetry readings and street demonstrations initiated by forces outside the working class, themselves brought hope and courage to the factories. In Poland between 1976 and 1980, the *indecisiveness* of the regime's harassment of dissidents raised popular confidence, and helped increase the dissidents' audience.

All kinds of circumstances, of course, can produce the vital condition: a subtle but real shift in the balance of confidence as between the people and the ruling class, and thus in the balance of real class power. State control loses its coherence and impetus by just a shade, and a sense of popular power gains fractionally.

All of this may occur 'spontaneously', in the sense that the shift is not directly attributable to the activity of any particular group or party. There is not necessarily any political generalisation involved, for the lifting mood of the masses is partial, fragmented, localised. By no means is the whole of society necessarily affected by the shift. Here a group of workers engages in a small trial of strength with its particular bosses, and gains a little ground; that encourages some others to try for their own particular small victories. The bosses are seen to concede a point here, retreat a step or two there; the popular response is not gratitude but an exploratory taking of note: 'they are being careful how they treat us, they're getting nervous'.

Needless to say, nothing in such developments means they must be a prelude to some radical social explosion. Unless at some point some focus of generalisation appears, confidence and militancy can rise in a fragmented form — and dissipate again without ever provoking a full-scale crisis. Or there may be generalisation, but in a shape that stays trapped within purely parliamentarist limits — as happened to the unofficial strike and shop stewards' movement of the 1960s and early 1970s in Britain.

To produce a 'revolutionary situation', something more is needed. Nonetheless, without that almost molecular growth of popular confidence and consciousness, itself arising out of the normal everyday processes of class struggle under capitalism, no major social movements are ever likely to spring up.

Hence the importance, in periods of 'normality', of attention to the small-scale 'guerrilla warfare' that goes on continually between the classes. In such localised and narrow struggles the militants of the classes are formed and train themselves, forces are assessed, the lessons of victory and defeat absorbed, the small seeds of large ideas are sown. Socialists who do not focus on these small struggles and organise within them condemn themselves to sterility.

THERE SEEMS always to be an element of the unexpected about the actual initiation of a major social crisis. Like the single shout that sets off an avalanche, a small event proves capable of setting in motion a movement of historic importance. What launched the 1871 Paris Commune was the French government's attempt, after the turmoil and privations of the Franco-Prussian war, to take back cannon bought with workers' subscriptions. The 1905 revolution in Russia started when the Tsar's troops fired on a peaceful and pro-monarchist demonstration led by a police agent, Father Gapon. The February 1917 revolution began with a women textile workers' demonstration. The revolution that destroyed the German empire in 1918 began with sailors refusing a suicidal order to take the battle fleet to sea against an obviously superior British navy.

Afterwards, historians will decode why that event, in that place and under those circumstances, proved to be the spark that set society alight. But, at the time, there is always an element of surprise.

It is the same with the events here. Who, in 1968, expected the students of Paris to detonate the largest general strike in world history? Certainly not the students, nor the workers or the state either. The Portuguese army captains who planned to topple the old regime never dreamed of the popular social forces their coup would release into independent action. The small group of workers who met in a Gdansk flat and decided to organise a protest at the sacking of a woman crane-driver would not have dared to hope, as they wrote out their handful of posters, that they were launching Solidarity. In Chile, what began as a defensive struggle against the lorry-owners' boycott was rapidly transformed, because of its mass scale, into an offensive.

Whatever the exact event, 'something happens'. The small occasion becomes a catalyst which, by a social chemistry that is never fully clear, produces a vast societal reaction. Huge masses of people erupt into active political life in ways that, only days or even hours before, seemed impossible. The effect is felt rapidly. Normal patterns of life are disrupted. There is a sudden swelling in the self-organisation of large numbers of the previously disorganised and passive. And, simultaneously, the ruling order is disorganised.

The opening stage of every great social movement springs society's locks and releases immense popular democratic impulses. Yet, commonly, the events that begin the process are not, themselves, formally 'democratic'. A group acts independently, but meets with a chorus of popular approval that echoes back, sometimes only weeks later, as the impulse they gave works its way through society. The actions and demands of a determined minority draw into collective action not only people like themselves (students in other cities, workers in other factories) but other classes too, other exploited and oppressed groups. Effective action by one favourably placed group is the signal for other movements to stream into the suddenly swelling river of popular revolt.

In such a situation there is an unleashing of what Lenin, writing on the 1905 revolution, called 'festive energy'.[8] The term is apt. The development of a revolutionary situation involves a great change in the psychology of millions of people. New hopes emerge. Previous habits of subordination and deference collapse. A new sense of personal and collective power develops. The 'common sense' of class society suddenly falters. Normal everyday social relations are transformed. Historic hierarchies — in workplaces, in the state, in schools and colleges, in families — are threatened or actually tumble. Old divisions between different groups of workers, national and ethnic groups, among peasants, between men and women are shattered and re-shaped by the development of new solidarities. Ordinary people find themselves performing tasks and assuming responsibilities from which society previously excluded them. New kinds of competence appear, new divisions of labour, new powers.

Popular confidence and imagination advance by leaps and bounds. With them, practical intelligence also rises: nothing is so mentally numbing as the habit of subordination. Every 'festival of the oppressed' involves a sudden release of collective pleasure. Perspectives alter, the horizons of possibility extend.

This kind of mass arising, the fundamental process in every potential revolution, is an indispensable condition of major social advance. Its transformations of consciousness, power, social relations, imagination are impossible except through such developments. For consciousness is inseparable from everyday social practice. New languages, symbols, artistic forms are adopted to express the new conditions; the flourishing of posters, symbols, newspapers, leaflets, badges and jokes bear witness to the profound shifts going on in the consciousness of millions. New moral principles are enunciated, old rules challenged.

In such circumstances, it is no wonder that existing authority is thrown into disarray, undermined and disturbed. The growth of popular confidence has its reverse aspect, in a collapse and inner division within the ruling class. Confidence is an essential prerequisite of effective rule. Now, within a short space of time, what was previously sacred and unquestionable becomes open to question, even laughable. Those who were self-assured now stutter, as those who bowed their heads stare them boldly in the face.

Every revolutionary situation develops through a whole series of local and partial acts. Often, what the Portuguese workers termed *Saneamento* — a cleaning out — comes at an early stage. Hated symbols of previous oppression tumble: policemen are disarmed, foremen and managers are locked out of workplaces, officials are booted from office, authoritarian teachers are challenged by pupils and students, statues and victory columns are pulled down. (In Poland, indeed, the rulers were compelled to accept new public monuments to their own previous crimes.) Those who survive the purging find a sudden need to 'conciliate', often conceding large-scale reforms, in the (secret) hope that the time of troubles will pass and their full authority will be restored.

Previous property rules are challenged. Premises are occupied. Existing uses of places and things are altered. Land is taken over, workplaces seized. In the process, sections of the population gain new social experiences as they enter and take control of areas of social life previously shut to them. The workers are in the boardroom, the crowd is in the palace, the confidential files are opened, the workers' commission is inspecting the warehouses. What was closed is opened, and note is taken.

New bodies determine issues previously beyond popular control. Transport and supplies now move under licence of a popular committee. The academic syllabus is questioned. Prices and supplies are now determined by popular forces, rather than by some unassailable 'natural laws'.

These partial, local advances also contribute to changing consciousness. Aspirations and demands develop further. What only shortly before would have been hailed as a great victory now seems insufficient. A large wage rise, formerly the occasion for a return to work, is now the occasion for further strikes. 'Settlements' break down as popular horizons expand and the limits of possibility are transformed by the new balance of power. Old demands and new ones appear together, in seemingly incongruous association.

Learning processes speed up. Long-established patterns of loyalty break down, and new allegiances develop. Political ties shift. In periods of days and weeks, broad sections of the people make more advances than previously they achieved in years.

Revolutionary socialist ideas, in such an environment, can make immense headway, for suddenly they conform to the real experience of large numbers of people. But the extent to which they do so is a function, not only of the rising imaginative and creative power of the mass movement, but also of the ability of organised revolutionary socialists to offer those ideas, and show how they may be realised in practice.

THIS suddenly increased fluidity of society's structures and the sense of joy and power it embodies is, in itself, insufficient to do more than make the foundations of class rule tremble. A widespread demand for change in society's institutions may, implicitly, be present in such an upsurge of popular activity, but unless it crystallises in new organisational forms it can dissipate rapidly, lacking any focus.

In many ways, that was the fate of the French movement of 1968, which rose like a brilliant firework, illuminating in its explosive fires much that was previously hidden, but spending its energies almost as rapidly. May and June 1968 saw a mighty upsurge of working-class militancy and revolutionary rhetoric, but the independent organisational achievements of the workers' movement were limited.

That fundamental weakness was a function of the relative strengths of different political tendencies within the workers' movement. The labour bureaucrats of the CGT and PCF worked hard to inhibit development towards independent workplace organisation, and to prevent autonomous link-ups being established between occupied factories and between striking workers and students. They were successful, largely because the influence of the revolutionary left within the workplaces was simply too small. As a precursor of a future socialist revolution, the May events in France offered drama and poetry, a mass *feeling* of excitement and fundamental change, but not much real organisational development. The French state was seriously shaken for a moment, but it was not confronted by even the outline of an alternative political system.

The May events reveal, on the one hand, the ready and even eager acceptance of fundamentally challenging ideas about contemporary social organisation among the widest layers of society, and thus the permanent *potential* instability of bourgeois rule. The underground world of popular critique and imagination is a feature of modern capitalism that conventional journalism and social science alike regularly ignore and deny. On the other hand, however, the degree to which those subterranean forces actually advance or retreat is determined in large measure by practical issues of class organisation. Where workers do not succeed in establishing their own genuine rank-and-file committees at the most elementary workplace level, let alone in linking them up into local, regional and national councils of workers' representatives, even an immense flowering of ideas and popular enthusiasm for social transformation can achieve little of permanence.

The degree of threat to the existing structure of power depends on how far the insurgent movement develops and strengthens new kinds of popular bodies. Movements that remain contained within the old organisational formats of bureaucratised trade unionism and parliamentarist politics cannot advance far.

In all our other cases, workplace forms of organisation were rapidly established during the early stages of revolutionary development. But in each case, union bureaucracies had less influence than in France. In Chile, it was notable that the best-unionised sectors were among the more backward in the massive movement that opposed the threats from the right: there the *cordones* were least developed. In Portugal, the initial weakness of the union structures created a space in which workplace organisation could grow — often in the teeth of direct opposition from the nascent union bureaucrcy. In Iran, the very weakness of the unions created the space in which the *Shoras* could develop. And in Poland, where the old 'official' unions were utterly bureaucratised and state-dependent, the workers' movement constituted itself precisely around the demand for the removal of these bankrupt and corrupt bodies.

But this observation poses a problem: how, in the conditions of Western capitalism, where the heart of the workforce is organised into unions, bodies moreover with extensive degrees of bureaucratisation, can an outcome like that in France be achieved? The ability of union burcaucrats to sabotage workers' movements has long been apparent. What matters, under these conditions, is whether — in advance of a major upheaval — there has already been the conscious development of a network of rank-and-file opposition and workplace-based trade unionism, influenced and led by revolutionary socialists.[9] It was the weakness of such a network which proved decisive in France. There were insufficient forces to contest for the leadership of the strike, to argue for democratising and opening up the occupations, for the establishment of links between workplaces, and against the return to work that the CGT officials pushed through.

From the beginning, the real weight of the forces of revolutionary socialism shapes the pattern and possibilities of a mass movement.

THE DEMOCRATIC workplace strike committee has provided the basic element in every significant working-class revolutionary movement of the 20th century. It is here that workers are first able to measure their growing power in direct confrontations with the capitalist class, and first able to assess their own capacity for self-organisation. Here, in the natural centre of the class struggle, a movement determines whether it shall challenge the power of capital, not simply over wages and conditions, but also over the control of discipline, distribution and production. At this most elementary level, too, the real ability of a revolutionary party to lead the working class is tested in practice.

The practical confidence of working people in their own ability to run society is developed not only on the large political stage of a struggle for state power, but concretely and immediately over a host of 'local' issues in the area they know best: at the very point of exploitation and production. A 'left' that cannot connect with and offer real leadership to struggles at this level condemns itself, in reality, to utter impotence, as the example of the Fedayeen and Mojahedin in Iran clearly reveals. When a workers' movement meets a check to its forward advance and is thrown backwards, as Solidarity was in March 1981, it is often from the workplace that it can regenerate and reorganise its forces — especially if there are socialist currents who perceive the possibilities and seize the opportunities. This the Chilean left and Poland's radicals alike failed to do.

Working-class self-emancipation remains a dream if ordinary workers do not realise it in their own experience. The manifold struggles at the base of society, often seemingly limited and partial in their aims, are the real taproot of the revolution. Those sections of the left who fall into the trap of 'ultra-leftism' always forget this, substituting their own desires and consciousness for those of the masses. If every revolutionary situation involves huge forward leaps in working-class confidence, it is nonetheless the case that each separate leap is conditioned by its starting point.

For many workers, the sign that new opportunities are opening up is measured not in terms of grand revolutionary generalisations, but in their feeling, for the first time, that they can unionise, that a bullying supervisor can be controlled or even better removed, that a wage rise or a cut in working hours is winnable. Their own upsurge consists first in getting to the point which more advanced and organised workers are already moving beyond. Without such elementary developments in their own confidence, organisation and power, how can they hope to reorganise the whole of society? In the initial variety of workplace struggles, many of the real advances and defeats of a potentially revolutionary movement are measured.

Any effective revolutionary party has to be able to respond to this unevenness, by encouraging forward not only the most advanced sectors of the movement, but also the more hesitant. Indeed, nothing determines in advance which part of the working class may play the part of 'vanguard' at any particular point in the struggle. Large battalions, in the big workplaces, possess a strategic power which may propel them into the leadership of a movement, as in Poland. Yet workers in smaller workplaces — perhaps more 'backward' in terms of union organisation — are sometimes less constrained by union bureaucracy, and thus more open to taking radical new initiatives. So it was in Chile. Those who begin 'further back' may often provide vital forward impulses to the whole movement. A *mass* movement grows through the interaction of its parts: differences and distinctions, thought of as weaknesses in 'normal' times, can become sources of strength when the whole class is on the march.

This variety in tempos and issues poses important tactical problems for revolutionary organisations. Success for the workers' movement is a matter of the development — uneven, contradictory, yet mutually self-reinforcing — of the great majority towards a consciousness of its power to remake society. In this respect, the 'advances of the backward' are as significant as those of the vanguard, and as vital to determining the overall pattern of the masses' challenge to existing society. Hence the importance — for a movement that aims to leap *beyond* the limits of trade unionism — of a continuing struggle *within* the unions, to win over the great majority.

AT SOCIALISM'S heart is the aspiration to workers' control of production. What marks these events is how easily, when faced with particular issues requiring practical solutions, strike committees could begin to convert themselves into instruments of workers' control. In France, outside a small number of particular workplaces, such developments did not go very far. But they were important in all the other events.

Of course, as the Iranian experience makes especially clear, by themselves workplace committees, even when they have developed into factory councils pressing for democratic control of the workplace, are anything but sufficient for success. A movement for workers' control can advance on two inter-related conditions. First, that workplace committees coordinate their struggles by establishing higher-level bodies on the basis of elected delegates. Such, at a fairly underdeveloped level, were the *Inter-Impresas* and the Setubal Committee of Struggle in Portugal; such, at an altogether higher level, were the Chilean *cordones*, the Polish Inter-Factory Strike Committees and the structures of *NSZZ Solidarnosc* itself. The second condition is that the movement fights directly for *political* power: workers' councils that do not become *soviets* in the full sense will crash on the reefs of the state.

Organisational creativity is one of the most vital aspects of a rising revolutionary wave. The development of factory committees and inter-enterprise councils conditions the parallel development of all manner of other popular bodies: tenants' committees, street committees, student organisations, peasant unions, soldiers' committees and so on. These all rise to challenge old authority and to begin to reorganise everyday life. Under the vital democratic impulses of a real revolutionary movement, too, old organisations are inwardly altered, their leaders are changed, their purposes and procedures are transformed. New political and organisational focusses for mass loyalty are created. Within these new structures, new leaders emerge, often from utter obscurity, to articulate new hopes and possibilities. The new bodies become essential elements of the newly emerging social order. Their defence and extension becomes synonymous with the whole process of popular advance.

The consolidation of a revolutionary situation in its first phase is measurable by the extent to which exploited and oppressed layers of the old society begin to develop a host of directly democratic institutions of their own in every field of social life, and to coordinate these under their own direction.

New popular institutions and the democratic social relations they embody provide the key bridge between the old society and a possible new social world. In those new institutions are vested immense loyalties and hopes, for — however partially — they represent the beginnings of a radically democratic and socialist order. It is the practical democracy characterising such new institutions, itself developed in struggle, which represents the emergence of a new *form* of social organisation. And on just that ground it offers a fundamental challenge to the hierarchical and authoritarian power of class society.

A revolutionary situation, insofar as it develops to this point, brings to the fore a conflict between utterly opposed *principles*. Now society is defined by a confrontation of opposites, a power stand-off which is inherently unstable. On one side, bruised and weakened, but by no means yet destroyed, are the institutions of class society in the hands of the ruling class. On the other, still forming and uncertain of the way forward, are the newly arisen popular democratic institutions. Each finds the other intolerable. Each, for its own principles to win, must by some means or another weaken and destroy the other.

This is what is meant by a situation of 'dual power'. For a period a fragile balance is maintained between two rival and incompatible powers, two sets of organisations, each struggling to assert its different principles, each opposed by the other. Such a situation of political crisis cannot last forever. 'Normality' — everyday production and distribution of necessities, the ordinary routines of social life — must, by one means or another, be restored. But that cannot occur until the contending parties have won and lost. The issue is, who will conquer whom?

Nothing, in such circumstances, is more dangerous to the popular movement than those reformist tendencies which deny the real character of the situation, attempting — in the interests of 'mediation', 'compromise' and 'balance' — to smooth over the antagonism that now structures all social relations. If, in such a juncture, no coherent revolutionary organisation insists both on calling things by their proper names, and on the necessity for the popular organisations to continue to march forward towards complete victory, the whole movement prepares its own defeat.

IN HER brilliant pamphlet on the lessons of the 1905 revolution, Rosa Luxemburg pointed out that in periods of revolutionary movement the distinction between 'political' and 'economic' issues breaks down. Whereas in 'normal' conditions reformism imposes a sharp demarcation between 'trade unionism', concerned with 'economic' questions, and 'politics' proper, a revolutionary workers' movement fuses the two in an entirely new and dynamic fashion.

> . . . the movement . . . does not proceed from the economic to the political struggle, nor even the reverse. Every great political mass action, after it has attained its highest point, breaks up into a mass of economic strikes. And that applies not only to the great mass strikes, but also to the revolution as a whole. With the spreading, clarifying and involution of the political struggle, the economic struggle not only does not recede, but extends, organises and becomes involved in equal measure. Between the two there is the most complete reciprocal action . . .
>
> In a word: the economic struggle is the transmitter from one political centre to another; the political struggle is the periodic fertilisation of the soil for the economic struggle. Cause and effect here continually change places; and thus the economic and the political factor in the period of the mass strike . . . merely form the two interlacing sides of the proletarian class struggle . . . And *their unity* is precisely the mass strike.[10]

These observations apply very powerfully to the great workers' movements of recent years. Indeed, it is notable how 'economic' and 'political' demands were often fused together in single lists. The practical experience of workers in struggle does not need to recognise any sharp dividing line between the two spheres — as indeed they should not, for the very separation is a product of capitalism, not some universal and a-historical necessity.[11] As soon as the struggle over living and working conditions touches on issues of *control*, in particular, the whole sphere of 'politics' and power is immediately confronted.

The interaction of 'politics' and 'economics' is also, as Luxemburg suggests, a key to the interaction between the various segments of the working class as a whole. A workers' movement is never completely homogeneous. At the very point where the vanguard of the movement may be reaching out, practically and in its imagination, towards the very pinnacles of political power, other sectors of the working class are still being drawn into action for the first time. The issues over which they first organise themselves and take collective action may be narrowly 'economic'. Nonetheless, in terms of their previous experience, their battles may have quite as transforming an effect on consciousness as the more 'advanced' issues being taken up by the leading militant sectors. Success in 'economic' struggles permits a rapid leap to the 'political' — and vice versa.

There is an *organisational condition* for breaking the barriers between 'politics' and 'economics'. As long as workers' struggles are contained within the crabbed limits of 'trade union' organisation alone — where 'trade', 'industry', 'membership' and the like maintain lines of sharp division within the working class, and where 'politics' is always treated as a separate sphere — it is also harder for workers' demands and movements to transcend reformism's favourite distinctions. It is the emergence of new kinds of democratic bodies — workplace commissions, workers' councils and the like — which permits this leaping across conceptual boundaries.

Those movements that developed their organisations further, federating different workplaces into some kind of workers' council for a whole locality, also went further in weaving 'economic' and 'political' threads together. How can we characterise the *cordones* of Chile, or the Gdansk Inter-Factory Strike Committee? Were they 'economic' or 'political' in character and aspirations? In truth, they were neither and both together, and this is what gave them their particular strength, and also what attracted the hatred of the ruling classes. They were embryos of workers' power, and that recognises no separation of spheres.

TO SPEAK concretely of a mass working-class struggle is, of necessity, to recognise complexity and unevenness, the interactions between the various parts and their relative contributions to the whole movement's decline. And that is by no means the end of the story.

For if the *tendency* of modern society is to split into two great camps, that tendency is never completely realised. Other classes than the proletariat and the bourgeoisie complicate the political landscape.

To the degree that a workers' movement can aspire to transform social relations, it has to be more than simply a workers' movement, as all the great revolutionary Marxists recognised. Socialism is more than a solution to the proletarian condition, it is the emancipation of all humanity from domination and oppression. Every genuine revolutionary movement reaches out to suffering humanity at large, and draws it behind its banners.

To the degree that this does not occur, the whole movement is weakened. The Polish workers' movement gained immense moral authority by its championing of the cause of the dissident intellectuals, of political prisoners, of the students, of the peasants, And it gained in practical strength both from their adhesion to its leadership, and from Solidarity members' readiness to use their industrial strength in support of general social and political issues. Solidarity became, because of its very generosity of spirit, a movement of general social liberation — and not as something distinct from its role as a workers' movement, but as a vivifying ingredient. By contrast, the fact that the Portuguese revolution never really touched the conditions of the northern peasantry was ultimately a significant source of weakness.

The issue is of fundamental political significance. If one wants an index of the weakness of the Iranian left in 1979, one has to look no further than their failure to campaign openly and proudly among the workers, in the *Shoras* and elsewhere, in unambiguous support of the rights of women to determine their own lives, of the rights of the religious minorities to pursue their faiths in complete freedom, and of the rights of the national minorities to secede from the Iranian state. A movement against oppression and exploitation that is divided and sectionalised is a movement more easily defeated. It is noteworthy that the first Chilean *cordon* was built, not in the heartland of an industrial district, but to unify the struggles of urban and rural workers. For the Gdansk workers, the final 'sticking point' in their negotiations with the regime was the freeing of the dissident intellectuals. In early 1981, an opinion poll conducted among Solidarity members in the factories revealed that the majority held two simultaneous views: that the leadership was 'too soft' in its dealings with the regime, and that the most pressing question of the hour was not their own struggle over Saturday working, but the right of peasant farmers to build their own Solidarity organisation.

A mass movement cannot help but draw into action behind it many oppressed and exploited groups from other classes. And the mood and combativity of peasants, small traders, students and so on cannot but affect layers of the working class closest to them, and thus affect the whole class movement. The issue is not whether these groups shall be involved in the movement or not, but on what terms, and to what end? A 'popular front', which holds back the advanced section of the movement to accommodate to its most conservative layers, heads to disaster. By contrast, a hegemonic working class tries to direct more backward and conservative 'middle layers' of society towards the solution of their problems through its own revolutionary methods; it seeks by its own determination and militancy to lead them forward to assert their own needs and demands in a revolutionary manner, and it offers them its own strength in support.[12]

This *in no way* means that the working class has to restrict its own struggles in order to win these groups away from the influence of the ruling class. As the experience shows, when the working class holds back it merely gives the ruling class the chance to reclaim the initiative and restore the confidence of these middle groups in its rule. On the contrary, it is only when the working class shows the utmost resolution in pursuing its own goals that the peasants, students, and other middle groups will be persuaded that revolutionary struggle can liberate them too.

The more advanced the workers' movement, the more it can urge its allies to adopt its own principles. The political form that represents the pinnacle of development of a combative and revolutionary working class — the workers' council — is, precisely because of its essential simplicity and openness to development, the form also suited to other oppressed and exploited groups. No wonder that the Iranian national minorities and peasants formed their own *Shoras*, or that the title of 'Solidarity', along with its democratic structures, was adopted by Polish peasants and students alike for their fighting organs.

NO revolutionary movement ever proceeds in a neat line from initiating upsurge to complete victory. Rather, it passes through crises of development, which challenge its existing politics, organisation and leadership.

The early stages of a popular upsurge are regularly marked by a sense of profound unity, in which oppositions and tensions are submerged. Commonly those who first leap to the head of mass movements are people of quite moderate politics, reformists of various stripes who have won some popular credentials in the pre-revolutionary phase. They rise to leadership, in part, because they are able to articulate the still cloudy and half-formed aspirations of newly awakened masses of people. The everyday life of workers under 'normal' conditions of class society does not promote self-confidence in public speech, but that capacity is more developed among 'intermediate layers' within society: among local councillors, union officials, sections of the intelligentsia, liberal clergymen, 'professional' workers of various kinds — in short, the non-commissioned officers of class society. Their conditions of life may engender a limited kind of oppositional politics, but their natural habitat is the activity of *mediation* between opposed social forces, of manoeuvering *within* the everyday institutions of capitalist society. They provide the staff, commonly, of reformist politics.

Such people, rising to initial leadership of a mass movement, regularly play the same part: they try to limit its forward momentum. Their activities and ideas come to represent the key *danger* to the development of the movement, once the initiating phase is over.

For an initial revolutionary upsurge does not immediately destroy the ruling class. This may be temporarily weakened and disoriented, but it still exists, desperate now to regain its lost ground and break the threat from the popular movement.

Yet in just such situations, reformist leaders urge the necessity of 'moderation', in the fond illusion that gains already won are secure while further general advance is unnecessary and even undesirable. Nothing, they urge, should threaten the new *modus vivendi* between the classes. Further 'disorder' would be dangerous. The surviving forces of the old regime must be conciliated and given confidence that tranquillity can be restored. In our earlier chapters, the voices propounding such views were very diverse: Communist and Socialist Party leaders, liberal intellectuals, former guerrillas, mullahs and bishops.

Always the implication of their argument was the same: nothing too much should be attempted; this is a time for consolidation; national interests require that workers' 'sectional' demands be restrained and oppressed nationalities be moderate; peasants should not expect too much land reform; women must not press their demands too far; we must work with and not frighten the progressive element among the ruling class, but isolate the reactionary minority; and so on and so forth. Reformist 'realism' elaborates a thousand reasons why the revolution must halt at this phase, why concessions to old forces are needed rather than confrontations with them.

And always the same practical conclusions followed: the very popular forces that pushed such leaders into prominence must now be tamed and de-mobilised. The *cordones* and the workers' commissions should be subordinated to the trade unions; 'wildcat' strikes are undesirable and anarchic; women should keep quiet; 'dangerous' demands should be avoided. Those who express these views represent the conservative side of every radical movement, they speak to fear and tiredness and underdeveloped imagination. They are the forces that derail potentially revolutionary movements, and open the way for reaction's victories.

But the demobilisation they preach is never simple and automatic. For the very emergence of an insurgent mass movement lifts the hopes and strengths of whole layers of the population, permitting emancipatory visions to grow. Large numbers of people value the sense of collective power they have developed, and do not want to lose it. They want to advance, not to be incorporated and retreat.

Within all such movements, sharp oppositions soon develop between the initial leadership and the rank and file. What regularly bring such conflicts to the fore are ruling-class attacks. As Marx remarked about the 1848 revolutions, a movement sometimes needs the 'whip of reaction' to stimulate it forward.

The events discussed here provide many examples of such whips cracking: the Gaullist demonstration in the Champs Elysées, the Chilean lorry-owners' boycott, the coup attempts in Chile and Portugal, Khomeini's attacks on the rights of women and of national and religious minorities, and the beatings inflicted on Solidarity activists at Bydgoszcz. Those events were matched, at more local levels, by all manner of smaller-scale offensives.

Some of those attacks succeeded; indeed, they brought the final dénouements of these various movements. The popular movement was disoriented, unable to gather its forces for a new struggle, and thrown back in defeat. The quite small-scale offensive on 25 November 1975 was sufficient to mark the end of the Portuguese revolution; Khomeini's challenges to the forces of the Iranian left produced confusion and capitulation; the military takeovers in Chile and Poland were able to smash independent working-class organisation. Yet none of these defeats was in principle inevitable.

For other challenges could also have had the same results, yet these produced a heightened level of militancy, and a partial re-composition of the popular forces. Souper's coup attempt in Chile led to a brief strengthening of the *cordones*. The Portuguese revolution was twice pushed to the left by attempted military coups. The arrest of two Warsaw Solidarity members in November 1980 not only produced a city-wide strike movement: the steelworkers went on to challenge their union leaders' softness and to raise new political demands.

Such crises provide the occasions when revolutionary and reformist tendencies have to battle for the real leadership of the movement. Such moments test their relative weights, and also offer opportunities for revolutionary parties to make important gains in influence. Equally, these are the moments when failures and weaknesses on the left are most dangerous in their consequences.

For the situation of dual power is strictly temporary. If a popular movement does not destroy its antagonists, it will dissipate its forces and prepare its own destruction. And the costs of that — as the examples of Chile, Iran and Poland in particular reveal — can be terrible.

What counts at such moments is whether new mass initiatives develop. For that to happen, the rank and file have to be won to new and clearer perspectives. The reformists' leadership has to be challenged *politically*, and large bodies of workers won to new kinds of independent action and organisation. A revolutionary movement advances, in Trotsky's phrase, through 'the active orientation of the masses by a method of successive approximation';[13] its political aims, hopes and attachments shift according to its response to practical arguments about how to respond to crises.

Here the question of the left comes once more to the fore. A breach with the destructive consequences of reformist leadership depends on whether an alternative perspective is clearly articulated and a different lead is offered. Advance by the movement depends on the presence and activity of a revolutionary party. Otherwise, the impulses in favour of further advance, which regularly flow up from below in such moments of crisis, risk being fragmented and dissipated, leaving the whole movement open to decisive attack by the ruling class.

In essence, that was indeed the fate of the different movements we have described. The left failed, because it never challenged reformism properly, and because it lacked adequate organisation.

THE CRUCIAL ISSUE facing every revolutionary movement is that of state power. Class society is constituted on the principle of exploitative rule by a minority, on the practical exclusion of the great majority from direct self-government and control over the conditions of everyday life. The institutions of the existing state are a direct barrier to popular rule.

Ever since Marx, it has been a central argument of revolutionary socialism that 'the working class cannot simply lay hold of the ready-made state machinery, and wield it for its own purposes'.[14] The existing state machinery — of parliamentary as well as of dictatorial regimes — stands directly in the way of the realisation of democratic working-class self-government. This is just as true where a leftist party is in office, as in Chile, as where the government is controlled by the right. Workers' control, workers' power — the heart of the socialist vision — stands opposed to the bureaucratic apparatuses of the state, whether of the army and police, the 'civil service', 'welfare state', and so on. To adopt any other position is regularly to disarm the workers' movement.

From this perspective, what more than anything else marks reformism is its *pro-statist* character. It takes the subordination of the mass of the population as a *principle*. In that sense, all the various manifestations of reformism are united around their strictly *counter-revolutionary* character. Parties, unions, churches, movements of the reformist left, all share this common feature: they oppose the breaking and dismantling of the state power. Chilean Communists praised the 'patriotism' of the heads of the armed forces, and betrayed the rank-and-file sailors who warned of the approaching coup; Portuguese Communists supported anti-strike legislation and opposed demonstrations against NATO; former Iranian leftist guerrillas supported the national state in Khomeini's fake 'anti-imperialist' struggle, even though that meant the destruction of the workers' councils; Polish bishops and even former heroic dissidents urged that the state's 'vital interests' should be left unscathed.

Challenges to this perspective did arise, from within the workers' movement. But they remained fragmentary. The revolutionary groups that opposed this perspective were tragically too small to make a difference. None of the larger radical or left groupings posed real alternatives and focussed popular dissatisfactions with the moderate leaders in a consistent revolutionary direction. The majority of the left missed major opportunities, fundamentally because of their confusions over the state.

In reality the left often accepted the main substance of the reformist case. They did not centre their politics on the practical achievements of the actual workers' movement, or the various other popular organisations that grew up beside the workplace-based committees. They did not discern in these the outlines of a new social order, and struggle for the full realisation of these incipient tendencies. To do so would have required a sharp political split with the reformists. Instead, they let their opponents disarm them.

Some accepted various 'stages' theories, whose implication was always that popular struggles should not go 'too far'. Faced with the reality of mass popular insurgency, left organisations insisted on the impossibility of an immediate strugle for workers' power. In Poland, the various groups of 'radicals' within Solidarity never really questioned the correctness of the leadership's insistence on a 'self-limiting revolution'. In Portugal, the various Maoist groups — like their antagonist, the Communist Party — held that only a 'bourgeois-democratic revolution' was possible in 'backward Portugal'. In Iran, such perspectives were held by all the significant organisations of the left.

Everywhere the practical implications were clear: either workers' struggles and organisations were declared partly irrelevant ('economistic' was a favourite label in such circumstances) or their importance was played down and no serious effort was made to develop and generalise them. The Socialist and Communist Parties in Chile never understood that the *cordones* had grown up independently of their leadership, and offered an entirely new way forward; Portuguese revolutionary groups under-estimated the significance of bodies such as the workers' commissions and the *Inter-Impresas*; the Fedayeen and Mojahedin failed to grasp the importance of the *Shoras'* struggle, and eventually abandoned them to destruction by Khomeini; Polish radicals never tried to coordinate the various impulses from Solidarity's rank and file.

Not one of these groups grasped the lesson that Marx drew from the 1848 revolutions, and Trotsky from 1905 and 1917, and which they called 'permanent revolution'.[15] 'Stages theories' ignore the significance of the working class: in a revolutionary situation workers' struggles against capitalist exploitation push the whole movement to the left, beyond the confining limits of 'democratic revolution', 'national liberation', 'political reform' and the like. In 'advanced' and 'backward' countries alike, modern revolutionary movements directly raise the question of socialist transformation, as an immediate issue. A left that does not *start* with a recognition of this fundamental theoretical point will fail and worse. For the very logic of the theory of 'stages' must at some point lead its holders to side with the existing state against workers' struggles. Whether in the name of 'the immediate need for production' (which always means: the need for bosses) or 'the national struggle against imperialism' or the 'need for compromise', they take their stand somewhere against the working class and its demands. So it was with sections of the left in Chile, in Portugal, in Iran and in Poland.

Those who cannot wake from the parliamentarist dream present the same problems. The most tragic case, in these pages, was the left of the Socialist Party in Chile. The socialism they preached was a 'socialism from below', a doctrine of self-emancipation.[16] Yet, despite the opposition between the workers' movement and the UP government, they continued to attempt to ride both horses. Indeed, the left peddled the same illusions in the state as the orthodox reformists. Mike Gonzalez quotes the MIR's tragically dreadful opinion about the generals in the UP government. Equally, the left-wing general secretary of the Socialist Party, Altamirano, declared, after Souper's 29 June coup attempt:

> Never has the unity between the people, the armed forces and the police been as great as it is now . . . and this unity will grow with every new battle in the historic war that we are conducting.[17]

Time and again, instead of pointing up the fundamental conflict between the working class and the state, and drawing practical lessons from this, the left denied what it knew. In Chile, the left never broke decisively with Allende's government, even when the latter was using military force to disarm and break up the *cordones*; faced with a major strike by copper miners, they took the state's side, and split the working class. In Portugal the MES used revolutionary language, but saw its role as a pressure group on the reformist parties; the 'orthodox Trotskyists', instead of calling for a clear political breach with the reformism of the Socialist and Communist Parties, peddled illusions in them. In Iran, the Mojahedin tried to create a bridge between Islamic statism and workers' control; the Fedayeen majority sided with the state against the *Shoras*, once Khomeini declared 'holy war' on the US embassy. The Polish radicals never publicly questioned the need to 'prop up the state'. In every case, faced with a situation in which the conflict between a rising workers' movement was in irreconcilable conflict with the existing state machinery, important sections of the left fudged the issue, or worse. Those who opposed them were too weak in numbers to make a difference.

In this way, the immense possibilities offered by these movements were not realised. These revolutionary rehearsals offered a brief and brilliant glimpse of the potential within an unchained workers' movement. But the rehearsals were never permitted to proceed towards the final act. What was missing, time and again, was a sufficient organised body of revolutionary socialists ready and able to counter the arguments of those who would lead these movements to defeat, and to offer an alternative lead.

THE MOST important cause oȋ the defeats recorded here was the failure of the organised left. That conclusion seems inescapable.

When Marx developed his ideas in the 19th century, he devoted little attention to questions of political organisation and consciousness within the working class. He seems, if anything, to have assumed that the experience of exploitation and struggle within capitalism would more or less automatically lead to the development of revolutionary consciousness and organisation.[18] The *permanence* of the problems of reformism within the working-class movement did not become fully apparent until the 20th century. The subsequent generation of revolutionary theorists — above all, Lenin, Luxemburg, Trotsky, Gramsci — had to face directly the issue of explaining and dealing with it. Problems of revolutionary organisation, strategy and tactics became of necessity much more central in Marxist theory.[19]

The 20th century has witnessed, on the one hand, an immense development of capitalism's productive forces, and above all of the working class. Ours has been a century of wars and revolutions, of immense class struggles on a scale Marx and Engels could only have guessed at. On the other hand, it has been a century, up till now, of defeats for the working class. In those defeats, the politics of reformism have played an absolutely central role.

Social Democracy publicly revealed its bankruptcy, from a revolutionary standpoint, at the outbreak of the First World War. It has regularly done so since: the parts played by the socialist parties in France, Chile and Portugal between 1968 and 1975 represented nothing new.[20] On top of that, the Communist movement, created as a direct challenge to the Second International's betrayals, ended — in the wake of the degeneration of the Russian Revolution — by collapsing back into nothing more than a second version of reformist politics.[21] The role of the various Communist Parties in the events described in our previous chapters is adequate witness to this.

This doubling up of the forces of reformism did not, however, immediately lead to a revival of classical, revolutionary Marxism: those who upheld that tradition remain a tiny, embattled minority. Rather, in the 1950s and 1960s, the most influential 'left' positions were attached to a sometimes insurgent left nationalism, whose specifically *class* character was always bourgeois. The outcome has been a considerable disorientation of the left internationally.[22] The effects are all too clear in our earlier chapters.

World capitalism today is plainly ridden with crisis. The ruling classes of the world threaten each other, and all of us, with the ultimate barbarism of nuclear war. The competitive defence of sectional interests, on which capitalism is founded, stands in the way of the assertion of collective needs, in an ever more unbearable fashion. Millions still starve, at a time when the potential for a unified world, capable of meeting the material needs of its entire population, has never been so great. Real growth, oriented to expanding human needs, is increasingly held back. Millions of workers, whose skills and energy might contribute to the resolution of humanity's pressing needs, are shut out of productive life by unemployment. Vast resources are wasted; practical imagination is repressed; disbelief in the existing order grows, if as yet without finding an adequate outlet. In these conditions, we have to expect larger and more explosive class struggles across the world. Their outcome will be fateful for the very future of the human race.

The errors of the left in the last two decades were not new: every one of them was a tragic repetition of earlier mistakes by socialists. The power of Marxism is greatest when it functions as the organised memory of the working class: the events described in previous chapters are a record of its absence. The question for the future is: will a more realistic revolutionary theory and practice now find means to develop and to attract adherents, or must the world's left suffer still more defeats before it recovers its historical and political sense?

Time and again, what was missing was effective revolutionary socialist organisation. That vacuum has to begin to be filled here and now, practically and realistically. There is no point in a handful of socialists proclaiming a new 'International', when their real forces on the ground are insufficient, in any single country, for them to give a real lead to a revolutionary movement. They might delude themselves, but nobody else. What are needed are more modest, but realistic, beginnings.

The problem of socialist organisation cannot wait until a popular upsurge begins. For Marxists to enter a revolutionary situation without even the *embryo* of a party is disastrous. The previous chapters provide enough materials to illustrate the consequences. Reformism, in a rising workers' movement, met no coherent platform of opposition. The most advanced sections, those whose practical experience drove them into opposition to the reformists, found no alternative pole of organisation. No one stood ready to intervene with different ideas in the debates and struggles within workers' organisations and to win new adherents to Marxist ideas. No network of revolutionary militants, their leadership capacities already put to the test of practice by workers in different industries, was organised to challenge the union bureaucrats, or to propose bold tactics and advances to their fellow workers. There was no revolutionary newspaper with an established audience, no organisation whose members had developed the practice of discussing and learning together from other international and historical struggles and who were able to sound warnings at moments of danger; as a result, ultra-leftist lunacies and reformist adaptations alike flourished too easily.

In such circumstances, the left remains disarmed. Certainly, all revolutionary situations take time to work themselves out, and offer immense opportunities for the rapid spread of revolutionary ideas and organisation. The tempo of development in such situations is enormously speeded up. But that very rapidity of development also means great issues are decided fast. It is likely to be too late to *start* developing effective revolutionary organisation. Success requires that small but decisive beginnings are made in advance. The Bolsheviks were able to lead the October 1917 Revolution because, in February, they already had a few thousand members with a collective tradition. Rosa Luxemburg's organisation, the Spartakists, was born only in the moment of the 1918 revolution, and lacked a coherent revolutionary strategy: it — and the world revolution with it — suffered a terrible defeat in January 1919.[23]

What makes a revolution possible is the energy, imagination and boldness of the working class. But victory comes only if, within that working class, there is a revolutionary organisation fighting for the right to lead, to provide theoretical and practical direction to the movement. The ruling class organises its forces, selects and forms its leaders, according to its principles; so do the reformists. Only idiots suppose that revolutionaries must not do likewise.

The events discussed in these pages point up the key task for socialists: the development of an international revolutionary current, rooted in the everyday struggles of the working class. Its absence was crucial to these defeats. The central task of socialists is to develop everywhere revolutionary parties genuinely capable of giving leadership to workers' and other struggles.

It would be foolish to suppose that the building of such parties will be easy, for there are no magic formulae. Modesty and realism are vital. Nothing is more useless than revolutionary posturing, the substitution of impressive slogans for the real work of organising, recruiting and developing what will initially be small groups of committed revolutionary socialists. There is a bourgeois caricature of revolutionaries as burning-eyed and impatient idealists. In reality, genuine revolutionary socialist politics has to be founded on a profound *patience*, a willingness to see success in the sale of a handful of newspapers, an argument won, a single recruit to Marxism made, a tiny branch founded in a great city, a contact established somewhere new. Lenin's slogan for the Bolshevik Party, in the middle of the 1917 revolution, was not a high-sounding rhetorical balloon, but something immensely more modest, down-to-earth and therefore effective: 'Patiently explain'.

Marxist organisation rests on a number of central principles, which have to be argued for, over and over again, and applied constantly in practice. They have to be continually developed and enriched in the light of new experience. Where they are forgotten, the left will drift without bearings, more historic opportunities will be missed, and defeats like those discussed here will be repeated.

First, because of its specific situation and capacities, the working class's struggle against its conditions of exploitation is the key agency for socialist transformation. No socialist strategy which is centred elsewhere can succeed.

Second, capitalism is a global system of social production, which shapes *every* country in the contemporary world. 'Socialism in one country' is a delusion. An adequate socialist politics must be consistently internationalist.

Third, socialist advance demands the overthrow of every single existing state, and its replacement by a system of democratic workers' councils and other popular bodies that seize and maintain control of all political, economic and social decisions. Necessarily this requires the extension to all non-exploiting classes in society of the fullest democratic rights, just as it necessarily involves strict opposition to all manifestations of racist, nationalist, sexist, religious or other forms of discrimination and exclusion.

Fourth, all forms of reformism and opportunism within the workers' movement have to be strictly combatted, whether they take the shape of trade union or labour bureaucracies, petty-bourgeois left intelligentsia, substitutionist and élitist political and/or religious groupings and so forth. Against them, what has constantly to be stressed is the necessity of independent rank-and-file working-class organisation and control.

Fifth, precisely because socialism is a struggle for human emancipation from all forms of oppression, all manifestations of imperialist control by one nation-state over other peoples have to be vigorously and unambiguously opposed.

Sixth, the pursuit of this strategy requires the creation of mass revolutionary socialist parties devoted to propaganda and agitation in line with these principles. Such parties must relate directly to workers' actual daily struggles against capital, however unromantic and inglorious these may initially appear; for the everyday struggle of labour against capital is the crucial seedbed for the overthrow of world capitalism as a system.

For at least two generations, the revolutionary left has been a tiny, struggling minority. For a long period we lived under the dark shadow of Stalinism and its corruption of Marxism. The long post-war world boom strengthened reformism's hold. It is now, however, becoming more widely apparent that both these traditions of 'socialism from above' are exhausted. They attract none but the tired; as visions of social transformation, they are bankrupt. So too are their fake substitutes, Maoism, guerrilla politics and left nationalism.

Socialism offers an ever more threatened human race its only hope for the rebuilding of the world. But only if socialists can learn from previous defeats and re-shape their theory and practice. In a world locked once more into crisis, where mighty popular revolts again promise to burst out, revolutionary Marxism, a consistent socialism from below, can now achieve its proper place, as the theory and practice of human self-emancipation.

Abbreviations used in the text

APOC: Anglo-Persian Oil Company, Iran

BUMIDOM: Migrant labour organisation, France

CDE: Opposition electoral front, Portugal

CFDT: Union confederation, France

CGT: Communist-controlled union confederation, France

CIA: US Central Intelligence Agency

CIL: Conference of workers' committees, Portugal

COPCON: Radical military command group, Portugal

CRS: Riot police, France

CRTSM: Revolutionary Councils of Soldiers, Sailors and Workers, Portugal

CUF: Business corporation, Portugal

CUT: Union federation, Chile

FER: Student organisation of OCI (see below), France

FGDS: Left federation, France

FO: Anti-communist union federation, France

JAP: Community organising committees, Chile

JCR: Trotskyist youth organisation, France

KOR: Committee for the Defence of Workers, Poland

KPN: Nationalist federation, Poland

LCI: Trotskyist group, Portugal

LOT: Airline, Poland

MAPU: United Popular Action Movement, Chile

MAPUOC: Right-wing breakaway from MAPU (see above), Chile

MDP: Left-wing political party, Portugal

MES: Movement of Left Socialists, Portugal

MFA: Armed Forces Movement, Portugal

MIR: Revolutionary Movement of the Left, Chile

MKS: Inter-Enterprise Strike Committee, Poland

MRP: Shanty-town organisation of MIR (see above), Chile

MRPP: Maoist group, Portugal

NATO: Western military alliance

NSZZ *Solidarnosc*: Independent Self-governing Union 'Solidarity', Poland

OAS: Right-wing paramilitary organisation, France

OCI: Trotskyist group, France

OPEC: Organisation of Petroleum Exporting Countries

PCF: Communist Party, France

PCI: Trotskyist group, France

PCP: Communist Party, Portugal

PIDE: Secret Police, Portugal

PPD: Political party, Portugal

PRP/BR: Revolutionary Party of the Proletariat/Revolutionary Brigades, Portugal

PRT: Trotskyist group, Portugal

PSU: United Socialist Party, France

PUWP: Polish United Workers Party

RAL-1 and RALIS: Radical infantry regiment, Portugal

SAVAK: Secret police, Iran

SFIO: Socialist Party, France

SUV: Rank-and-file soldiers' organisation, Portugal

SWP: Socialist Workers Party, Britain

TAP: Airline, Portugal

TKK: Solidarity co-ordinating committee, Poland

UDP: Maoist popular front, Portugal

UNICIDADE: Proposed unified union federation, Portugal

UP: Popular Unity left coalition, Chile

ZOMO: Riot police, Poland

Notes

Introduction

1. The Founding Rules were drafted by Marx. For the original text, see Karl Marx, **Political Writings**, volume 3 (Penguin: Harmondsworth 1974) pages 82-84.
2. For a critical socialist survey of some of these, see Ellen Meiksins Wood, **The Retreat From Class** (Verso: London 1986).
3. As we write, the still embattled black workers' revolution in South Africa has yet to reach its climax. Though we do not consider it here, that bitter and magnificent struggle reveals many of the same possibilities and many of the same problems we discuss in the following pages. See, for example, Alex Callinicos, 'Marxism and revolution in South Africa', **International Socialism** 2:31, spring 1986.

Chapter one: FRANCE 1968

NOTE ON SOURCES: The main source of information used in this account is the contemporary press — in particular **Le Monde, Le Figaro, L'Humanité, Voix Ouvrière, The Economist** and **The Times** — plus a number of works published at the time and largely based on eye-witness reports, interviews and the ephemeral literature of the period, in particular: T Cliff and I Birchall, **France the Struggle Goes On** (London 1968); P Seale and M McConville, **French Revolution 1968** (Harmondsworth 1968); A Hoyles, **Imagination in Power** (Nottingham 1973); **Paris: May 1968** (Solidarity Pamphlet No 30; Bromley 1968). Also valuable were the special issue of **Partisans** (No 42, May-June 1968), and the serialised '*Mai-Juin au Fil des Jours*' which appeared in **Lutte Ouvrière** issues 19-39 (November 1968-April 1969). The analysis presented here derives largely from Cliff and Birchall (with a small retrospective reduction of euphoria); I also learnt much, despite political reservations, from the publications of the **Lutte Ouvrière** tendency.

In 1968 a great deal was written and translated extremely rapidly; grammar and proof-reading often seemed to be luxuries for which we didn't have time. In quoting from contemporary documents I have therefore taken the liberty of correcting a few obvious slips and misprints.

1. **The Economist**, 18 May 1968, especially pages xi, xii, xiii, xiv, xx and xxxii.

2. A Gorz, 'Reform and Revolution' in R Miliband and J Saville (editors), **The Socialist Register 1968** (London 1968) page 111. (Gorz's article was based on a lecture series originally delivered in Sweden in April 1966.)

3. For a short bibliography, see J Gretton, **Students and Workers** (London 1969) pages 312-17.

4. 1 June 1968.

5. For more details see I Birchall, **Workers Against the Monolith** (London 1974) chapters 6, 9 and 10, and A Werth, **De Gaulle** (Harmondsworth 1965).

6. **The Economist**, 25 May 1968; Seale and McConville, page 154.

7. Seale and McConville, page 155.

8. G Lefranc, **Le Mouvement Syndical** (Paris 1969) pages 173-76.

9. **L'Humanité**, 7 May 1968.

10. Hoyles, page 16; Cliff and Birchall, page 23.

11. **The Economist**, 18 May 1968.

12. G Pompidou, **Pour Rétablir une Vérité** (Paris 1982) page 223; Gretton, page 41.

13. Cliff and Birchall, page 12 (the paragraph cited was by Tony Cliff).

14. Lefranc, pages 222-23.

15. G and D Cohn-Bendit, **Obsolete Communism: The Left-Wing Alternative** (Harmondsworth 1969) page 118.

16. Seale and McConville, page 33.

17. **Le Monde**, 3 May 1968.

18. **Paris: May 1968**, page 1.

19. Jean-Jacques Lebel in **Black Dwarf**, 1 June 1968.

20. Seale and McConville, page 87.

21. See UNEF/SNESup, **Le Livre Noir des Journées de Mai** (Paris 1968).

22. **Daily Mirror**, 22 May 1968.

23. Pompidou, pages 184-85.

24. **Paris: May 1968**, pages 11-12.

25. Hoyles, pages 17-18 and 64-72.

26. Hoyles, pages 21-22.

27. Hoyles, pages 22-23.

28. **Le Monde**, 26-27 May 1968.

29. **L'Humanité**, 29 May 1968. (Some accounts speak of nine million strikers, some of ten million. Obviously the circumstances made an accurate count impossible. Even the lower figure is quite unparalleled in working-class history.)

30. Roger Smith in **Black Dwarf**, 1 June 1968.

31. They were also, of course, following in the tradition of the factory occupations of May-June 1936. See J Danos and M Gibelin, **June '36** (Bookmarks, London 1986).

32. Hoyles, pages 41-42.

33. **Le Monde**, 22 and 28 May 1968.

34. **L'Humanité**, 27 May 1968.

35. **Le Monde**, 28 May 1968.

36. **L'Humanité**, 28 May 1968.

37. **Le Monde,** 21 May 1968.
38. E Mandel, *'Leçons de Mai 1968'* in **Les Temps Modernes** numbers 266-7, translated as 'The Lessons of May 1968', in **New Left Review** 52, 1968.
39. See further details below.
40. **New Left Review** 52.
41. J-Ph Talbo, **La Grève à Flins** (Paris 1968) page 23.
42. Hoyles, pages 32-33.
43. **Lutte Ouvrière** 5, August 1968.
44. Cliff and Birchall, pages 36-39.
45. Seale and McConville, page 123.
46. G and D Cohn-Bendit, pages 81-82.
47. See **Lutte Ouvrière** 9, 18 September 1968.
48. **Le Monde,** 21 May 1968.
49. **Le Figaro,** 30 May 1968.
50. Seale and McConville, page 168 (100 *centimes* were roughly 10p at 1968 prices).
51. **Le Figaro,** 30 May 1968.
52. At Saint-Nazaire a striker claimed that the prefect was no more than a mail-box for transmitting workers' decisions to Paris (**Le Figaro,** 30 May 1968); at Caen all access to the town was blocked for 24 hours (Mandel, **New Left Review** 52).
53. This account of Nantes is based on Seale and McConville, pages 166-68 (based on **Cahiers de Mai,** number 1, 15 June 1968); Hoyles, pages 32 and 44-46; report by Pierre Bois in **Le Figaro,** 30 May 1968.
54. Cliff and Birchall, pages 17-18.
55. J Besançon, **Les Murs ont la Parole** (Paris 1968) page 25.
56. See J Pesquet, **Des Soviets à Saclay?** (Paris 1968).
57. Seale and McConville, pages 130-33.
58. **Le Monde,** 23 May 1968.
59. **Daily Mirror,** 23 May 1968.
60. See a leaflet issued by nurses and doctors who investigated such hostels, cited by Hoyles, pages 19-20.
61. A Quattrochi and T Nairn, **The Beginning of the End** (London 1968) page 67.
62. **The Economist,** 15 June 1968.
63. Talbo, page 17.
64. **Lutte Ouvrière** 21, 11 December 1968.
65. Bureau pour le Développement des Migrations intéressant les départements d'Outre-mer — office for the development of migration involving overseas departments.
66. **Le Monde,** 1 June 1968.
67. **Partisans** 42, May-June 1968, pages 84-85.
68. Talbo, page 85.
69. Cliff and Birchall, page 35.
70. Besançon, pages 169 and 83.
71. A Touraine, **Lettres à une Etudiante** (Paris 1974) page 109.

72. See **The Times**, 13 May 1968.
73. Hoyles, page 33.
74. Seale and McConville, pages 134-37.
75. **Le Monde**, 22 May 1968.
76. Seale and McConville, pages 107-108; Besançon, page 107.
77. Seale and McConville, pages 104-105.
78. G and D Cohn-Bendit, page 79.
79. Hoyles, pages 43-44; for a collection of posters see **Atelier Populaire — texts and posters** (London 1969).
80. For an anthology see Besançon.
81. Besançon, pages 42 and 87.
82. Pompidou, page 197.
83. **The Economist**, 1 June 1968.
84. **Le Monde**, 29 May 1968.
85. **L'Humanité**, 25 May 1968.
86. According to Les Evans, **Intercontinental Press**, 10 June 1968; I have been told that printworkers in Southern England also refused, but I cannot document this.
87. **Le Monde**, 1 June 1968.
88. **Le Monde**, 9 May, 15 May, 17 May and 19-20 May 1968.
89. **Le Monde**, 15 May 1968.
90. **Le Monde**, 17 May 1968.
91. **The Times**, 31 May 1968.
92. **Le Canard Enchaîné**, 19 June 1968. (A fuller report was printed in **Action** (14 June 1968), but this issue was seized by the authorities.)
93. **Partisans** 42, May-June 1968, pages 188-90.
94. Pompidou, especially pages 190-205.
95. Pompidou, page 201.
96. See **The Times**, 16 June 1982; **Le Monde**, 22 June 1982.
97. See **Le Monde**, 30 June, 3 July, 9 July 1982.
98. Editorial in **Le Figaro**, 30 May 1968.
99. **L'Humanité**, 10 July 1968.
100. See I Birchall, **Workers Against the Monolith**, especially chapters 9, 10 and 13.
101. **L'Humanité**, 3 May 1968.
102. **L'Humanité**, 15 May 1968.
103. CGT statement of 9pm, 16 May, published in **L'Humanité**, 17 May 1968; see also interview with Georges Séguy, **Le Monde**, 19-20 May 1968.
104. Gretton, page 181.
105. **L'Humanité**, 29 May 1968.
106. **Lutte Ouvrière** 30, 12 February 1969.
107. **Lutte Ouvrière** 25, 8 January 1969.
108. **L'Humanité**, 8 June 1968.
109. **Paris: May 1968**, page 10.
110. Statement at press conference, cited in **Partisans** 42, May-June 1968, pages 131-32.
111. Broadcast on *Europe 1*, cited in **L'Humanité**, 10 June 1968.

112. L'Humanité, 15 May 1968.
113. F Mitterrand, Ma Part de Vérité (Paris 1969) page 105.
114. J Lacouture, Pierre Mendès-France (Paris 1981) page 474.
115. C Estier, Journal d'un Fédéré (Paris 1970) page 234; see also Mendès-France's own account in P Mendès-France, Choisir (Paris 1974) pages 138-39.
116. *Aficionados* may like to consult the family tree of French *gauchisme* published in M-A Burnier, Histoire du Socialisme 1830-1981 (Paris 1981) page 99.
117. See G and D Cohn-Bendit, pages 199-245; for Cohn-Bendit's debt to the libertarian ex-Trotskyists of Socialisme ou Barbarie, see G and D Cohn-Bendit, page 18.
118. See Lutte Ouvrière 5, August 1968.
119. Paris: May 1968, page 42.
120. Hoyles, page 17.
121. Hoyles, page 21.
122. Voix Ouvrière 26, 20 May 1968.
123. Voix Ouvrière, the PCI and the JCR established a permanent co-ordinating committee between their three organisations and issued at least one joint leaflet (Partisans 42, May-June 1968, pages 73 and 126); but this was only a small step towards the unity that was needed.
124. See Lutte Ouvrière 5, August 1968, for failure of the National Union of French Students to join a mass demonstration organised by the PCF and the CGT.
125. Le Monde, 1 June 1968.
126. Gretton, page 196.
127. Seale and McConville, page 212.
128. The Economist, 8 June 1968.
129. Lutte Ouvrière 37, 2 April 1969.
130. Estier, page 243.
131. Seale and McConville, page 212.
132. Partisans 42, May-June 1968, pages 190-93.
133. The Economist, 22 June 1968.
134. See article by Marc Ullman in The Times, 29 May 1968.
135. The Economist, 29 June 1968.
136. Lefranc, page 247.
137. L'Humanité, 6 June 1968.
138. See G Pompidou, cited in Lutte Ouvrière 26, 15 January 1969.
139. Cliff and Birchall, pages 32-33, based on reports in Lutte Ouvrière 2, 3 July 1968, Analyses et Documents No 156, Nouvelle Avant-Garde No 1, Action No 5.
140. See various statements in Lutte Ouvrière 30, 12 February 1969; in retrospect I think the revolutionaries may have been tactically mistaken in refusing to run candidates, although at the time I did not question the advocacy of boycott.
141. L'Humanité, 2 July 1968.
142. L'Humanité, 22 June 1968.

143. See Gretton, page 269.
144. Alain Krivine won 1.1 per cent of the poll in the 1969 presidential election; 2.69 per cent went to Krivine and Arlette Laguiller in 1974; 2.30 per cent was for Laguiller in 1981. The groups banned in 1968 all rapidly reorganised under new names.

Chapter two: CHILE 1972-3

1. The railways carried one-third of total national freight, the other two-thirds going by road. There was a nice extra irony in the fact that the government had announced, not long before the strike, its intention to expand the road transport industry.
2. In fact he was member of a small extreme right-wing terrorist organisation called *Patria y Libertad* (Fatherland and Freedom), with avowed sympathies for the theorists of fascism. *Patria y Libertad* had been involved in the murder of General Schneider late in 1970 — Schneider was sympathetic to Allende — and in a series of violent incidents after that. From October 1972 it was actively involved in the preparation of the military coup, and its leaders, Pablo Gonzalez and Roberto Thieme, became vocal champions of the military regime after 1973. Ironically, both turned against the Pinochet regime later. *Patria y Libertad* found its social base among the young of the wealthy families and in those lower middle-class sectors caught between the big battalions, such as the small shopkeepers and lorry-owners.
3. The policies of Popular Unity are described in detail in Ian Roxborough, Phil O'Brien, Jackie Roddick: **State and Revolution in Chile** (Macmillan, London 1977) (hereafter Roxborough, 1977), chapter 4. See also Ann Zammit (editor), **The Chilean Road to Socialism** (Brighton 1973).
4. The basic indicators can be found in Roxborough, 1977, pages 131-32. For a fuller treatment see S Ramos, **Chile, una economia de transicion?** (Chile, 1972).
5. The debate around Chile has been discussed in detail in M Gonzalez, 'The Left and the Coup in Chile', in **International Socialism** 2:22, winter 1984, pages 45-86.
6. See F Casanueva and M Fernandez, **El Partido socialista y la lucha de clases en Chile** (Santiago, 1973). Also C Altamirano, **Dialectica de una derrota** (Siglo XXI, Mexico 1977).
7. The argument rests on the fact that the right was unable to agree a joint candidate for the 1970 elections, and in fact presented two. Alessandri, representing the National Party, spoke for the landowning interests and the major financial concerns. After major internal ructions, the Christian Democrats presented Radomiro Tomic, regarded as on the left of the party. In the event, the votes divided fairly evenly between the three, with Allende receiving 36 per cent, Alessandri 34.9 per cent, and Tomic 27.8 per cent.
8. See Monica Threlfall, 'Shantytown dwellers and people's power', in P O'Brien (editor), **Allende's Chile** (Praeger, New York 1976) pages 167-91. Also J Giusti, **Organizacion y participacion popular en Chile** (FLASCO, Santiago 1973).

9. MAPU was formed in 1968 and became a member of the Popular Unity coalition. Christian Left was formed in 1971 around Frei's ex-minister of agriculture, Jacques Chonchol.

10. See Gonzalez, pages 65-68. See too the very good analysis by Tom Bossert, **Political argument and policy issues in Allende's Chile** (University of Wisconsin Press, 1976).

11. In fact the copper companies had done extremely well under Frei. His policy of 'Chileanisation' of the mines meant that the Chilean state bought shares in the companies, at inflated prices, and became responsible for all future investment. This investment was financed by more foreign borrowing. Meanwhile, the big copper multinationals still controlled the market and the world price.

12. The full list of firms nationalised is set out in Roxborough, 1977, pages 90-93.

13. The full text of the Statute is in Roxborough, 1977, page 104. For Allende's own explanation of the Statute see Debray, **Conversaciones con Allende** (Mexico 1971) pages 116-17.

14. See Allende, **Chile's road to socialism** (Harmondsworth: Penguin, 1973) chapter 9, pages 90-100. Joan Garces, a key adviser to Allende, presented this case in **Chile Hoy** with his argument on 'dual power in the state'; see Garces, **El estado y los problemas tacticos del gobierno de Allende** (Siglio XXI, Mexico 1973).

15. On the government's economic performance during its first year, see Roxborough 1977, chapter 4. Also P Sweezy in **Monthly Review**, December 1973, pages 1-11.

16. The US had also played its part, cutting off all aid other than military assistance (which increased in volume) and calling in Chile's external debt. On the role of the US, see **The ITT Memos: Subversion in Chile** (Spokesman Books, Nottingham 1972); P Agee, **Inside the company: A CIA Diary** (Penguin, Harmondsworth 1975); and the report of the US Senate Select Committee 1975, **Covert Action in Chile: 1963-1973**.

17. On the question of the land, see I Roxborough, 'Agrarian policy in the Popular Unity government' (University of Glasgow Occasional Paper, 1974) and D Lehmann, 'Agrarian reform in Chile 1965-72' in D Lehmann (editor), **Agrarian reform and agrarian reformism** (Faber, London 1974). On strikes and the balance of politics in the working-class movement, see **Correo proletario**, number 2: London, November 1975, pages 4-5.

18. These comments were made by Radomiro Tomic and quoted in the **Morning Star**, 7 August 1972.

19. See Bossert, on the whole discussion. The responses of MIR and MAPU are in the collections of documents published by **Politique Hebdo** (Paris) in 1974, and Roxborough 1977, chapter 4.

20. See MAPU (**Politique Hebdo**) chapter 2. MAPU's confusion was deeper because it claimed throughout to be a revolutionary party based on Marxism-Leninism (see the minutes of its 5th Plenum in **El segundo año del gobierno popular** (Santiago, November 1972)). MIR vacillated wildly in its responses (see **Punto Final**).

21. See **Chile Hoy** no 3, 30 June/6 July 1972, page 6. Vergara was to reappear and make almost identical comments after the Lo Hermida incidents (see note 26), in his capacity as under-secretary for the interior.

22. The whole discussion is reproduced in the magazine **Chile Hoy** no 1, 16-22 June 1972, pages 4-6. I shall be quoting from this extremely good weekly review (edited by members of the Socialist Party but containing full and continuous debate) from this, its first number, to its final edition on 30 August 1973. **Chile Hoy** and the MIR journal **Punto Final** provide the fullest and most accurate account of the Chilean process. Articles from **Chile Hoy** have been published in an anthology edited by Pio Garcia, **Las Fuerzas armadas y el golpe de estado en Chile** (Siglo XXI, Mexico 1974). In relation to this period in general, see Altamirano, especially chapter 4.

23. See **Chile Hoy**, no 6, 23-30 July 1972, pages 10-11.

24. This is not to say they were ignored; **Chile Hoy** and **Punto Final** were to discuss the *cordones* almost continuously from now on. See **Chile Hoy** no 8, 4-10 August 1972, pages 4-5. The first programme can be found in Roxborough 1977, pages 170-71, and in Allende.

25. See O'Brien page 31. See also Hurtado Beca, 'Chile 1973-81' in Gallitelli and Thompson (editors), **Sindicalismo y regimenes militares en Chile y Argentina** (CEDLA, Amsterdam 1982).

26. See **Chile Hoy** no 9, 11-17 August 1972, pages 6-7 and no 10, 18-25 August 1972, pages 6-7.

27. See for example E Gonzalez' interesting analysis in **International Socialist Review** (New York) October 1973.

28. See P Santa Lucia, 'Industrial workers and the struggle for power' in O'Brien, page 140-41. Also **Chile Hoy** no 8, pages 6-7 and no 11, where Miguel Enriquez, secretary-general of the MIR, gives his view on pages 32 and 29. For the MAPU view see MAPU (Paris, 1974) chapter 2, B.

29. See **Chile Hoy**, no 8, page 6.

30. 'Indeed by 1973 the only remaining bourgeois democrats in Chile were Allende, the Communist Party and a section of the Socialist Party', writes C Kay, 'The Chilean road to socialism: post mortem' in **Science and Society**, summer 1976, page 224.

31. **Chile Hoy** and **Punto Final**. See Marta Haernecker's summary of the strategies of the right before October in **Chile Hoy**, no 21, 3-9 November 1972, pages 15-18.

32. Sources of information on this period are, as usual, **Chile Hoy** and **Punto Final**, on which most books base their accounts — see for example M Raptis, **Revolution and Counter-Revolution Chile** (Allison and Busby, London 1974).

33. Quoted in **Punto Final**, no 170, 7 November 1972, page 6.

34. **Chile Hoy**, no 19, 20-26 October 1972, page 5.

35. On battles in the media, see the outstanding work of Armand Mattelart and his group at CEREN, published in the magazine **Cuadernos de la Realidad Nacional**. Some of this is to be found in the collection of essays published by Harvester Press, **Multinational corporations and the mass**

media (1978). See also M Gonzalez, 'Ideology and culture under Popular Unity' in O'Brien, pages 106-127.

36. **Chile Hoy**, no 19, page 5.
37. On the strategy of the right, see Ian Roxborough, 'Reversing the revolution: the Chilean opposition to Allende' in O'Brien, pages 192-216; also J Petras and M Morley, **How Allende fell** (Spokesman, Nottingham 1974).
38. **Punto Final**, no 170, page 6.
39. **Punto Final**, no 170, page 6.
40. **Punto Final**, no 170, page 6.
41. **Chile Hoy**, no 20, 27 October-2 November 1972, page 30.
42. See Roxborough 1977, pages 167-8 and 172-4. Also Raptis, pages 103-4.
43. See, for example, Bossert and **Correo proletario**.
44. See Allende, pages 192-3, for example.
45. An argument reproduced, for example, in the pamphlet **Chile: trade unions and the resistance** (London: Chile Solidarity Campaign 1975) page 11: 'the cordones could be seen as an extension of the CUT at local level'!
46. **El segundo ano . . .** page 383.
47. Bossert, page 221.
48. See **New Chile**, London, no 2, January 1973, pages 2-3. See also MAPU, **Chile 1973: ni reforma ni revolucion** (La Pulga, Medellin 1973) page 18.
49. See Garces, pages 214-17, who lays emphasis on the interviews with General Prats, army commander, in **Ercilla** (quoted page 217) and **Chile Hoy**. Garces asserts, for example, that 'the army men who agreed to collaborate with the Allende government were not the kind of military men the reactionary right imagined them to be'!.
50. **Chile Hoy**, no 22, 10-16 November 1972, page 32.
51. **Chile Hoy**, no 22, page 32.
52. See the document quoted in **Chile 1973**.
53. **Chile Hoy**, no 22, 10-16 November 1972, quoted in Garces.
54. **Punto Final**, no 170, 7 November 1972, page 3.
55. In **Chile Hoy**, no 58, page 5.
56. These are the views of Bosco Parra, leader of the Christian Left, given in an interview with **Punto Final**, no 171, 21 November 1972, pages 6-7.
57. The speaker is Gabriel Aburto in **Punto Final**, no 172, 5 December 1972, pages 4-5.
58. The urgency of the discussions can be sensed in the documents of the different parties at the time — journals such as **Chile Hoy** and **Punto Final** and **Puro Chile** as well as the newspapers of the various organisations — **El Siglo** (CP), **La Aurora** (SP), **El Rebelde** (MIR), and the intense debate conducted in each of them.
59. Lenin, confronting a similar moment in the course of the Russian revolution, presented in his **April Theses** an incisive and thorough analysis of the particular tasks, building the party on the strength and combativity of the mass organisations, but above all through winning the battle for the political leadership of the movement. 'As long as the government yields to the influence of the bourgeoisie, it is the task of the revolutionaries to

present a patient, systematic and persistent *explanation* of the errors of their tactics, and *an explanation especially adapted to the needs of the masses'* (**April Theses**, page 9, my italics).

60. A debate reported in full in **Punto Final**, no 173, 16 January 1973, Documentos section, pages 1-22.

61. See E Gonzalez.

62. In an interview in **Punto Final**, no 183, 6 May 1973, page 4.

63. P Santa Lucia, page 147.

64. P Santa Lucia, page 148.

65. See Roxborough in O'Brien, pages 205-7.

66. See Roxborough 1977.

67. The examples are legion — the political commission of MAPU, for example, argued on 12 February 1973 the need to 'demand of the government a revolutionary response' and to build 'a revolutionary pole within UP' (in **Chile 1973**, pages 54-55). In the May debate, the leader of the MIR's workers' organisations insisted that the *cordones* should be led by the CUT etc.

68. See, as one particularly crude example of this argument, C Kay, 'The making of a coup' in **Science and society**, 1974 — reproduced in the Edinburgh Solidarity Campaign Bulletin, **Chile Hoy**, 1974, no 2, page 9. For the opposite argument see H Prieto, **The gorillas are amongst us** (Pluto Press, London 1974) pages 34-36.

69. See Prieto.

70. **Punto Final**, 3 July 1973, page 13.

71. See **Punto Final**, no 183, 8 May 1973, *'La toma de Constitucion'*.

72. **Punto Final**, no 182, 24 April 1973, page 4.

73. Described in **Punto Final** as *'Un congreso fuera de onda'* (A congress out of its time), no 187, 3 July 1973, page 9.

74. See **Punto Final**, no 185, 5 June 1973, pages 16-18.

75. P Garcia, quoting from **Chile Hoy**, no 55, 6 July 1973.

76. From P Garcia, see also Santa Lucia.

77. Prieto, page 37.

78. Prieto, page 39.

79. See **Punto Final** and **Chile Hoy**. The Socialist Party leadership boasted that the working class had no arms — see **Chile Hoy**, nos 58 and 59.

80. Altamirano said, after the 29 June attempted coup: 'Never has the unity between the people, the armed forces and the police been as great as it is now . . . and this unity will grow with every new battle in the historic war that we are conducting' (cruelly quoted in **Le Monde**, 16-17 September 1973). He echoed the words of the Communist Party's general secretary, Luis Corvalan, in early August at a major rally in Santiago; sadly for him his speech was published in the September 1973 issue of **Marxism Today**, journal of the British Communist Party.

81. **Punto Final**, no 189, 31 July 1973.

82. Roxborough 1977, page 176.

83. See Gonzalez in O'Brien, pages 118-21.

84. Reproduced, with tragic irony, in the British Communist Party's journal **Marxism Today** in September 1973.

85. See the interview with MIR secretary-general Miguel Enriquez in **Punto Final**, no 189, 31 July 1973, pages 4-7.
86. See Gonzalez, 1984.
87. See the British Communist Party's pamphlet, **Chile: Solidarity with Popular Unity**, London.
88. It is one of the paradoxes of the Chilean experience that the huge body of writing and analysis of the Chilean process 1970-73 has been conducted since the coup, in the main with the objective of justifying or legitimating one or other perspective during the UP period. In the immediate aftermath of the coup, however, the emphasis was on the savagery and barbarism of the coup and the days and weeks that followed. Of the many accounts the following can be mentioned: **Chili: le dossier noir** (Gallimard, Paris 1974); R Silva, **Evidence on the terror in Chile** (Merlin, London 1975); the magazine published by the Chile Solidarity Campaign (UK), **Chile Fights**, from late 1973 onwards; **Chile: The story behind the coup** (NACLA, New York 1973); and the key speech by E Berlinguer, secretary of the Italian Communist Party, in **Marxism Today**, February 1974.

Chapter three: PORTUGAL 1974-75

NOTE ON SOURCES: Much of the information for this chapter was obtained directly. I was myself in Portugal at various times during the years 1975-76, and have returned there several times since. I have interviewed many militants who took part in the events of the revolution, and to all of them special thanks are due. The most useful book to be published since is Phil Mailer, **Portugal: The Impossible Revolution?** (Solidarity, London 1977). Its weakness is that Mailer is a libertarian who argues on principle against all parties and trade unions. The most readable account of the coup of 25 April 1974 is **Portugal: The Year of the Captains** (**Sunday Times** Insight Team, 1975). Also worthy of mention are Douglas Porch, **The Portuguese Armed Forces and the Revolution** (Croom Helm, London 1977).

1. Luis Solgado de Matos, **Investimentos estrangeiros en Portugal** (Lisbon 1973).
2. Interview with Augistinho Roseta, Easter 1984. Roseta, a student leader in the late 1960s, worked for many years as an official of the textile workers' union. He was a conscripted officer (*Miliciano*) in 1974-75.
3. Quoted in Antonio de Figueiredo, **Portugal: Fifty Years of Dictatorship** (Penguin, Harmondsworth 1975) pages 231-2.
4. Quoted in Figueiredo, page 233.
5. Mailer, page 44.
6. Charles Downs, 'Residents commissions and urban struggles in revolutionary Portugal', in Graham and Wheeler, **In Search of Modern Portugal** (University of Wisconsin 1983).
7. **Portugal: The Year of the Captains**, page 120.
8. Interview with Roseta.
9. Details are in Maria de Lourdes, Lima dos Santos and others, **O 25 de Abril E as Lutas Socias Nas Empresas** (Porto 1976).

10. The slogan 'O fascisme nao passara' (fascism shall not pass), raising memories of the struggle against fascism during the Spanish Civil War of the 1930s, was frequently heard on demonstrations during 1974. It need not concern us here whether the Caetano regime was truly fascist, or an authoritarian dictatorship, but the image of Portugal's struggle against fascism developed a powerful emotional charge which sometimes stood in the way of deeper political analysis.

11. Gallagher, **Portugal: A Twentieth Century Interpretation** (Manchester University Press 1983) page 172.

12. Richard Robinson, **Contemporary Portugal** (Allen and Unwin, London 1979) page 136.

13. Carlos N, a metalworker in the Rocha yards at Lisnave, interviewed in 1984.

14. **Portugal: The Year of the Captains**, page 152.

15. Interview, in 1984, with worker at Plesseys and member of the workers' commission in 1974.

16. Interview with Roseta.

17. Figueiredo, page 238.

18. Reprinted from **Combate**, no 7, 27 September 1974. For a detailed account of the action in Lisnave, see Maria de Fatima Patriarca, 'Operaios da Lisnave de 12 Sept 1974' in **Analise Social**, no 56 (Lisbon 1978).

19. Published in **Causa Operario**.

20. Full text published in Mailer.

21. Both groups were affiliated to the United Secretariat of the Fourth International, where the differences between them provoked a furious row.

22. From an article in the French paper **Libération**, republished in 'Portugal: A Blaze of Freedom' (**Big Flame**, London).

23. Downs, page 163.

24. A useful analysis of the Portuguese Socialist Party is by Ian Birchall, 'Social Democracy and the Portuguese Revolution', in **International Socialism** 2:6, autumn 1979.

25. Returns from a Ministry of Labour questionnaire gave the following reasons for takeovers in Lisbon: abandonment 44.3 per cent; contract violation 15.4 per cent; managerial incompetence 11.5 per cent; unlawful sackings 11.5 per cent; fraud 9.6 per cent; bankruptcy 7.0 per cent (quoted by Nancy Bermao, 'Workers' management in industry', in Graham and Wheeler (editors), **In Search of Modern Portugal** (University of Wisconsin 1983).) See also Jack Hammond, 'Workers' control in Portugal: The revolution and today', in **Economic and Industrial Review**, no 2, November 1981.

26. Quoted in Tony Cliff and Robin Peterson, 'Portugal: The last three months', in **International Socialism** 1:87, March 1976 ('Robin Peterson' was a pseudonym of the present author).

27. Denis MacShane, **New Statesman**, 18 July 1975.

28. See Robin Peterson, 'The failure of workers' power in Portugal', in **International Discussion Bulletin** no 5 (Socialist Workers Party, London 1977); also Paul Sweezy, 'Class struggles in Portugal', in **Monthly Review**, September 1975, pages 19-22.

29. Quoted in Mailer, page 229.

30. Mailer, page 231.
31. Tony Cliff, **Portugal at the Crossroads** (a special issue of **International Socialism** 1:81-2, September 1975) page 39.
32. Richard Robinson, page 242.
33. Gunter Walraff, **The Undesirable Journalist** (Pluto Press, London 1978) pages 13-14.
34. **Expresso**, 9 August 1975, quoted in Cliff, page 29.
35. Mailer, page 275.
36. **Expresso**, 9 August 1975, quoted in Cliff, page 29.
37. Jorge, a soldier serving in the RTM regional transport barracks in the north, interviewed in August 1980.
38. Interview with a member of the secretariat of SUV on 23 September 1975, published in **Os SUV em luta**, translated in **Imprecor**, no 35.
39. Interview with Jorge.
40. **Os SUV em Luta**, in **Imprecor** no 35.
41. Jeanne Pierre Faye, **Portugal: The Revolution in the Labyrinth** (Spokesman, Nottingham 1976) pages 49-50. The fear that Portugal would become another Chile was shared by most of the revolutionary left outside Portugal, including the International Socialists.
42. Charles Downs, 'Community Organisation, Political Change and Urban Policy: Portugal 1974-6' (PhD thesis, University of California 1980).
43. Even the British section of the Fourth International characterised the events of 25 November 1975 as an 'insane adventure' by 'ultra-left groups' (see its paper **Red Weekly**, 4 December 1975).
44. Marshall and Ferreira, **Portugal's Revolution: Ten Years On** (Cambridge 1998).

Chapter four: IRAN 1979

1. For this period, see Shaul Bakhash, **Iran: Monarchy, Bureaucracy and Reform under the Qajars, 1858-1896** (Ithaca Press, London 1978) and N Keddie, **Religion and Rebellion in Iran: The Iranian Tobacco Protest of 1891-1892** (London 1966).
2. E G Brown, **The Persian Revolution of 1905-1909** (Cambridge 1910) and A Kasravi, **Tarikhe Mashroteh Iran** (The History of the Constitution of Iran) (Farsi, Tehran 1976).
3. Ramy Nima, **The Wrath of Allah** (Pluto Press, London 1983) chapter 1.
4. On land reform, see A K S Lambton, **The Persian Land Reform 1922-1966** (Clarendon Press, Oxford 1969) and E J Hoogland, **Land and Revolution in Iran 1960-1980** (University of Texas Press 1982).
5. On industrialisation, see J Bharier, **Economic Development in Iran 1900-1970** (Oxford University Press, New York 1971) and Fred Halliday, **Iran: Dictatorship and Development** (Penguin, London 1979).
6. Halliday, pages 127-28.
7. Nima, page 15.
8. Halliday, pages 147-58.
9. Ervand Abrahamian, **Iran Between Two Revolutions** (Princeton University Press, Princeton 1982) pages 435-40.

10. Halliday, pages 173-83.
11. Nima, page 51.
12. For industrialisation in this period see Halliday, chapters 5-7 and J Bharier, **Economic Development in Iran, 1900-1970** (Oxford University Press, New York, 1971) chapter 13.
13. The Tudeh Party, despite its Russian links, has no direct connection with the Iranian Communist Party of the 1920s. On communism in Iran, see Sepehr Zabih, **The Communist Movement in Iran** (University of California Press 1966). Also Abrahamian and **Historical Documents: The Workers, Social Democratic and Communist Movement in Iran** (Farsi, Mazdak Publications).
14. Abrahamian, page 446.
15. Shariati's mosque, *Hoseiniye Ershad*, was closed and bricked up by SAVAK in the late 1960s. Shariati himself, after years in one of the Shah's prisons, died in London in 1977 of a heart attack — in reality as a result of his tortures in prison.
16. US News and World Report 26 June 1978, cited in Fereydoun Hoveyda, **The Fall of the Shah** (Weidenfeld and Nicholson, London 1979) page 6.
17. Abrahamian, page 520.
18. **Khabar Kargar** (Workers News, Journal of the Tehran Industrial Plants), number 6, February 1980 (Farsi, Tehran), and **Akhbareh Mobarezateh Tabagheye Kargar** (News of Workers Struggle), published by the Fedayeen Guerrilla Ashraf Deghhani Group (Farsi), April 1980.
19. 'Profit-sharing schemes' were the fourth point of the Shah's twelve-point 'White Revolution' programme of 1963.
20. By 1976, an estimated 50,000 foreigners were working in Iran as skilled technicians and managers at the same time that there was massive unemployment among Iranian workers.
21. Assef Bayat, 'Workers Control', MERIP **Report** 113 (Middle East Research and Information Project, London) March-April 1983. See also Assef Bayat, **Workers and Revolution in Iran** (Zed Books, London 1987).
22. In 1942 the Central Council of Trade Unions in Iran was formed. By 1946 it had 400,000 members. All through the 1940s and 1950s workers played a crucial part in the struggle against the repressive state, and a general strike played a key role in oil nationalisation.
23. Bayat.
24. Chris Goodey, MERIP **Report** 88, June 1980.
25. **Paygham Emrouz** (radical daily newspaper, Farsi) 5 March 1979.
26. **Keyhan** (Iranian daily newspaper, Farsi), Reports on workers and industries, 1 October 1979.
27. **Paygham Emrouz**, 1 March 1979. The repetition of 'sick pay' in points 7 and 13 appears in the original.
28. **Ayandegan** (radical daily newspaper, Farsi) 31 March 1979.
29. **Ayandegan**, 19 April 1979.
30. **Ettellaat** (daily newspaper, Farsi) 28 April 1979.
31. **Ayandegan**, 11 April 1979.
32. **Paygham Emrouz**, 6 March 1979.

33. Bayat.
34. **Keyhan,** 9 August 1979.
35. **Khabar Kargar,** October 1979.
36. Cited by Fred Halliday in **MERIP Report** 88, June 1980, page 4.
37. The Paykar was the third largest organisation on the Iranian left, after the Fedayeen and Mojahedin. They represented a Maoist anti-Islamic break-away from the Mojahedin. Their organisation was the most active in the workplaces. The organisation was to be dissolved after heavy losses in Khomeini's jails.
38. Since Khomeini came to power, many members of the Baha'i faith have been executed for their religious beliefs.
39. Bayat.
40. During the revolution there were four distinct political lines within the Iranian left:

    ONE: The majority Fedayeen, the result of the 1979 split, went under the leadership of the Tudeh Party. They saw Russia and the Eastern bloc as socialist; they looked for a non-capitalist road to development for Iran; and they supported the Islamic Republic and Khomeini's regime until 1984 as an anti-imperialist force.

    TWO: The Fedayeen minority, along with three smaller organisations (*Cherikhaye Fedayee Khalghg Ashraf Dehghani,* the *Rahe Fedayee* and the *Rahe Kargar*) also saw Russia and the Eastern bloc as socialist, but did not support the Islamic Republic and Khomeini. After 1980 the first of the three groups was reduced to operating only in Kurdistan, while the other two merged to become the *Sazemane Kargarane Enghelabi.*

    THREE: The third position was taken by the various Maoist organisa-tions. These looked to the political teachings of Mao to provide a new democratic revolution in the Third World, which they saw as subordinated to capitalism through social imperialism and economic dependency. The most significant was the Paykar, which had split from the Mojahedin in 1975, at the same time rejecting Islamic ideology. Others were the *Razmandegan, Ettehadiehe Kommonistha, Arman Baraye Azadieh Tabagheh Kargar, Ranjbaran, Toofan* and *Sahand.* Most, including the Paykar, suffered heavy losses under Khomeini and were dissolved. In 1982 *Sahand* merged with *Komoleh* in Kurdistan to form the Communist Party of Iran (*Hezbe Komoniste Iran*). This still seeks a bourgeois democratic 'stage' of revolution as a precondition for socialist revolution.

    FOUR: The final group were organisations which rejected Russia as socialist, while differing in their analysis of its actual status. Among these, two Trotskyist groups supported the Khomeini regime: the HVK and the HKE, both affiliated to the Fourth International. The rest opposed Khomeini, including Communist Unity (*Vahdate Komonisty*), *Ghiam, Zamane Noe, Andishe va Enghelab* and a third affiliate of the Fourth International, the HKS.

    Among the opposition were also the Kurdish Democratic Party of Iran (the pro-Russian national liberation movement for Kurdistan) and the Mojahedeen Islamic guerrilla organisation.

Chapter five: POLAND 1980-81

NOTE ON SOURCES: Much of the material for this article is taken from two previous books: **Solidarnosc: From Gdansk to Military Repression** (written with Kara Weber), a special issue of **International Socialism** (second series) 15, 1982; and **Festival of the Oppressed: Solidarity, Reform and Revolution in Poland 1980-1981** (Bookmarks, London 1986). Particular thanks are due to numbers of Solidarity members in Poland who generously gave me their time; they must remain anonymous, but I learned enormously from their comments and experiences.

1. Details of the crisis, its pattern and its causes, are discussed at length in Part Two of Colin Barker and Kara Weber, **Solidarnosc: From Gdansk to Military Repression.**
2. For a general review, see Chris Harman, **Class Struggles in Eastern Europe** (Pluto Press, London 1983).
3. This is brought out well in the lively narrative of Stan Persky, **At the Lenin Shipyard** (New Star Books, Vancouver 1981).
4. A Kemp-Welch (editor), **The Birth of Solidarity: The Gdansk Negotiations, 1980** (Macmillan, London 1983) page 53.
5. Interview in **Women's Voice** 46, November 1980.
6. There is an especially valuable review of many of the political lessons of the Workers' Council experience in Donny Gluckstein, **The Western Soviets** (Bookmarks, London 1985).
7. Jadwiga Staniszkis, **Poland's Self-Limiting Revolution** (Princeton University Press, 1984) page 45; Alain Touraine, **Solidarity: Poland 1980-81** (Cambridge University Press, 1983) page 38.
8. The strategy was spelled out in a 'secret' speech to security police officers in Katowice by Andrzej Zabinski, the local party secretary, in December 1980: see Timothy Garton Ash, **The Polish Revolution: Solidarity 1980-1982** (Cape, London 1983) page 150.
9. **Labour Focus on Eastern Europe**, 4:4-6, page 15.
10. **The Guardian**, 28 March 1981.
11. **The Guardian**, 19 February 1981.
12. Cited in Mary Craig, **The Crystal Spirit: Lech Walesa and his Poland** (Hodder and Stoughton, London 1986) page 203.
13. **Financial Times**, 26 March 1981.
14. Mary Craig, page 204.
15. This is brought out in Ray Taras, **Ideology in a Socialist State: Poland 1956-1983** (Cambridge University Press, 1984).
16. For professional people, in particular, it is acceptable to be a non-party member; it is less acceptable to be 'ex-party'.
17. Paul G Lewis, 'Institutionalisation of the Party-State Regime in Poland' in Bronislaw Misztal (editor), **Poland After Solidarity: Social Movements versus the State** (Transaction Books, New Brunswick 1985) page 43.
18. Kazimierz Brandys, **A Warsaw Diary, 1978-1981** (Chatto and Windus/ The Hogarth Press, London 1984) page 209. There was also a call for resistance to 'judaisation' of Polish 'national culture' from a newly regis-

tered Catholic body, the Polish Academic Union (PZA): Jan Toporowski, 'Poland: Cliffhanger Democracy', **New Statesman**, 12 June 1981.

19. See chapter four of Colin Barker, **Festival of the Oppressed: Solidarity, Reform and Revolution in Poland, 1980-1981** (Bookmarks, London 1986); also Michael Szkolny, 'Revolution in Poland', **Monthly Review**, 33:2, June 1981; and the considerable materials collected in Bogdan Szajkowski, **Next to God . . . Poland: Politics and Religion in Contemporary Poland** (Frances Pinter, London 1983).

20. Szajkowski, page 94; Peter Raina, **Independent Social Movements in Poland** (London School of Economics/Orbis Books, London 1981).

21. See the extraordinary memoir of Gdynia port worker J Gajda, 'August 1980 As I Saw it' in Wladyslaw W Adamski (editor), **Sisyphus Sociological Studies, Volume 3: Crises and Conflicts, The Case of Poland 1980-1981** (PWN — Polish Scientific Publishers, Warsaw 1982) (extracts in Barker, pages 65-66).

22. Ludwik Hass, a veteran Polish Trotskyist, described this as a 'real class operation': 'Die Tragödie von Solidarnosc sind der Berater!' (interview with Ludwik Hass by Ernst Haenisch), **Klassenkampf** 10, March-April 1982. My thanks to Ian Birchall for a translation.

23. Details in the two memoirs by Jadwiga Staniszkis, 'The evolution of forms of working-class protest in Poland: sociological reflections on the Gdansk:Szczecin case', **Soviet Studies** 33, 2 April 1981 and by Tadeusz Kowalik, 'Experts and the Working Group' in Kemp-Welch (editor).

24. Much of Marxism has still to come to terms with this important element within 20th-century capitalism. This class has played a major role in 'Communist' countries, in the 'national' movements in the backward countries, and not least in the labour movements of the West. It is variously delineated in Leon Trotsky, **History of the Russian Revolution** (Gollancz, London 1965), pages 184-85; Tony Cliff, 'Deflected Permanent Revolution', **International Socialism** (first series) 12, spring 1963; and Alex Callinicos, 'The "New Middle Class" and Socialist Politics', **International Socialism** (second series) 20, summer 1983. It is the very root of tendencies to 'substitutionism'.

25. Martin Myant, **Poland: A Crisis for Socialism** (Lawrence and Wishart, London 1982) page 189.

26. Touraine (page 142) is surely wrong in interpreting this as a decision for a 'centralised offensive, capable of forcing the regime to retreat' as against action from the rank and file. For no such offensive was envisaged by the leadership.

27. Staniszkis 1984, pages 112-13.

28. Interview with **Niezaleznosc**, 18 September 1981, cited in Staniszkis 1984, page 13.

29. Lawrence Weschler, **Solidarity: Poland in the Season of its Passion** (New York: Simon and Schuster, 1982) page 85.

30. Touraine, page 78.

31. **Labour Focus on Eastern Europe** 4:4-6, spring 1981, pages 26-32.

32. **Tygodnik Solidarnosc**, 25 September 1981.

33. Text in Stan Persky and Henry Flam (editors), **The Solidarity Source-book** (New Star Books, Vancouver 1982).

34. Interview with Gdansk Polytechnic Student Solidarity paper, **Servis**, 24 July 1981.

35. Cited by Harman, pages 249-50.

36. Touraine, page 72.

37. Kowalik, page 154.

38. Their document was printed in English as Network of Solidarity Organisations in Leading Factories, **Position on Social and Economic Reform of the Country** (Gdansk, 5 September 1981).

39. Notably Maciej Madeyski from Warsaw: see Barker and Weber, page 66.

40. Staniszkis 1984, page 25.

41. **Robotnik**, August 1981.

42. Leszek Szymanski, **Candle for Poland: 469 Days of Solidarity** (Borgo Press, San Bernadino 1982) page 34.

43. **Tygodnik Solidarnosc** 21, 21 August 1981.

44. **Tygodnik Solidarnosc** 22, 28 August 1981.

45. Ash, page 250.

46. **Labour Focus on Eastern Europe** 5:1-2, spring 1982, page 15.

47. 'One Year After August — What Shall We Do Next?' **Robotnik**, September 1981, translated in **Labour Focus on Eastern Europe** 5:1-2, spring 1982, pages 15-19.

48. Staniszkis 1984, page 22.

49. The complete text of the programme, adopted at the congress, is translated in **Labour Focus on Eastern Europe** 5:1-2, spring 1982.

50. Touraine, page 142.

51. **Sunday Times**, 20 December 1981.

52. Information from a Polish informant.

53. **The Guardian**, 20 October 1981.

54. Seen in some of the many opinion polls that flourished through this whole period: see David S Mason, 'Solidarity, the Regime and the Public', **Soviet Studies**, 35:4, October 1983.

55. **Washington Post**, 20 December 1981.

56. See Zbigniew Kowalewski, 'Solidarnosc on the Eve', **Labour Focus on Eastern Europe**, 5:1-2, spring 1982.

57. Kowalewski.

58. Kowalewski, pages 28-29. It is perhaps worth noting the degree to which the Lublin Group's ideas recapitulated the early theories, and errors, of Gramsci and the Turin Factory Council theorists: see Gluckstein, especially chapters 9 and 10.

59. Szymanski, pages 55-56.

60. See for example the statements by Zbigniew Bujak and Adam Michnik, cited in Barker, pages 148-49 and 188-89.

61. Informant from Warsaw.

62. **Labour Focus on Eastern Europe**, 5:1-2, pages 15-19.

63. See Harman, pages 240-41 and Barker, pages 157-58.

64. 'Realists' can be very unrealistic in revolutionary situations: Jacek Kuron of

KOR, who was in prison during the Gdansk talks, commented afterwards: 'If I had gone there I would have told them expecting to get independent trade unions was too much. I really believed it was impossible. In fact, I knew it was impossible.' Denis MacShane, **Solidarity: Poland's Independent Trade Union** (Spokesman Books, Nottingham 1981) page 134.

Chapter six: PERSPECTIVES

1. For further discussion of this elementary, but crucial point, see for example Nigel Harris, **Of Bread and Guns** (Penguin, London 1983).
2. The more developed the character of capitalist development, the more true this was. Thus France and Poland demonstrate this shift more markedly than Chile or Iran. Indeed, especially in Iran, the top layer of white-collar workers — technical managers, and the like — were used by the regime to undermine workers' control in the factories.
3. It is also notable that, with the striking exception of the Iranian revolution, the 'woman question' did not feature very significantly in any of these events. In Poland, women workers were largely excluded from the Gdansk occupations in the summer of 1980, except where they were delegates to the MKS or performing traditional 'service' roles as cooks and the like. The reason given was the danger of military attack on the shipyards, etc. To date, no significant women's movement has developed in Poland, and this ruling went largely unchallenged. My informant, a woman shipyard worker, thought the ruling correct — though she herself simply wangled her way into her own workplace occupation . . . On the other hand, the '21 Points' put forward by the workers' movement in Gdansk included a call for improved nursery and maternity facilities — as *class* demands.
4. Karl Marx and Friedrich Engels, **The German Ideology** (Progress, Moscow 1964) page 86 (translation modified).
5. Hal Draper, 'The Two Souls of Socialism', in **International Socialism** 1:11, winter 1962-63.
6. V I Lenin, **Left-Wing Communism: An Infantile Disorder**.
7. Jacques Danos and Marcel Gibelin, **June '36: Class Struggle and the Popular Front in France** (Bookmarks, London 1986).
8. V I Lenin, **Two Tactics of Social Democracy**.
9. There is an excellent discussion of these problems, as they appeared in the upheavals at the end of the First World War, in Donny Gluckstein, **The Western Soviets** (Bookmarks, London 1985).
10. Rosa Luxemburg, **The Mass Strike** (Bookmarks, London 1986) pages 50-51.
11. Marx traced this separation — in his language, between 'civil society' and 'state' — as long ago as 1843. See 'On the Jewish Question', in Karl Marx, **Early Writings** (Penguin, Harmondsworth 1975) pages 233-34. It is tragic to note that Solidarity's intellectual leadership sought to restore the significance of that division as a principle in their politics.
12. Gramsci's notion of 'hegemony' has been utterly perverted by Eurocommunist interpretation. His thought never pointed to the right-wing

concessionary politics of the 'popular front' and the 'broad democratic alliance'. See Chris Harman, 'Gramsci versus Eurocommunism', in **International Socialism** 1:98 and 1:99, May and June 1977. If one seeks a simple illustration of what Gramsci meant, it is not to be found in the capitulation of 'historic compromises' with capital, but in the Bolshevik adoption of 'All land to the peasants' as a slogan of the proletarian revolution.

13. Leon Trotsky, **The History of the Russian Revolution** (Gollancz, London 1965) page 18.

14. Karl Marx and Friedrich Engels, 'Preface' to the 1872 edition of the **Manifesto of the Communist Party**, written in the light of the experience of the Paris Commune.

15. Karl Marx and Friedrich Engels, 'Address of the Central Committee to the Communist League (March 1850)' in Karl Marx, **Political Writings**, volume 1 (Penguin, Harmondsworth 1973); Leon Trotsky, **Results and Prospects** (1906) and **The Permanent Revolution** (1930).

16. Mike Gonzalez, 'The coup in Chile and the left', in **International Socialism** 2:22, winter 1984.

17. **Le Monde**, 16-17 September 1973, quoted in Ralph Miliband, 'The Coup in Chile', **Socialist Register 1973**, page 474.

18. There is a useful discussion of aspects of this in Carol Johnson, 'The problem of reformism and Marx's theory of fetishism', in **New Left Review** 119, January-February 1980.

19. See especially Chris Harman, 'Party and Class', in **International Socialism** 1:35, winter 1968-69; and John Molyneux, **Marxism and the Party** (Bookmarks, London 1986).

20. There is an excellent recent survey in Ian Birchall, **Bailing Out the System: Reformist Socialism in Western Europe 1944-1985** (Bookmarks, London 1986).

21. For a succinct review of the process, see Duncan Hallas, **The Comintern** (Bookmarks, London 1985) and — for the period since 1945 — Ian Birchall, **Workers Against the Monolith** (Pluto, London 1974).

22. Hence the necessity of posing the question (and providing the heart of an answer) in John Molyneux, **What Is the Real Marxist Tradition?** (Bookmarks, London 1985).

23. See Donny Gluckstein, **The Western Soviets**; also Donny Gluckstein, 'The Missing Party'; Alex Callinicos, 'Party and class before 1917'; Donny Gluckstein, 'A rejoinder to Alex Callinicos' in **International Socialism** (second series), issues 22, 24 and 25, winter, spring and autumn 1984.